The Great Days of the
COUNTRY RAILWAY

The Great Days of the COUNTRY RAILWAY

David St John Thomas
and
Patrick Whitehouse ARPS

DAVID & CHARLES
Newton Abbot   London   North Pomfret (VT)

Frontispiece:
The Line to Llanidloes. An
engineman's view of the former
Cambrian Mid Wales line taken
from the footplate of a then brand
new LMS post war Class 2 2-6-0
leaving Tylwch station just south of
Llanidloes in 1950. This was a
passing loop with the section
switched out thus fully locked and
signalled for one side only with
signals pulled off for both directions.
With road transport available to
most people by this time, it was
inevitable that passenger services
over this beautiful piece of line
would eventually succumb which
they did on 31 December 1962.
Some freight traffic ran from Moat
Lane to Llanidloes until 4 May
1964.

The authors wish to express their
grateful thanks for the special help
by John Powell in the preparation of
material for this book.

British Library Cataloguing in Publication Data

Thomas, David St. John
  The great days of the country railway.
  1. Railways – Great Britain – History
  I. Title   II. Whitehouse, Patrick
  385'.0941   HE3018

  ISBN 0-7153-8775-8

First published 1986
Second impression 1986
Third impression 1987

Book designed by Michael Head

Typeset by Typesetters (Birmingham) Limited
Smethwick, West Midlands
and printed in Great Britain
by Butler & Tanner, Frome and London
for David & Charles Publishers plc
Brunel House   Newton Abbot   Devon

Published in the United States of America
by David & Charles Inc
North Pomfret   Vermont 05053   USA

CONTENTS

Country Terminus. Malmesbury
station at a date unknown but
probably in the 1920s or earlier.
This is very much a period GWR
station with its buildings constructed
in local stone and fitting carefully
into the adjacent landscape. On the
platform are the huge milk churns of
the time – one of the jobs soon
learned by the new junior porter was
how to trundle them into the van. On
the right is a gas cylinder wagon
carrying its own station name –
Malmesbury – gas lighting was very
much the norm. The track is very
unusually laid with flat bottom rails.

1
INTRODUCTION

Long, sleepy intervals between trains when it seemed always a Sunday afternoon; some passengers arriving early not knowing how long to allow and on no account wishing to be late; comradeship between the staff often following their fathers and uncles in the service; gardens lovingly tended; buildings and other arrangements usually unnecessarily lavish as though the promoters expected much more traffic than materialised; parcels offices reeking and sounding of the farms they served; booking offices issuing a high proportion of tickets to a few, nearby destinations but also occasionally to places throughout the kingdom; growing tension at the month's end as the pile of paperwork – the accounts – had to be balanced. That was the country station, throughout the British Isles. There was a powerful common denominator, including also of course mail bags, the daily pouch in which the takings were sent to district headquarters, a trickle of customers leaving or collecting merchandise of all descriptions, the screeching of the local goods stopping with the station truck opposite the parcels office, the smell of oil, used in the signal lamps, trimmed daily, if not also for platform lighting.

But even within the same region, different stations had sharply differing characters, traffics and traditions. The idyllic station that perhaps first comes to mind is that at which trains in opposite directions passed each other in the station loop. That meant at least one of their engines whistling on approach since the signal (board or stick) was kept 'on' to ensure the driver did not enter too rapidly the loop on which he was bound to halt. Then the signalman who had possibly been tending his garden for the past hour and a half became as busy and as central a character as the orchestra's conductor. But not all country stations were on branch or single lines; some of the most remote were in fact on trunk routes with fairly continuous through traffic though, since this was given priority by the timetablers, platform staff might have even longer intervals between services that called.

Even junctions were of different kinds: those where you left the main line to join the branch train waiting in the bay; those indeed where there might be two or three country trains waiting; those between one branch line and another where there would again be long quietnesses though slightly extended periods of activity once things began to happen. Most stations had at least one goods siding and signalbox coming under its stationmaster's jurisdiction, but some were of course devoid of points and signals, some indeed – the halts – even without booking office, gentlemen's or anyone with whom you could exchange the time of day or

Joint Exercise
Father booked all twenty-four or so passenger trains between 7.15am and 8.20pm every day, and had to obtain permission from the District Office to go into Melton for a hair-cut! His only clerical assistance was what his young sons could manage to do. The first train in the morning, and the last at night to Grantham conveyed the milk – some 50 or so churns from 'our' station each time. Making out milk waybills, with carbon copies, was a good exercise for schoolboys' handwriting. Good, too, was the booking of tickets, and seeing the last train off, after father had gone to some parish or church meeting!

The great days were when the hounds met in the vicinity of the Joint Line. On those days the hunt specials would arrive with so many horse-boxes that they had to be unloaded on to the platforms while standing on the running line. It was all hunting pink then, with the ladies in side-habits. They would commandeer all the four-wheel milk barrows as mounting steps. After the formal meet, the undulating countryside would soon be ringing to 'tally-ho!' At three or four o'clock in the afternoon the dirt-splashed hard-riders would be making their way slowly back to the station along the many bridle-paths to load up for home. – R. T. Munns on the GNR and LNWR joint ex Market Harborough.

Trains Crossing. Ardlui, the last stop before a fifteen mile long slog up Glen Falloch on the West Highland line to Fort William. The signal arm has just been pulled off for the Glasgow train headed by two ex LMS class 5 4-6-0s while the westbound train waits impatiently behind a B1 class 4-6-0 double heading a K2 2-6-0: this is late, very late as the B1 is a replacement for a BR Standard 4-6-0 which failed before Dumbarton with a broken pin on the right hand side valve gear radius rod. The hills beyond Ardlui reward the passenger by giving some of the finest views of the line.

Boredom

Whatever the grandeur of the country railway when conditions were normal, it could be sheer hell for passengers on packed summer Saturday trains climbing slowly uphill, hours late, windows steamed up, rain beating on the roof.

'Will we ever get there, mummy?' screamed the kids. Woebetide any enthusiastic passenger who corrected an optimistic answer.

Long waits for crossing with a lavatory visible on the opposite platform added to the inconvenience of travel in non-corridor coaches, which at peak times the Great Western cheerfully provided for some three-hour journeys in North Wales and from Taunton to Ilfracombe.

And hunger. 'If you don't give him one of your prunes, I can't be responsible for what he does,' pleaded an anxious mum on an Ilfracombe-bound train decidedly not making the journey the best part of the holiday.

ask to be guided through the complexities of the timetable.

Then, again, some stations were beautifully situated as though nature had worked extra hard to create the perfect environment, the buildings, gardens, seats, signals and the rails themselves forming a spectacle as pleasing as any other the district offered, and being sold on postcards at the village post office along with views of the time-honoured tourist attractions. Others were windswept, bleak, forbidding; others again in such deep cuttings that the sun shone on their platforms only briefly in winter. Some stations were actually in the middle of the towns and villages that bore their names, though many had only a few houses and farms – and if lucky a pub – immediately around them, a footpath beside the road and maybe another through fields optimistically pointing the way to local civilisation.

Between regions there were enormous variations in habit, culture and even lingo. There were the sharp differences between the railway systems themselves, their buildings, signals and platform furniture telling of the people who financed and operated the lines and who had to draw what strength they could from the kind of countryside they served. Even to sit on a Furness Railway seat was a world apart from placing oneself on a Highland one, while few people had the agility to manipulate equally skilfully the luggage carts of the different railway companies. As to lingo, the passenger from Southern England would genuinely have difficulty in understanding the porter within a score of miles of say Newcastle-upon-Tyne or Glasgow and would be safer relying on his own interpretation of the timetable. The harsher the local culture, the harsher the railway station and the trains serving it, while at the opposite extreme if tourists of a civilised nature were expected to form an appreciable part of the traffic, no effort was spared to render the railway environment welcoming. The railway at once unified Britain and emphasised its repertoire of regional individualities. In Ireland it did just the same.

Had you never left railway property, you could enjoy the full range of regional experiences of scenery, culture, language – even food, for the sandwich, the basic thickness and type of bread used, varied with the place and the local labour used in its making.

The railway was always the railway, trains for example taking the left hand track, engines whistling when signals were at danger and needing periodic pauses for drinks, while passengers only joined or alighted at recognised stations and halts, and paid different fares according to the class travelled, their age or the time of day or when the return journey was planned . . . and a whole variety of matters that railway users have always taken for granted – as they have accepted the basic fact that the railway world is a different world – but would be perplexing to the man from outer space. The railway, moreover, was universal. It went everywhere.

Almost all of it was built in the first two generations after man first began travelling faster than the speed of an animal, on the Liverpool & Manchester of 1830, the first inter-city railway. The speed of building

was incredible. How can one resist repeating that within twenty-four years, the largest English towns left without trains were Hereford, Yeovil and Weymouth? And that the thirty years 1830–1860 saw more fundamental change in our society, brought about by the railway's 'creative destruction', than any such period later, notwithstanding two world wars?

In the first place the railway was very largely the country railway because Britain and Ireland were still agrarian nations. Most of the routes between cities, and between cities and ports, ran deep through the countryside, giving employment and service that revolutionised the local way of life without standardising it one region with another. Though many more people lost their fortune than made it through investment in railways, in the early part of Victoria's reign, most of those who did become really wealthy took the railway route. Greed encouraged competition, and rival routes opened up new belts of countryside, halving the price of coal for rural industries and doubling that of the milk that could now be sent a hundred or more miles to its market (so ending the necessity to keep large milking herds within the cities). The countryside benefitted not merely from the Victorians' desire for dividends, but also from their lack of basic understanding of the economic nature of a railway. A railway to them was always a railway, seen as having almost limitless potential. So branch lines that had scant chance of paying, however economically they had been built, were given the full treatment with palatial stations, often two tracks where one would have done, or bridges and earthworks prepared for two even if only one were laid. Signalling and much else was unnecessarily elaborate but gave valuable rural employment.

Wye Valley Junction. Monmouth Troy station on 29 July 1932 with a train for Chepstow (right) in the platform. Straight on then curving to the left is the branch to Ross on Wye. At that time a further branch ran through Usk to join the North to West line; this was the second casualty, being closed on 30 May 1955. The first to Coleford was long ago – on 1 January 1917. The Ross and Chepstow sections closed on the same day, 5 January 1959. This could scarcely be a more typical Great Western country junction, buildings, corrugated iron shed, lamps, cast iron lettered station nameboard, platform trolley, steeply inclined semaphore bracket signal, signalbox and notice which reads 'PASSENGERS are requested to CROSS the line by the BRIDGE'. Not to mention the high domed 0-4-2 tank and wooden bodied auto trailer.

So full-scale trains calling at full-scale stations crossed and criss-crossed the kingdom, in England the system having a far greater density than anywhere else in the world, except possibly Belgium. By the time some narrow-gauge and more rudimentally-built lines under the Light Railway Acts had been added by the very early years of the twentieth century, virtually nowhere was more than walking distance from a station. It was not quite the same in the more remote areas of Wales, Scotland and Ireland, though taking the population into account if anything the over-provision was greater in Ireland than England. In all countries within the British Isles, the vast majority of the population could, if they desired, walk to the station for a train to their capital city. Everywhere the national newspapers were delivered on the morning of publication, and instantaneous news came across that underestimated railway adjunct, the electric telegraph.

So far from standardising everything, the railway encouraged special-isation and individuality – in agriculture, horticulture, brick-making, brewing and every type of industry, tourism and (though the Victorians did not use the name) commuting. Local industries rose to national or regional importance – or collapsed under competition. Exports in-creased, yet even the smallest goods yard received consignments from the Empire, weeds whose predecessors' seeds came in Australian wool bundles being among the visual evidence still to be seen at places where the rails have long receded.

Victorian Country Junction. An early photograph probably taken well before the turn of the century at Newbury, Berkshire, the junction of the Didcot, Newbury & Southampton Railway and what later became the Great Western's line to the West Country. The engine is one time Pembroke & Tenby Railway 2-4-0 Pembroke rebuilt by the GWR as its No 1361. Built as early as 1866 this was a standard Sharp Stewart design (No 1712); it was the only P&T engine to have worked far from its native soil and was in regular service on the DN&S. Note the bridge rail still in use and the splitting distant signal for the branch.

11

Local View. Hayfield station on the Midland & Great Central Railway joint line from New Mills Central around the mid 1900s. The train is completely Great Central being hauled by a Class 3 (LNER class F1) 2-4-2 tank No 574 built at Gorton works in 1889 and withdrawn in 1946. The card, a typical 'local view' of the period clearly shows the working of a country station, adequate passenger facilities, stationmaster's house, coal and merchandise sidings plus a small single road engine shed and water tower. In those early days a 'permanent' branch engine would be shedded here though based at Gorton for washouts and minor repairs. Economies later would see the men out of work or transferred to the junction shed. The line closed as late as 5 January 1970.

Sell It!
Fish or other perishable merchandise refused or left on hand, or of which from any other cause delivery cannot be effected, and which requires immediate disposal, must be sold by the Agent or through some recognised person, such as a salesman or broker. Where, however, without loss of market or risk of depreciation disposal instructions can be obtained, by telegraph or telephone, this course must be followed. If the merchandise is sold, the Company are required by the Standard Terms and Conditions of Carriage to do what is reasonable to obtain its value; an account of the quantity and proceeds must be taken, and the case immediately reported to Headquarters and sending station. – Under the heading of 'Perishables which cannot be delivered must be sold' in the 1931 *GWR General Directions to Agents.*

Above all the railway was a business, the weekly receipts of major companies published in the national Press being the most significant barometer of trade. Credit squeezes are not the prerogative of our century. Every stationmaster, if not his staff, knew the good times and the bad times and, as competition increased and following the early railway industrial disputes labour became more expensive, there was an even greater exhortation to attract traffic and save money. It is too easy for us, nostalgic about the neat country station and its steam trains, to forget that like a shop or factory the railway was set up to earn its owners a profit – directly or indirectly. With the larger companies, it was all about locking away savings in the expectation of steadily-rising dividends. Though the prospectuses always spoke about the inevitability of their forecasts being surpassed, deep in the countryside there must have been those who had their doubts; but then they would mainly have been the local landlords, farmers, merchants and mill-owners who had most to gain from the opening up of their valley, and who would not have been out of pocket in total if their locally-sponsored line was eventually sold to the main-line company at half price. Many branches were so built and acquired.

Everything the railways did was with a view to increasing income and reducing expenditure. Extra trains were only provided when there was a sound case in trade for providing them. High fares were charged until it was obvious that extra income could be obtained from cheap ones. If many villages first saw electric lighting at their station, it was because the railway thought this was the best investment on its shareholders' behalf. Generally country trains, engines and carriages, became those that had spent their first decades on inter-city services, but when the Great

12

Western introduced brand new branch-line sets it was thought to be sound financial as well as public-relations policy – a precursor of BR's recent decision that it is no longer economic to run yesterday's discarded main-line outfits over branches, but cheaper to introduce new specially-designed sets. Of course, the economic understanding was often primitive, boards of directors acting more out of prejudice than based on even simple cost accounting, while within its first generation the passenger railway settled down to a conservatism of operating practice that served everyone badly.

As we shall see in more detail, improvements were more frequently forced on railways than volunteered by them. But in the annals of the numerous separate railways that served Britain before the amalgamation into the Big Four in 1923, the name of one always stands out for its aggressive business practice: the Midland. A relative latecomer among the trunk routes, it was forever pushing into its neighbours' territories and introducing new practices. Country people, on the whole being more poorly paid than their urban counterparts, came especially to benefit from it – even though they lived well beyond its system. It introduced comfortable, cheap, universal third-class travel.

To begin with, third-class passengers, beside having to travel in open trucks with hard, wooden planks for seats, were restricted to slow and usually inconvenient trains, those making long journeys perhaps being overtaken by an express that started hours later than their train. To encourage the mobility of the working class, in 1844 Gladstone introduced an Act compelling railways to run at least a daily all-stations train over every route at an old penny per mile. Such trains were acknowledged as 'Parl' or 'Gov' at the head of the appropriate timetable columns; on some lines some third-class trains were provided addition-ally at an extra farthing a mile. In 1872, the Midland, whose aggression was already upsetting its neighbours, especially the well-established, stately London & North Western, suddenly announced that third-class passengers would be accepted on *every* train. Two years later, it announced the abolition of second class and the reduction of first-class fares to the pennyhalfpence level of second class. One year later again, it decided to upholster third-class carriages.

Protest though they might, and the Great Western and London & North Western certainly regarded it as an affront to well-ordered society, the other railways could not ignore this. While second class lingered on many lines, third-class passengers were now universally welcomed rather than tolerated – and rapidly accounted for the lion's share of passenger receipts. In practical terms, this meant that families paying an annual visit to relations would now go by train rather than walk a dozen miles or more, while working-class men began attending funerals of distant relatives, and the railway provided a really practical step to town for those seeking a higher standard of life. It encouraged the spread of Sunday school outings and individual trips to sea and moor, a Christmas shopping expedition to the nearest town, and paved the way for the spread of long-distance excursion services. Britain's population was up

Mishaps
Passengers were probably safer in a country train than in their own homes, but minor accidents abounded. It was not unusual for every one of a dozen or so crossing stations on a branch line to experi-ence a derailment within the course of a couple of years.

Nearly always it was an odd goods truck or two jerked off the road in a violent shunting move-ment – or on those devilish catch-points provided especially gener-ously on GWR routes of stiff gradients. An engine slipping could cause sufficient backward movement to throw a truck.

In the goods yard, old track-work taken too quickly could see the pony truck or bogie of the shunting locomotive slip between the rails. Then came the question whether or not to try a local, off-the-record remedy or ask control to send the breakdown train. Unofficial efforts of course often made things worse.

Trains passing signals at danger were rarer occurrences, though a few readers will recall a Tavistock train overshooting into the up platform where another train was waiting when one of the present author's farewell to staff news-paper reporting partly coincided with the new district manager paying an official visit to Prince-town. But until the end, an occa-sional descending loose coupled freight would get out of control – while others broke in two – the back perhaps making mincemeat of closed level-crossing gates.

Such accidents seldom en-dangered life – the railways' road delivery services caused far more fatalities – but tidying up was slow and expensive. 'The train to Aberystwyth is the bus outside', said the station announcement at Carmarthen. Sadly, a single-decker bus usually coped more than adequately.

Brecon & Merthyr Junction. One of the most complicated areas of railway geography in South Wales was that around Merthyr and eastwards across the valleys where many pre grouping companies, each tapping coal mining districts, met up with the LNWR's Heads of the Valleys line. Into all this from the north came the Brecon & Merthyr Railway splitting at Pontsticill Junction to run westwards to Merthyr (via a joint line with the LNWR) and south east to Deri Junction where it met the Rhymney Railway head on. Traffic was still heavy in 1950 when this early evening photograph was taken; it shows a southbound train double headed by 0-6-0 pannier tanks Nos 5793 and 4635 both of Merthyr (88D). Like so many other country junctions, Pontsticill was the home of a railway hamlet with the station house conveniently attached to the signalbox.

Where Two Lines Met. Great Malvern station in 1950 when the Midland branch to Tewkesbury and Ashchurch was still worked by that company's engines – an 0-4-4 tank for the passenger service and a Class 3F 0-6-0 for the freight. No 58071 still carries Salter safety valves on top of the dome and the condensing pipe to the water tank for use over the Metropolitan Widened Lines section of London Underground. It was a Tewkesbury engine – sub shed to Gloucester 22B. The notice hanging from platform awning still reads 'To LMS Trains for Tewkesbury and Gloucester'. The branch closed on 1 December 1952.

from 16,000,000 to 28,000,000 in the first forty years of the railway age; the demand was there. Again, country people especially welcomed the railway and used it more than cityfolk, though throughout the British Isles you would not be thought unusual never to have ridden on a train.

The railway inevitably fostered an urban economy. Most country stations literally sent away far more passengers than arrived, for cities and towns swallowed much of the rural population, particularly as rural-based industries were overtaken by larger urban ones. Emigration was also substantial in many areas, such as Cornwall and throughout Ireland.

Hundreds of miles of country railway, and dozens of once-isolated stations, were absorbed into the new cities and suburbs. This alone meant that the railway companies saw the remaining true country railway as being less important. Additionally, traffic declined at some places deep in the countryside, especially where the basic industry had been lost – such as the local brewery giving up the ghost because of competition from the mass-produced Burton-on-Trent brew. Even before the first world war there were indeed occasional rural line and station closures, though on balance accessibility still improved.

A system that enabled you to travel or send parcels and goods between stations within walking distance of almost everywhere in England, and close to the majority of the population of Wales, Ireland and Scotland; a system that was cheap, safe, and regulated by standard safety and other rules monitored by the Board of Trade (pre-nationalisation railways genuinely were a happy mixture of private enterprise and government control of a kind our own generation seems incapable of rediscovering) and enjoyed *Bradshaw's* all-embracing monthly timetable and the Railway Clearing House to list facilities nationwide and apportion income on through transits: clearly the word 'Great' in this book's title is not unjustified. Britain's railways were the wonder of the world, much of which of course acquired systems from us.

But just which were the most golden days? That is a rather more complicated question than perhaps most people expect.

Like so much else in Britain, the country railway was very class orientated. What should have been its greatest days, when only it could provide a service faster than that of a horse, was often marred by monopolistic behaviour and a patronising attitude to all but the richest. To be sure, opening day was a grand occasion: speeches and a trial ride for the rich, light refreshments for the ordinary folk, a triumphal arch for all to admire. And, as we have seen, dairy farming immediately became more profitable, while mail and papers were received more promptly and rapidly expanded in scope, and cheap mass-produced groceries and other products captured an ever increasing share of business.

But train services were usually sparse, run for the railway company's convenience rather than the public, and while the station usually became the most important trading post in village and small country town, it was quickly evident that its real potential was not going to be realised. Though occasional excursions to the seaside became memorable events,

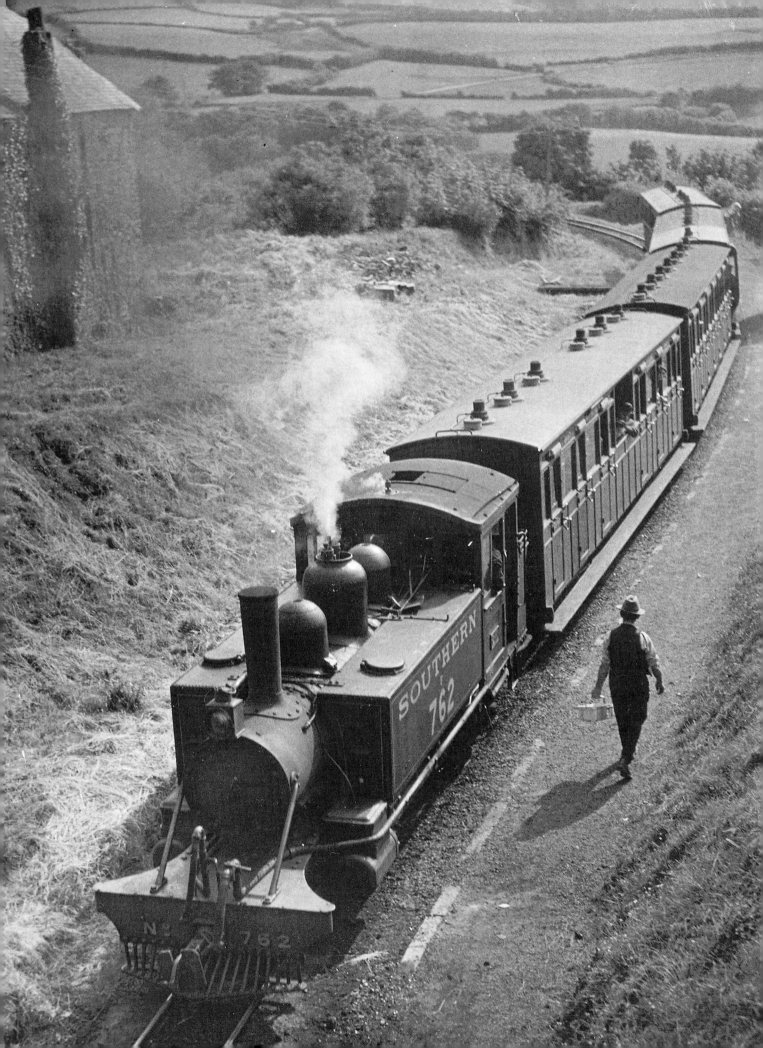

Special Excursion. Pentewan Railway 0-6-0 saddle tank Canopus (Manning Wardle 1547/1901) with a train of china clay wagons (cleaned and fitted with benches) forming the annual (free) Sunday school excursion in 1915. This train ran regularly until the line's closure on 2 March 1918.

Views From The Train

Credit has never been given to the railway companies for the 'creation' of the many fine views which came into existence only with the construction of the lines, but for which they would never have existed.

Many of these views rank with the finest in the country. Among the best known and most popular is from the sea-wall, between Dawlish and Teignmouth, built at the foot of Devon's towering red cliffs and lapped by the blue waters of Torbay. The coastal views here from the train are unsurpassed in the British Isles, and there is never enough room for all those, young and old, who try to crowd the corridors, and for whom it may mean either the anticipation of pleasures to come or the last remembrances of a wonderful holiday in the West. *GWR Magazine*

generally only the richer quarter or third of society actually went by train. Newspaper correspondence columns were filled with complaints about poor connections, excessive charges and arrogant officials – and any proposal for a new line that would result in competition was eagerly received. It is interesting to speculate how much less duplication of route there might have been had the main-line companies looked after their customers better in the early years, had even the Midland's lead in encouraging third-class travel come earlier. Certainly we can note that often there was a greater rejoicing when a town's second railway was opened than when the first steam engine arrived thirty or more years before.

So what should have been their greatest days were usually disappointing ones. Indeed, hardly a rural railway enjoyed its most generous service until well into the twentieth century. Competition resulted in many improvements from the 1870s on, and generally services improved steadily in the last third of the century until by 1900 there was an amazing range of facilities such as through coaches to branch line destinations from London and other large cities, and cross-country connections that took the occasional (perhaps only once a day) express racing down many secondary routes long since removed from the map. Improvements continued until 1914, and for many people these early years of the century will always be the golden ones, with a generosity of

Opposite:
Basking in the Summer Sun. An unusual engine for Britain in the form of Baldwin built 2-4-2 tank No E762 Lyn at Parracombe on the Lynton & Barnstaple narrow gauge section of the Southern Railway. An idyllic scene photographed in the early 1930s and impossible to replace; the engine simmering beside the new cut grass close to an ivy clad cottage whilst a punnet of fruit is carried down the 'platform' for the guard.

On The Run

Thomas Hardy's *Tess of the d'Urbervilles* includes a splendid description of the way in which a Wessex stationmaster realised he had a criminal on the run.

For over a century, the station provided the exit for lovers, murderers and swindlers. Sometimes they made it, the stationmaster glad to take their fare. Sometimes local knowledge helped, turning up with a small group of shoppers going to market and buying a local ticket with a view to re-booking likely to cause less concern than presenting oneself as the only passenger bound for the outside world. The constable enquiring after the train had gone would be bound to ask what tickets had been issued.

The strangler sharing an unstaffed Cornish halt with an unsuspecting lady passenger made a wise choice. He slipped into the autocar close by her innocently making them look like man and wife, while police were searching the nearby station. Not that he was free long.

Passengers without money or tickets at stations near mental hospitals naturally caused suspicion though they were fairly frequent. Eloping lovers might join different coaches of the same train at different stations, not speaking until safely aboard the express from the junction.

Prisoners were of course regularly conveyed by train, and for many years accounted for a significant income on the branch to the GWR's highest station above sea level, Princetown. Inevitably there were escape bids and races round freight yards.

The country station closed at night and all day Sundays afforded many men on the run – and tramps – privacy, comfort and food. Many a signalman found his larder raided when opening up and heard a cough from the locking frame.

alternatives not to be seen again, a stability, permanence, dignity (call it what you will) that many of us have been striving to regain ever since. But fascinating though the pages of *Bradshaw* are for this period, when you come to study the everyday rather than glamorous detail, you are usually shocked by just how few country trains ran. And when you read books and diaries of the day, you realise that even the better-to-do businessman then possessed a patience that would quickly disappear in the motor age. In 1910 it was not thought unusual to have to spend three hours at a junction town waiting for one of the four or five daily trains; by 1925, if there were no train the journey would be finished by bus.

And so, curiously, you come to the view that it was the arrival of the motor vehicle that forced railways to provide a better service and enjoy their greatest days before the passengers were sucked away from them and the freight went by lorry. Because total business was still increasing, the railways were able to meet the threat of road competition with increased frequencies on most rural routes. Many services now started earlier in the morning and especially continued later into the evening, notably on Saturdays. Villages past which trains had run non-stop were now given halts. A greater proportion of the community began to travel, though as services improved the country railway increasingly became a working-class institution, for the country gentleman now began being ferried by his chauffeur and, for those who could afford it, a car journey to or from the main-line station was quicker than a branch-line connection.

The greatest traffic, passenger and freight, was generally carried on the country railway in the years immediately before and after the first world war and immediately after the second. Some lines such as the Highland to the Further North in the first world war, were at their peak of activity as the result of military traffic, and both wars of course brought their strain with scarce resources and extra traffics. But in any event the strains of wartime meant indifferent service and certainly not the greatest days. Economic depression and road competition hurt many rural lines in the 1930s, but there was a vigorous fight for traffic, indeed survival, including pampering favoured customers and playing to the gallery. So the Great Western not merely ran the world's fastest and longest non-stop trains, but the largest number of through summer Saturday services in its history and a weekday seasonal service from Torbay to the Mortonhampstead line that passed non-stop through the junction at Newton Abbot. But then the standard of service varied dramatically between the wealthier and tourist parts of Britain and the hard-pressed more pedestrian backbone. In the rural Midlands, North and Scotland, most passengers would by no means rejoice at the standard of service they were offered. The golden era had seemed to end in 1914 and was not about to be restored.

Had it not been for hostilities, thousands of miles of branch lines would surely have closed (or at least have lost their passenger services) in the 1940s. The 1930s saw sufficient casualties to set the trend. Conversely, had narrow-gauge systems like the Lynton & Barnstaple

(closed 1935) survived until the outbreak of war, they would probably have lingered on for a further decade – and in the case of any narrow-gauge then probably have been saved as a tourist attraction for today. The wartime railway was pretty grim in town and country alike; only those who had to travel did so, but everyone was involved in comings and goings of service people to the front. Such had been the lack of investment that it was often the same trains running over some of the same rails that took a second generation of young men to the front in France. Three-coach trains that between the wars perhaps carried a score or at most two of passengers on all except the busiest market and fair days now had forty *standing* passengers per coach.

The aftermath of 1945 was very different from that of 1918. For the first time the average family had money to spend on travel, including an annual holiday. The railways were shortly to be nationalised, to be owned by the people, who expected a decent service. Yet despite the severe difficulties of the 1930s, the railway remained as a common carrier and even the new Transport Commission accepted traditional Victorian attitudes, while the 1930 Road Traffic Act, which gave the railways substantial shareholdings in bus companies, forbade them to operate

Central Wales Line. LMS Class 5 4-6-0 No 45190 takes the 7.15pm from Llanelli to Shrewsbury train into Knucklas on 5 June 1964. This one time LNWR route gave that company access to South Wales cutting across country from Craven Arms via Builth Road (where it met the Cambrian), Llandovery and then over Great Western metals to Pontardulais, thereon to Swansea over its own tracks. There was an LNW section from Llandilo to Carmarthen though this was regarded as a branch. Complete closure was attempted in 1963, but because of protests a passenger only service was retained though running to Swansea over ex Great Western metals via Llanelli.

19

Bishop's Castle Railway

	Week Days only			
	Y			
	am	am	pm	pm
Craven Arms &				
Stokesay............ dep	7.50	11.25	3.10	6.55
Horderley.................. „	8.00	11.35	L	7.05
Plowden.................... „	8.10	11.45	3.25	7.15
Eaton .... „	L	K	L	L
Lydham Heath .... „	8.23	11.58	3.38	7.25
Bishop's Castle .... arr	8.30	12.10	3.50	7.35

	Week Days only			
	Y			
	am	am	pm	pm
Bishop's Castle .... dep	7.00	9.00	12.35	5.40
Lydham Heath .... „	7.08	9.10	12.45	5.50
Eaton .... „	L	L	L	K
Plowden .... „	7.18	9.25	12.55	6.00
Horderley.................. „	7.25	9.35	1.05	6.05
Craven Arms &				
Stokesay.............. arr	7.35	9.45	1.15	6.17

K—Calls at Eaton on Fridays.
L—Calls on informing the Guard.
Y—Bishop's Castle Fair days only.

BCR Timetable

their own buses. Here was a curious mix that led to the belated greatest days of the country railway as late as the 1950s and early 1960s.

Services were then generally more frequent, quicker and more comfortable than in previous eras, and a high proportion of travellers were attracted by bargain fares. As we will see later, at the end the only thing missing was a worthwhile number of passengers, yet the terminal rundown in traffic generally began later than most people assume. Because of the dramatic growth in tourism in the post-war years, for example, British Railways' peak summer Saturday carryings were not reached until 1958, though their share of the cake had been declining for about five years. Though there were notable exceptions, freight usually disappeared faster than passengers, and in their last years many branch lines were wholly passenger affairs – as are many of today's survivals.

Certainly the public first became aware of the charms of the branch line after 1950, railway enthusiasts and those who just appreciated the different way of looking at the countryside steadily accounting for a higher proportion of the passengers competing for the front seats of the new diesel multiple-units that enlivened many services from the late 1950s. And this is the period richest in photographic and other record.

But then, of course, there is a quite different yardstick. Were the great days of the country railway the many, many ordinary ones on which everything happened like clockwork, the only variations being the usual daily, weekly and seasonal ones as the branch line reflected the tempo, the ebb and flow of local, agricultural-based life? Or were they the days when something special happened, the village and market town station performing yeoman service in making some grand event possible – or keeping lifelines open when snow had closed the roads? The days 500 passengers from Blyth and Morpeth were welcomed by a band for the annual Bellingham fair, or Keswick station was full to overflowing for a conference, or 6,000 passengers went up the Plym Valley line for a walk across Dartmoor, were indeed great ones. Signalling and sidings

normally surplus to requirements were used to the hilt. No seats were
spare, no railwayman went home feeling he had not earned his keep.
Virtually every line had its exceptional traffics and moments and great
was the drama of trying to fit a quart into a pint pot, of locomotives
lifting maximum loads over tough gradients, of express services on
routes where everything normally stopped everywhere. Then, again,
there were the great days when little-used branches suddenly became an
alternative artery when main lines were blocked. Who would not be
excited at the prospect of seeing the Cornish Riviera Limited backed into
the refuge siding over points locked by hand in order to cross a down
train from Bristol at Christow on the Teign Valley?

Much of the attraction of the country railway lay in its regularity.
Patterns were repeated, sometimes with the same locomotive classes and
traffics, for generations and more. Again, only the rhythms of local life
made a difference, fertilisers for example always boosting inward freight
in the late winter and early summer. And abnormal events including
special trains of all kinds were the more remarkable for punctuating this
pattern than had the exception been the rule. Nobody was surprised to
see an extra train at a London terminus, but deep in the Kent
countryside the arrival of a hop-pickers special was quite an event. So
even the very last trains of exceptional locomotives and loads have gone
into rural and railway history as something worth recalling.

Here we invite you to share and relive the great days of all kinds. The
emphasis is on the post-war period when most lines were at their busiest

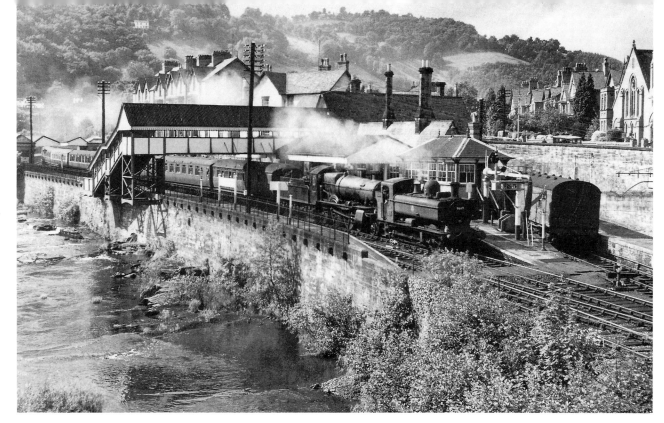

Saturday Special. Llangollen station on the GWR route from the Cambrian Coast on 4 September 1954. Running through is a return Butlin's holiday camp train which has come down from Pwllheli and is composed of ex LNER stock. This was a commonplace working at that time and was in the service timetable as a Birmingham relief train. The engines are 0-6-0 pannier tank No 9669 and an unknown Manor, both of Croes Newydd shed (84J). It is probable that 9669 was a Bala sub shed engine helping out with a heavy train or a weary Manor.

within years of closure or castration, but we also reflect earlier golden periods. Equally it is more on the everyday when the country railway was going about its time-honoured, unconscious way of serving the local community of which it became a colourful part, but special occasions of all kinds also have their part.

And what a lot there is to celebrate! The smooth rails pointing ever onward to the horizon, winding gently, climbing slowly, even in dramatic terrain, often hugging the banks of rivers and commanding the very best views. The variety of stations and the people that manned them, like the stationmaster who was usually the first man in his community to have reached the top by promotion from the ranks. By no means born a gentleman, he was often as ill at ease commanding his assortment of local characters from the porter who could barely write to the lonely signalman in his box as he was with the schoolmaster and parson in village life and politics. And if the next stations and grandiose viaducts were pleasing to the eye in themselves, the passage of the country train made the blood throb through the veins. Until dieselisation, few country trains were purpose built, rakes of yesteryear's main-line carriages bringing back memories and adding their touch of variety, while locomotives told their own story. Even the routine crossing of trains on single-line routes had its aroma, while connections at junctions – especially those junctions deep in the country which were just a meeting of branch lines – were endlessly fascinating. So was watching the traffic being carried, talking to passengers and guards, hearing how villages differed in lifestyle and outlook – about the local hopes and fears, the memories of which all were proud. Above all, the general fun of it, at least a touch of which we try to recapture especially in some of the shorter pieces in these pages.

Country branches were ever the repositories for small, elderly and superannuated steam locomotives, eking out their final days on relatively undemanding jobs appropriate to their size. In the 1930s, only one railway was producing new locomotives specifically for lesser branch lines; the GWR built a considerable number of 14xx 0-4-2 tanks, 2251 class 0-6-0s, 57xx 0-6-0 pannier tanks and 90xx 4-4-0s. One could hardly call them modern in concept, and indeed the 90xx 'Dukedogs' with their double frames could only be described as an anachronism at this period. Some LMS designs gravitated to the branch lines, notably the Class 3MT 2-6-2 tanks of Fowler and Stanier heritage, but this was largely because their disappointing performance fitted them for little else. They were doled out widely in small numbers.

Elsewhere the old engines soldiered on but gradually disappeared to their own Valhallas. Some went faster than others; in Scotland, with St Rollox the dominant works, the G&SW lines were progressively denuded of the home product by the old enemy, the Caledonian. The Hull & Barnsley found itself in a similar position at the hand of the North Eastern. Takeover of the Midland & Great Northern Joint by the LNER brought the early decimation of Melton Constable and its flock in favour of Doncaster, Stratford and Gorton engines. Even depots brought up to do Crewe's bidding felt the draught as Midland and L&Y engines were brought in for the middle range of duties with the early demise of the products of Webb, Whale and Bowen Cooke. Elsewhere, one might have thought that pregrouping engines were tethered to their native heaths.

Not until 1946 were the first thoroughly modern engines built deliberately for work on weight-restricted country branches, in the form of Ivatt's Class 2MT 2-6-0s and 2-6-2 tanks on the LMS. The LNER was beginning to think along somewhat similar lines, but was forestalled by nationalisation. The Southern was amply endowed with small pregrouping engines displaced by electrification and saw no need to build; the Bulleid 'Leader' design ostensibly had a role in this field, but its weight was hardly bearable on the highways, let alone byways.

So locomotive depots serving rural branches had much of a museum air about them. Some sheds, indeed, remained entirely stocked with pregrouping engines at nationalisation in 1948. On the LMS, examples were Penrith (with 10 LNWR 'Cauliflower' 0-6-0s), Highbridge (8 Midland 0-4-4 tanks and Class 3F 0-6-0s), Forfar (20 Caledonian 4-4-0s, 0-6-0s and 0-4-4 tanks), and Forres (nine 4-6-0s, 4-4-0s, 0-6-0s and 0-6-0 tanks of Caledonian and Highland origin). But it was on the LNER and Southern that this was seen to the greatest degree; big sheds such as Boston (50 engines), Brighton (54) and Tonbridge (66) were entirely stocked from the pregrouping mould, while others missed this category by no more than a whisker. Smaller depots with all-pregrouping allocations were almost too numerous to mention; the Isle of Wight system, Eastbourne, Three Bridges and a host of others come to mind. At the opposite end of the scale there was a handful of small depots from which pregrouping types had been banished entirely; Uttoxeter and Macclesfield, each with eight engines, were examples. Often engine classes were allocated in penny numbers in seeming random fashion.

A few engine classes did migrate spectacularly in the search for greater capability on country lines. One thinks immediately of Scotland, where the Great Eastern B12 4-6-0s took over the chief workings on the Great North of Scotland routes, and the Great Northern K2 2-6-0s which pounded over the West Highland line. Even the LNWR penetrated north of the Border – even if not very far! – with three Webb 2-4-2 tanks working the Lockerbie branch from Dumfries for some years and the steam railmotor which took up residence at Beattock for the Moffat branch. In this cross-Border osmosis it is perhaps surprising that Scottish engines rarely took root south of Carlisle; the only examples that spring to mind were not for branch line work but were a pair of Caledonian 0-4-0 Pugs which finished up in Burton-on-Trent and Shrewsbury. A few of Drummond's LSWR L12 4-4-0s took haven in the LB&SC's shed at Brighton, while in return some of the 0-6-2 rebuilds of Billinton's E1 0-6-0 tanks ventured into the West Country.

Nationalisation, and the adoption of the LMS policy of providing modern locomotives for the whole spectrum of power requirements, did much to erode the timeless look of rural branch lines before the axe was wielded over them under the Beeching holocaust. Of the 999 BR Standard engines built, no fewer than 430 were 2-6-0 tender and 2-6-4 and 2-6-2 tank engines in power class 4MT or below, while the corresponding LMS designs were also produced in considerable numbers for 'foreign' lines. They did some main line work, of course, but they were the mainstay of a host of branch lines the length and breadth of the land. A 2-6-4 tank rested from its far from exhausting labours in hauling a one-coach train, in the tiny one-engine shed at Killin, while 82xxx 2-6-2 tanks went to live on the Somerset & Dorset. 77xxx 2-6-0s battled with Pennine gradients over Stainmore Summit to their Kirkby Stephen home, and 84xxx 2-6-2 tanks took over the Seacombe – Wrexham service from Great Central engines. The pregrouping types went rapidly to the wall, displaced by new engines and falling traffics, and the sheds they inhabited did not escape the axe. The bigger mixed traffic locomotives invaded some remaining areas; Crieff saw Class 5s on two-coach trains that had been the preserve of nothing bigger than 4-4-0s or 0-4-4 tanks, with the indignity of working tender-first in one direction. The rural branches were beginning to look faintly ridiculous in their declining years, but not even the arrival of diesel railcars could save many of them.

23

Brecon & Merthyr Train. Great Western 0-6-0 Pannier tank (one of the first of the class with the improved cab) No 8778 takes the 7.06pm train out of Torpantau station in the summer of 1950. The engine carries a BR type shed plate (86A Ebbw Junction) but the number is still on the front buffer beam, GWR style, while the coaches are in chocolate and cream. The notice in front of the tablet collection post indicates a speed restriction of 15mph. The shingle sided signalbox is a relic of the Brecon & Merthyr Railway. The line closed to freight on 1 January 1959 and to passengers on 31 December 1962.

Branch Tank. Dolgelly, ex Cambrian Railways in August 1939 with a Great Western push and pull train from Barmouth standing in the platform behind Collett 0-4-2 tank No 4865 sub shedded at Penmaenpool, in a somewhat dirty external condition; a GWR roundel can just be seen on the tank sides. This was a market town to seaside town working; the ex Cambrian line met the Great Western's cross country tracks from Ruabon to the east of the station. Note the fire devil under the water tower to prevent freezing in winter, it would share its coal stocks with the stove in the adjacent signalbox just out of the picture.

Opposite:
A Beyer Beauty. Midland & Great Northern Joint Railway 4-4-0 No 33 waits for its turn of duty outside Melton Constable shed about 1933. Built in 1888 the engine is typical of its makers – varieties of the class could be seen as far away as Australia. Of particular interest are the tender windshield, the automatic tablet catcher on the cab side to the left of the polished numberplate and the Midland type power class 1 on cabside.

24

Midlands Junction. A very LNWR scene around 1934.
Superheated Precursor class 4-4-0 No 5300 Hydra *at Kenilworth Junction carrying express headlamps but with non corridor stock. It is probably the 4.41pm semi-fast from Leamington (LMS) and Warwick to Birmingham (New Street) via Coventry and a regular working for this class at that time. Express headlamps were carried as the train ran non stop from Coventry to Birmingham.* Hydra *was then a Rugby engine and this would be a filling in job. Closed to passengers on an intermediate station basis on 18 January 1965, the branch now has a new lease of life taking most fast trains from Birmingham to the old Great Western route at Leamington via Coventry, leaving the once busy tracks via Knowle and Warwick (GW) for suburban traffic.*

25

Ancient and Modern. Warwick shed in June 1950 when the new LMS designed Ivatt 2-6-2 tanks were about to take over the cross country push and pull trains to Rugby or Daventry and Weedon from the ex LNWR 2-4-2 tanks: both engines are fitted for this type of working and are shedded here. On the left is No 41228, on the right No 46749. The older class had been on these workings for over fifty years, the new was to last only nine as Leamington – Weedon closed on 15 September 1958 and Leamington – Rugby on 15 June 1959. Was it really worth it?

Southern Mixed. The North Devon & Cornwall Junction Light Railway was built as late as 1925 (partly over the course of a narrow gauge mineral line) to join Halwill Junction, the diversion point for the then Southern Railway lines to Bude and Wadebridge, to Torrington, the end of a branch from Barnstaple. It came too late in the day and lasted only until 1 March 1965. In later years it was worked by E1/R 0-6-2 tanks and trains were generally mixed. No 32696 nears Torrington on 20 May 1949.

Morning Train. An ex LB&SCR A1X class 0-6-0 Terrier tank works back to Havant across the timber trestle bridge spanning Langstone Channel and approaches the main line junction for the Hayling Island branch at Havant. Note the signalbox perched on the bridge side controlling the swinging span. All traffic ceased on 4 November 1963.

26

2
EXPLORING BY TRAIN

The process was always the same. How to fit in as much branch-line travel as possible without interminable waits minus food or drink at draughty stations.

Of course, there were refinements. You wanted to cover *all* lines, not missing spurs used by one daily train or even by one only on summer Saturdays. Daylight was imperative and some routes deserved sunshine more than others. Some mountain lines in particular were known to be better 'done' in a certain direction. And while steam might be a prerequisite for lines with stiff gradients, more could be seen of others forward or back through the driver's compartment of a diesel. Sometimes cheap fare restrictions reduced flexibility. Then you had to determine which connections might be lost through late running and minimise the upset if things went wrong. Finally, some places to be visited demanded a couple of hours beyond the station gate, and time also had to be left for inspecting interesting junctions and termini.

Every railway and country lover already had a working knowledge of geography, but a glance at the map might still be desirable. Then the timetable. What memories! Like a computer, you went searching through the simple permutations of YES/NO until a suitable combination of yesses emerged. There was some judgement about whether 15 or 78 minutes were preferable in Whitby or Barnard Castle, but basically you knew how soon parents or guest house would release you, where and when you wanted to go.

It was just very difficult to achieve what you wanted! Even branches with half a dozen to ten daily trains ran few of them at times you could be around, and then there might not be a main-line connection, at least not in the direction you wished to go. Where there were only two or three daily trains, your whole itinerary had to be fixed around one of them. Lines with a quite impossible schedule were frankly a relief, at least in the days that Britain had so dense a railway network that only a handful of the most dedicated could hope to travel it all. So many of us never did get by train to Fawley or travel by some of the more exotic lines on the outskirts of Glasgow, or joined those who it seemed only travelled in darkness on one or two short sections in South Wales.

The impossible was give-uppable; the difficult challenging. So you started producing your own mini-timetable, having no idea what would work best, if at all. Three or four possible starting directions each with several suitable trains optimistically suggested a dozen or so feasible possibilities, but half these would fail at the first connection, and most of

> **'We Do Have Passengers'**
> 'Do I have the train to myself?' asked the passenger of the guard (whose face looked as though it had been chiselled out of red marble) as the single coach was leisurely hauled toward Hatherleigh by a brand new BR standard 2-6-2 tank locomotive.
>
> 'Yes,' said the guard. 'But you can't count on it. On Wednesday we took Mrs and Miss Thomson to Halwill. They were going to Bude, you know. They'll be back sometime next week.'
>
> After a puff on his pipe, he added thoughfully: 'We do have passengers, you know.'

Marbles

The signalman's lot on the Taff Vale in early days was very mixed. Uniform included a 'John Bull' hat, a frock-tail coat, and moleskin trousers for long wearing – plus of course the truncheon that justified the first signalmen everywhere being called 'bobbies'. Promotion did not come from letting passenger trains down the valley on time if that meant an unnecessary delay to coal. But on a Monday morning all trains were sometimes in danger of delay because over the weekend boys short of marbles purloined the ball bearings encased in iron boxes that was part of the signal-rodding system. Setting the road became almost impossibly hard.

Opposite:
Sussex Junction. In May 1948 only five months into Nationalisation, little is changed at Robertsbridge. A Schools class 4-4-0 has just passed on its way to Hastings connecting with the 5.50pm train to Tenterden Town headed by Kent & East Sussex Railway No 3, a Stroudley Terrier (once LB&SCR No 70 Poplar) in malachite green. A Southern Railway totem is affixed to the concrete lamp standard and the station nameboard reads 'Robertsbridge change for Kent & East Sussex Line'. Today No 3 is back at work on its own home ground working for the restored K&ESR, still with its headquarters at Tenterden.

the rest peter out at some further junction. To get on a branch off a branch, you might have only two possibilities. And both of these might involve an unacceptably long 'lay over', inevitably at the least desirable place. So suppose one went by two expresses right to the other side of a possible piece of territory and wandered back by a series of branch lines? If you were too late to catch the better connections provided for people going to work, then the most difficult part of the itinerary might be tackled along with those coming home – but beware of trains that ran at different times in the unstated school holidays.

Is it right that all this is in the past tense? Can you not still explore much of the best of valley and coast by train? Yes, but true branches off branches are now rare. To practice real timetable wizardry, you must now go to parts of Europe, especially rural Italy, and then you will quickly realise how much we have lost in Britain. Incidentally, language is little barrier to the understanding of a timetable if you have the basic art.

So back to the great days of the country railway and the past tense. The timetable, cussed as it might be in its layout and much of its detail (just how did the three routes from Aberdeen to Elgin relate?), had always to be the explorer's servant, ultimately tamed. You might swear at it, close it in despair, but always depended on it – at home, work, in hotels, and while actually travelling. Because of the long slugs of time taken to prepare a complicated branch-line day's itinerary, often arrangements could only be finalised at the last minute. That often meant thumbing through the timetable, markers in various pages, notes getting increasingly untidy, in friends' houses or hotel lounges. Much was the mirth among those who only went by train as quickly as possible to get from A to B. 'But why delay the agony?' And, 'If you want to keep riding, why not go to London and spend the day on the Inner Circle?'

Off to bed, only to have a new idea and start afresh. Indeed, the best ideas, the best combinations of routes, were born out of familiarity and a chance to let the subconscious work on it. That might mean a nocturnal change of taxi and eating arrangements. And so finally to sleep.

What excitement when you arrived at the station for the first train. Of course, unless you were lucky enough to have a 'runabout', even deciding how best to ticket a complicated day's itinerary was another matter, perhaps only finalised with the help of a friendly booking clerk. Singles were the fares to avoid, workmen's those that might give you an early hitch to a distant starting point easy on the pocket. Day returns generally only covered journeys substantially in demand, but provided there was time you might sneakily rebook, using a series of such tickets for what in effect was a continuous journey. Two tickets covering portions of a through journey do not have the same validity as one through ticket, said the ticket regulations, meaning that you could not have cheap day returns in stages when there was no throughout cheap day ticket. Perhaps we did not notice. Monthly returns were still much better than singles. But then there were many special offers, some well advertised, some mysteriously kept under the counter. Penrith's

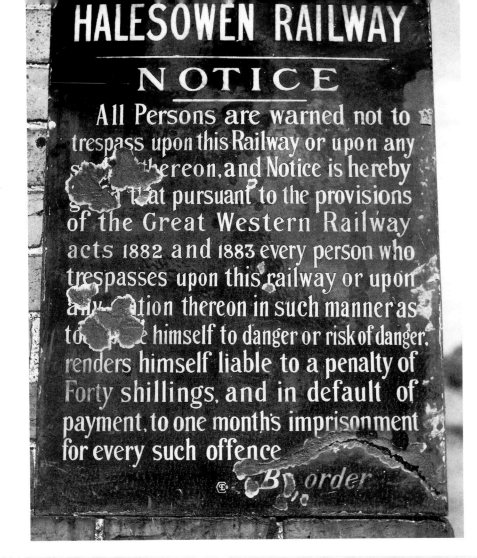

HALESOWEN RAILWAY

NOTICE

All Persons are warned not to trespass upon this Railway or upon any s... ...thereon, and Notice is hereby g... ...at pursuant to the provisions of the Great Western Railway acts 1882 and 1883 every person who trespasses upon this railway or upon any ...tion thereon in such manner as to ...e himself to danger or risk of danger, renders himself liable to a penalty of Forty shillings, and in default of payment, to one month's imprisonment for every such offence

By order

Discovery! Although battered by itinerant stone throwers and rusted into the bargain, this notice is evidence of the type of find possible when travelling station by station to research a piece of railway. The blue enamel notice has probably gone the way of all things material, but may well have ended up as a collector's treasure. It was found on Hunnington station's single platform in 1949 and is the only artefact known to this author showing ownership of the Halesowen Railway, a Midland and Great Western Railway joint line in Worcestershire linking the former's West of England tracks with the latter's Black Country system. Closed to regular passengers since 1919, the railway carried freight for the Austin works at Longbridge along with special workmen's trains (unadvertised) mornings and evenings. Hunnington station served the Blue Bird toffee factory while the line's ultimate fate was sealed by the construction of a by-pass road and the M5 motorway: it closed on 6 January 1964 although the workmen's trains were gone by 1 September 1958.

Bank Holiday Excursion. One of two exciting branches from Penrith was the one time North Eastern Railway route to Darlington via Kirkby Stephen and Barnard Castle – carrying coke traffic for the furnaces of the west coast. The line shared the bay platforms with the Keswick trains and on 6 August 1950 the NER services were still in the hands of the successful J21 class of 0-6-0, originally built as two cylinder Worsdell/von Borries compounds. Normal trains were all stations locals but August Bank Holiday Sunday shows a return excursion to Redcar, double headed with non corridor stock. The leading engine, No 65090, of Darlington (51A), has been specially fitted with a form of coupling release gear for banking freight up the hilly route to Stainmore summit. The use of the slip coupling ceased soon after this. The train engine was also a Darlington J21, No 65119.

booking clerk insisted that Penrith–Carlisle–Newcastle–Darlington–Barnard Castle–Penrith could only be done with a series of singles, and a small fortune was shelled out before a discreet duplicated notice was seen at Barnard Castle's booking office stating that this circular journey could be done in either direction, starting anywhere, for about a third the sum. BR duly paid a refund. All regular explorers naturally hoarded all the leaflets and excursion brochures they could, developing a knowledge that they willingly shared with other travellers and occasionally putting even booking clerks right.

There remained a gambling element. Sooner or later, for instance, you would find yourself without a ticket for an intermediate part of a return journey. Did you say nothing and hope that a ticket collector would not pop into your compartment before you reached the point at which your next ticket started, or go and tell the guard (if there was a corridor by which to reach him)? And by what alternative routes might your return ticket(s) be valid? Guards were generally pretty tolerant, more interested in having someone to chat with than in making extra paperwork. Most railwaymen of all kinds were welcoming, pleased to see you take an interest in their affairs, only BR's late 1960s nonsense about steam being psychologically disturbing to the staff producing a significant minority who took exception to an invasion of their private world. If you were the only passenger, as between Tillynaught and Banff, or Yelverton and

Great North of Scotland Junction. Craigellachie, where the Speyside branch followed the peaty river through Blackboat and Cromdale, Grantown and Nethy Bridge to Boat of Garten, to meet the Highland Railway's original main line from Forres to Aviemore. For many years the motive power over this line, serving so many whisky distilleries, was solely in the hands of GNoS 4-4-0s of classes D40 (1899) and D41 (1893). Class D40 No 62262 of Keith shed (61C) waits at the junction with the Speyside goods on the morning of 2 August 1954. Soon there will be a flurry of excitement with the branch passenger train arriving to make connection with the main line on the opposite side of the island platform. The Aberdeen bound train will have a B1 class 4-6-0 at its head, but only three years back this would have been an ex Great Eastern B12 4-6-0, one of a number sent up to Scotland by LNER in its later years. GNoS signals guard both main and branch line.

Princetown, you might almost expect a choice of being upgraded gratis to first or riding on the locomotive.

Tickets became especially complicated when during a holiday you took several different but interlocking itineraries using also one or more cars. Thus you might (and at least one person did!) park your own car at Craigellachie, hire one at Elgin, and still use a taxi between stations in Grantown-on-Spey. Apart from the fact that spouses might tolerate only one such day in a week's holiday, rendering a runabout ticket too expensive, it was always a pleasure to do business at the booking offices of out-of-the-way places.

And so aboard the train, usually at the front, the better to count passengers waiting at intermediate platforms, the less likely to be invaded. How you could enjoy your own company in a non-corridor compartment labelled to seat ten or twelve! Window open, shoes off and feet up on the seat opposite, itinerary and timetable, refreshments and reading matter organised nearby, cases and coat on the seats further away to discourage other passengers, your private room ambled along seldom at an average of more than thirty miles an hour, filled with the sounds and smells of the locomotive – and occasional sounds and smells of the countryside, too. Ecstacy alongside the Cambrian cliffs, past Bala Lake or Bassenthwaite or through the Spey or Eden valleys.

Paradoxically, though never could you enjoy your own company

31

**Stations Signalled
As Terminal Stations**

Drivers of trains when approaching any of the following stations must understand that the signal or signals taken off to give them permission to enter, simply give permission to run into the station, and not through it, and they must be prepared to stop at any point in the station the circumstances of the case may render necessary, unless the line is clear, and any signals applicable to the line on which they are running are taken off, giving them permission to leave the station at the other end:

Burnham, Wells, Glastonbury (for Wells Branch Line), Wimborne, Highbridge, Templecombe Upper, Templecombe Lower.

S&DJR Appendix to Working Timetables, 1933

Coastline. One of the more lovely views from a train in mid Wales is that running along the shore from Barmouth to Dovey Junction, the last section following the banks of the wide river estuary. The Coastline, as it is called, is sharply curved with short, steep gradients and this one time section of the Cambrian Railways has always been popular with enthusiasts as well as holidaymakers. Summer Saturdays often meant double heading because of increased loads; here one of the earlier batches of Churchward's small-wheeled 2-6-2 tanks of class 45XX double heads a Collett 2251 class 0-6-0 with an up express (though stopping at all stations bar halts as far as Welshpool) to the Midlands and London.

more, you also had other rich companionship: with the locomotive and train and the countryside, of course; with staff, driver and fireman during those long pauses for water and when crossing at single-line loops; with the guard when visiting his van to look at the parcels; and sometimes even with other passengers. Welsh miners, Scottish fishermen, crofters from the Western Isles, car workers in the Midlands, school children and shoppers, parsons and priests all had an interesting tale to tell when you had their attention in such a gentle environment. Business, education, entertainment, romance were there for the taking, social interludes being especially welcome on a generally solitary journey. What did happen to that Welsh lass travelling home from Swansea University where she was reading geography to do revision before the finals? There were twenty animated minutes semi-express climbing the final section to Hirwain, where the itinerary demanded a change for the steep descent to Merthyr. Such was the leisurely pace of secondary-line trains that there was ample time to buy a ticket, place luggage on the Merthyr train and return for more chat before her train continued on its way to Aberdare.

It was in another Welsh valley, climbing from Newport to Dowlais Top on the way to Talyllyn Junction that one passenger in a non-corridor compartment demonstrated the ultimate in keeping the populace out. A comedian, indeed a very funny man, like a significant contingent of branch-line passengers he was on his way to a funeral – his father's, in Aberystwyth, a cross-Wales journey then perfectly feasible there and back in the day with quite reasonable connections, now out of the question by public transport. Not wishing the conversation to be interrupted, on seeing a crowd going to market waiting at a wayside station, instantly he removed some of his clothes, hung his socks in the window and generally dishevelled himself. By the time passengers started peering between the socks, his naked toes were doing a ritualistic dance and he was feigning a violent cold. With standing room only in the rest of the train, one or two passengers got as far as opening the compartmnt door with only two people in it – but quickly withdrew. Better to stand next door than suffer this.

Wales was especially fun by branch line, railwaymen taking intense pride in their job and always willing to tell a yarn to someone interested in railway matters and the locality in which they lived and worked. It was on that little-used line with a curiously unbalanced service for decades on end from Swansea Riverside to Brecon that the guard was asked where another roll of film might ultimately be bought. 'No problem; indeed not.' At the very next halt the driver was told he would have to wait while the passenger slipped to the chemist down the street – by no means the only case of 'shopping by train'. Wales was enjoyable for Welsh people, steep valleys and dramatic mountains, for lengthy single lines carrying occasional expresses – and also because it was mainly Great Western.

Do not for a moment think that that meant the railway was well run, even punctual. Few parts of Britain's railways regularly ran so late as the

32

Cambrian Double Header. A reward for exploring the coast line by train, in August 1939, was the sight of this motley collection of Great Western coaches headed by two ex Cambrian Railways 0-6-0s, Nos 894 and 892 at Dovey Junction. What was even more exciting was a ride on 894 all the way to Barmouth, a schoolboy's dream. In those days, this section could provide Dukedogs, Dukes, Cambrian, Dean and 2251 0-6-0s and 45XX tanks.

Mini-Holiday		
Monday 18 May 1952, 311 miles		
Teignmouth	dep	8.25
Paddington	arr	12.15
	dep	5.10
Wolverhampton	arr	8.00
Tuesday 20 May, 244 miles		
Wolverhampton	dep	9.00
Shrewsbury	arr	9.35
	dep	10.35
Moat Lane Junction	arr	12.17
	dep	12.25
Llanidloes	arr	12.42
	dep	1.54
Moat Lane Junction	arr	2.09
	dep	2.45
Brecon	arr	5.24
	dep	6.15
Bargoed	arr	7.55
	dep	8.06
Cardiff General	arr	8.58
Wednesday 21 May, 131 miles		
Cardiff General	dep	12.08
Carmarthen	arr	2.11
	dep	3.20
Aberystwyth	arr	5.54
Thursday 22 May, 323 miles		
Aberystwyth	dep	9.55
Dovey Junction	arr	10.35
	dep	11.10
Barmouth	arr	12.15
	dep	1.12
Ruabon	arr	3.20
	dep	3.52
Shrewsbury	arr	4.27
	dep	5.03
Teignmouth	arr	11.30
Expenses, total £13 1s 3d		
Rail fares	£7	3s 9d
Hotels	£4	0s 6d
Meals &c	£1	11s 10d
Papers, cloakrooms &c		5s 2d

former Cambrian lines, with their long steeply-graded sections and trains of dramatically different loads according to the season and day of the week. With through coaches and connections from two London termini and Midland systems, double-heading involving pulling up to give the second machine a drink, short platforms involving more drawing up, some loops at which passenger trains crossed having only one platform, and awkwardly-sited signalboxes giving signalmen long walks to hand over the token, it was all calculated to go amiss and inevitably did (and still does) on summer Saturdays.

But Great Western trains were always lovable. You could not take your eyes off the green engine, though the benefit of their cleanliness (as the result of burning best Welsh anthracite) was enjoyed in the carriages. You could sit safely in them, unlike those of the former Midland and North Western branches in Wales, without wondering what was happening to your clothes. The carriages were generally of more recent vintage on Great Western than other branches, and not just because the GW built some special branch-line sets and ran the first diesel car fleet, but because – thanks to representations from local dignitaries with weak bladders – there was almost always at least one modernish corridor coach even if the rest of the train were non-corridor. Admittedly one thinks of holiday Wales, Pembrokeshire and Cambrian Coast, where the GW was out to give a good impression, and where through trains from Paddington set the standard. But even on the GWR valley lines there was a cleanliness that seemed to go with a purposefulness – and a universal interest in the photographs adorning all compartments taken by the railway's official photographers in between capturing the latest developments at engine depots and goods yards. It was notable that while railwaymen elsewhere usually regretted the Grouping, most of those who worked for the Welsh companies taken over by the GW welcomed it - if only for the more powerful motive power it brought.

The contrast was nowhere greater than Blaenau Ffestiniog in the years the Festiniog was closed. The GW branch from Bala Junction climbed through spectacular mountain scenery which could be readily enjoyed through the window, open or closed. After surveying the Festiniog's mineral-incline feeders, still bringing down large quantities of slate, mainly then for despatch by the London Midland Region, you walked into an altogether less desirable world at the latter's station. A cloud of sooty dust rose as you threw your bag on the seat, and you quickly became dirty. No proper cleaning had been done it would seem for months, and fleabites next day were hardly surprising. Worst of all, even when through the filthy tunnel, you opened the window at your peril, and certainly could not enjoy the beauties of the Conway Valley through it even after using a quarter of a toilet roll to remove the worst dust.

It was the short-lived North Eastern Region that first realised the commercial value of the new diesel multiple-units and advertised diesel trains in its timetables and brochures in the same way that years before

Great Western from Blaenau. One of Collett's Great Western 0-6-0 pannier tanks built specifically for passenger working, No 7442 of Bala shed (sub to Croes Newydd 84J) makes its homeward way north of Trawsfynydd in July 1954. This wild and mountainous line was built to tap the once prosperous North Wales slate industry at Blaenau Festiniog where it met (but not joined until 1960) the LNWR branch from Llandudno Junction via the Conway Valley and the narrow gauge Festiniog Railway. After closure on 4 January 1960 (28 January for freight) the upper connection was constructed to enabled trains to run to and from the nuclear power station at Trawsfynydd.

Five-Day Runabouts, 1953

Monday, 179½ miles

Teignmouth	dep	9.10
Taunton	arr	10.14
	dep	10.20
Bridgwater	arr	10.41
depart by bus to Glastonbury		
Glastonbury	dep	2.51
Templecombe	arr	3.49
	dep	4.15
Evercreech Junction	arr	4.40
	dep	4.48
Highbridge	arr	5.46
	dep	6.12
Taunton	arr	6.40
	dep	7.10
Teignmouth	arr	8.20

Tuesday, 165 miles

Teignmouth	dep	10.00
Weston-super-Mare	arr	11.52
	dep	1.45
Yatton	arr	2.02
	dep	2.05
Clevedon	arr	2.12
	dep	3.48
Yatton	arr	3.55
	dep	4.00
Weston-super-Mare	arr	4.15
	dep	4.48
Teignmouth	arr	6.40

Wednesday, 202¼ miles

Teignmouth	dep	9.10
Bristol Temple Meads	arr	11.21
	dep	12.00
Bath Spa	arr	12.17
Bath Green Park	dep	2.58
Evercreech Junction	arr	3.56
Walk to Castle Cary		
Castle Cary	dep	5.40
Taunton	arr	6.37
	dep	7.10
Teignmouth	arr	8.20

Thursday, 155¼ miles

Teignmouth	dep	9.10
Taunton	arr	10.14
	dep	11.05
Chard	arr	11.45
	dep	12.05
Chard Junction	arr	12.13
	dep	12.21
Yeovil Junction	arr	12.49
	dep	12.58
Yeovil Town	arr	1.02

continued opposite

Bradshaw had indicated what classes of passengers were carried. Not merely were the seats and windows clean, but you could enjoy a view of the railway itself, forward and back. Especially where the scenery was dull, this gave new fascination to country-train travel. You quickly realised how little of the railway itself you can take in from an ordinary train. And the way passengers compete for the front or back seats on the diesel multiple-units of the 1950s and 1960s shows just how wrong BR is to yield to alleged union pressure in abolishing glass partitions behind driver's compartments on the new generation of diesel units.

So, much though you might regret not having heard steam power fight its way up the bank on slippery rails at Robin Hood's Bay – when leaves added to the hazard even a two-coach train occasionally did not make the summit – you were pleased to have the chance of enjoying most of the North East's secondary and tertiary lines by DMU. Services were more frequent and faster, as well as infinitely more comfortable, than previously, and in addition to cutting the costs dramatically the DMUs attracted back many people who had abandoned rail travel.

On a typical day from Scarborough to Hull, for ever seeing level crossings open in front of the train to Hornsea, by taxi to Withernsea just in time to see the daily freight of six wagons arrive, along the double track (except where one section was removed for use overseas in the *first world war*) back through Botanic Gardens to Hull, and to York, where the North Eastern's general manager, D. S. M. Barrie, was on the platform. The Hornsea and Withernsea lines were under closure threat, there had been a public outcry, and Mr Barrie had ordered a further investigation to see if costs could be sufficiently cut. Of course the lines should have been singled years before, beyond their divergence at Botanic Gardens, and with proper investment one signalbox could have replaced the umpteen at level crossings, allowing the profitable running of commuter and tripper trains. But unthinkable that branch line infrastructure would be sorted out while there was still semaphore signalling on part of the East Coast main line. The branch line cause was hopeless, government legislation, union demands and much more adding nails to the coffin.

If you returned to the North East nearly a quarter of a century later and travelled on the same DMUs over lines still in service, the impression was the same. By then the staff levels had been severely cut, signalling reduced to the barest necessity, but the rest of the world had also moved on, garages and cafes going self-service, department stores cutting their staffs by half, and comparatively the railway thus seemed as wasteful as ever. Hartlepool–Darlington–Bishop Auckland–Darlington–Whitby–Middlesbrough, and never more than a score of passengers on the two-car DMU. And, just as a generation before, inevitably, you were just too late, the refreshment room just having closed, the bookstall shortened its hours, the station just become unstaffed and therefore lacking a lavatory. Some interesting traffic has always just ceased, the man who could tell you the best stories of the great days just retired. Yet the Middlesbrough–Whitby line could so easily have followed the other two routes to Whitby and most of the rest of the branch-line network of the former North Eastern into oblivion, and depressing though continual contraction is, you welcome the occasional service that has been intelligently arranged and promoted, and note that while the traffic may not be large it is ever persistent.

Almost every country railway that has survived has witnessed this persistence, if not some positive revival of business, and now as twenty, thirty or even fifty years ago note that those travelling by train would for the most part be unlikely customers for a bus. They would either not travel at all or do so by car. With such a loyal base of business, what might have happened had more of yesteryear's routes survived? Would Hunstanton and Minehead have seen increasing business, as have intermediate stations served by the frequent, fast trains with mini-

continued.		
Yeovil Pen Mill	dep	3.59
Taunton	arr	5.07
	dep	5.30
Teignmouth	arr	6.40
Friday, 40¼ miles		
Teignmouth	dep	10.00
Newton Abbot	arr	10.11
	dep	10.32
Heathfield	arr	10.42
	dep	10.45
Exeter St David's	arr	11.40
	dep	12.05
Teignmouth	arr	1.27

Rail fares £2 16s 6d or 678d for 742¾ miles

FESTINIOG RAILWAY - BLAENAU.

Meeting of the Gauges. A local postcard issued in 1936 and postmarked 3 November shows the railway scene at Blaenau Festiniog with both standard and narrow gauge trains. At the top is an ex LNWR 18in goods 0-6-0 (not yet on the duplicate list and carrying a cast smokebox numberplate) about to depart with a Llandudno Junction train via the Conway Valley branch. Next to the engine is an observation car, one of three built by the LNWR and one of which survives preserved by the Bluebell Railway. Below 0-4-0 + 0-4-0 double Fairlie tank Taliesin takes a Festiniog Railway train Portmadoc bound. Both lines are still there today with the Festiniog as one of Britain's premier tourist lines.

Suffolk Branch Line. The Great Eastern Railway's Holden designed 0-6-0s dating from 1893 and designated Class J15 by the LNER were contenders for the longevity stakes and could be found on most East Anglian country lines ten years into nationalisation, generally very dirty indeed. No exception to this rule is No 65467 of Framlingham shed (sub to Ipswich 32B), fitted with a windshield on the tender, seen leaving Marlesford station for Wickham Market on 25 May 1951 with the 12.48pm mixed train. The coaches are former GE corridor brake third and composite.

Great Eastern Junction. The very last 2-4-0 tender locomotives to run in Britain were Holden's Class E4s, all stationed in East Anglia. One of the branches adorned by these little engines in 1952 was that from Fordham Junction to Mildenhall, trains running from Cambridge. The last survivor of the class (No 62785, now preserved in the National Collection) ended its days as Cambridge (31A) pilot. No 62783 comes off the branch on to the main line in April passing an unknown GER J17 class 0-6-0 waiting at the bracket signal.

buffets between Aberdeen and Inverness, a route that once seemed on the point of closure? What could not have been achieved with a modicum of investment, common sense and drive?

But such thoughts have always been only one of the smaller strands of interest in the exploration of rural Britain by train. Always the railway winding smoothly forward along its own narrow, tightly-fenced in world, yet very much part of the greater scene, has induced satisfaction, joy, and greater understanding of what a land we live in – one of the few parts of the world generally to have been positively improved by the intervention of man. Sometimes there were special trains carrying crowds of local people to fairs and markets; other times specials over normally-closed routes in the company of fellow enthusiasts. All occasions, even noisy closure celebrations, had their pleasure, but it is the ordinary days of lone travelling by all-stations trains that most live in the memory. Exhausting but fun days like Cheltenham–Swindon Town via the M&SWJ–Swindon Junction–Kemble–Cirencester–Kemble–Tetbury–Kemble–Chalford (change to auto-car)–Gloucester–Kemble, more pleasurable than seeing the same hours' worth of famous films. That had to be a Saturday with the lunch time train from Swindon to Cirencester, a through service which switched platforms and gave time to buy cheap day tickets to both branch termini. At Cirencester a quick walk round the town and time to discover a copy of the 1865 Great Western rule book for six old pence. Less time to see picturesque Tetbury, but a promise from the guard that he would delay departure by five minutes. The same guard shouting to an empty countryside as the train ground to a halt on the return because of an open door: 'I can see

Reincarnation: In their latter days the Highland Jones Goods 4-6-0s were regular performers over the line to Kyle of Lochalsh, but all had gone before the second world war. Fortunately, the LMS had preserved No 103 at St Rollox works, and from 1959 the Scottish Region of BR with the encouragement of its then general manager James Ness, restored this engine and the Caledonian single wheeler No 123 to full working order for special trains. This, however, was something different as No 103, seen here at Achterneed station on 20 May 1960, was working the 5.45pm regular passenger trains from Inverness to the Kyle in connection with the BBC TV Railway Roundabout series. It worked back next morning taking the mixed train as far as Dingwall then double heading a Stanier Class 5 over the main line back to Inverness.

Opposite:
Trains crossing at Glenfinnan on the West Highland Extension amidst the splendour of the mountains overlooking Loch Shiel. All the activities of the country railway are here with the engine of the Glasgow – Mallaig train at the platform taking water while the guard supervises the unloading of parcels. In the background a Mallaig – Glasgow train, double headed by a North British Glen 4-4-0 and a Gresley K2 Loch class 2-6-0, coast into the loop.

Overleaf:
Two Glens from Fort William. On 8 and 9 May 1959 the ex North British Railway Glen class 4-4-0s once again held their own over West Highland metals working the 5.45am out from Glasgow and returning from Fort William with the 2.56pm. This was the last time that the class was to run regular service trains over the line; The engines were specially rostered in connection with the BBC Railway Roundabout TV series. Nos 62496 Gen Loy and 62471 Glen Falloch pause for water at Crianlarich Upper from 5.17pm (booked time) to 5.23pm on 8 May. It was a day to remember, captured in this unique colour photograph.

you. Don't you fool me. Come here at once, jumping out like that . . . I'm no fool; I know you're not there. The door just swung open, damn you.' And surprisingly heavy traffic down the Stroud Valley where the auto-train serving halts by numerous old woollen mills is still missed.

Going away from the railway to explore new towns and villages was part of the justification for using it. After all, once all distant visitors to Wells Cathedral came by train, difficult though the Somerset & Dorset made it to get there from sister Bath. Tintern (where the station is preserved as a little oasis of former civilisation to which many pay as regular pilgrimages as to the Abbey itself), Bolton Abbey, Robin Hood's Bay, Symonds' Yat and dozens of other beauty spots had their own railway adjunct provided to a suitable standard. Once the afternoon train arriving at any picturesque and historic village would bring a group of passengers ready to 'do' it. They would quickly disperse, visiting cliffs or lake, church and country house or garden, perhaps recognising each other and talking for the first time in the tea room and having a much more social return journey, swapping notes, guide books and hints about how to make the best of other visitor spots. Most moorland lines carried hikers out in the morning and back at night, perhaps by a different route, special walkers' tickets offering a wide choice of opportunities and giving thousands of people their first encouragement to take cross-country trips, some even involving a ferry crossing as between Exminster and Topsham.

Eating was another important part of exploration by train. The railways themselves generally fed you well. Occasionally, such as down the Somerset & Dorset or Midland & Great Northern, through glorious West Highland scenery or perhaps for a short section between junctions by the Cambrian Coast Express, there was the luxury of a restaurant car. Was the food really as good as it lingers in the memory? Full lunches were served in the restaurants at many major stations, while there were still well over thirty railway-owned hotels, most of them part of the fabric of stations from which country trains or at least country connections started. Even where the railway was not owner, there was frequently a special entry for passengers (as through an extended greenhouse at Keswick) to hotels that had been built in celebration of the arrival of trains last century. Scotland was especially strong on good hotels beside stations, the 1894 Murray's *Handbook for Travellers in Scotland* still being reliably useful in the 1950s and 1960s. It naturally assumed you were touring by train and was more helpful to those doing so than more recent publications, telling you how to catch the best views, which hotels to use and which to miss – only the steamship services on salt and freshwater lochs having by then been substantially curtailed. And at almost every junction and town of importance, there was the welcoming, always warm refreshment room. Never did orangeade quench the thirst so thoroughly as in that on the station on the marshes at Dovey Junction, or a decade earlier (when they first came off the ration) biscuits hit the spot so satisfactorily as during an early-morning change at Bodmin Road.

What extraordinary value it all was! Until well into the 1960s, if you took advantage of some cheap tickets, you were upset to pay more than an old penny a mile while, even including one restaurant car or other full-service meal, catering could be done in style for about half a pound per day. For that 1d and 10s you were treated royally, for at least half the miles had a compartment to yourself, were greeted enthusiastically everywhere, and found all station facilities generous if not ludicrously extravagant. Even if you were too mean to buy a newspaper from the bookstall, there would be plenty of free (if mainly advertising) literature to be picked up. The scenery was gratis.

Everyone had his favourite journey in the repertoire of memories. The writer recalls arriving off a sleeping car at Perth in the summer of 1962, Murray's *Handbook* and blue-covered Scottish Region timetable as guides, working out the itinerary off the cuff. No other passengers alighted from the Inverness restaurant-car express at Ballinluig, or travelled in the single coach hauled by a two-year-old diesel along the picturesque banks of the Tay (the guard pointing out the best fishing reaches) to Aberfeldy, where the stationmaster agreed to delay the return departure by five minutes to give time for exploration on foot. At a pinch there could be a bit longer, he explained, though that would shorten the guard's lunch break at the intermediate station of Grandtully, where the 'mixed' train was allowed 12 minutes lest shunting had to be performed. It never did, so the guard used the time to cross the yard and eat at home while the train waited at the platform. Back at Ballinluig, the diesel shunted round its single coach and prepared for another trip (without any passengers) while a second lightly-loaded restaurant car express for Inverness shot through, less than an hour after the first. Beside the fire in the porters' room, while a third such train was awaited, a ganger boasted: 'You couldn't have done what you've just done last year.' Services were much improved for the 1962 season. Only lacking were the passengers. Only nine partook the fine lunch in the restaurant car of the third train. A fresh fruit salad was chopped up for all to see; 'Don't carry a can-opener,' said the chief steward. And now a bird's eye view of the Pass of Killiecrankie, thanks to Murray's *Handbook* for catching the right angle, over the summit at 1484ft and down the Pass of Druimuachdar, 'by far the wildest scene through which any rly. passes in this country,' and calling but doing little business at almost all stations on to Aviemore, (where the restaurant car came off) and in an otherwise empty front carriage via Nairn and the original coastal entrance to Inverness. Even though services were still being 'improved', it was obvious it could not last. But it was not to be missed while it was there.

Opposite above:
Country Restaurant Car. The afternoon Inverness – Euston train waits at Aviemore station from 6.38pm to 6.52pm on Whit Monday 1950. It is headed by two ex LMS Class 5 4-6-0s – both somewhat grimy – but with the old company lettering still decipherable on the pilot engine. The third class diner is laid for tea and is a standard LMS part kitchen car. An open composite next to the train engine provides first class restaurant seating. Note that there is only one 'No Smoking' bay. Behind the first coach is an ex Caledonian Pickersgill 4-4-0.

Kelvedon and Tollesbury (Light Railway)–(One class only)

M			Week Days only	
			am	pm
—	**Kelvedon**.............. dep		10.10	5.48
½	Feering Halt		10.13	5.51
2¾	Inworth		10.20	5.58
3½	Tiptree		10.29	6.07
4	Tolleshunt Knights............		10.33	6.11
6½	Tolleshunt D'Arcy.............		10.45	6.23
8½	**Tollesbury** .... arr		10.50	6.28

M		Week Days only		
		am	pm	pm
—	**Tollesbury** .... dep	8.30	12.50	6.37
2	Tolleshunt D'Arcy.............	8.38	1.05	6.50
4½	Tolleshunt Knights............	8.44	1.11	6.56
5	Tiptree	8.54	1.35	7.07
5¾	Inworth	8.57	1.38	7.10
8	Feering Halt	9.05	1.46	7.18
8½	**Kelvedon**.................. arr	9.09	1.50	7.22

E Except Saturdays
S Saturdays only

Tickets (single only) and Local Tickets are issued on the train

LNER Timetable, 1946

Opposite below:
Cornish Local. An ex LSWR O2 class 0-4-4 tank runs alongside the River Camel near Grogley Halt with the 4.40pm from Padstow to Bodmin North on 10 September 1960.

TRAINS IN THE MARCHES

THREE COCKS AND THE HEREFORD, HAY & BRECON

One of the more isolated junctions in the Welsh Marches was Three Cocks, where the tracks of the old Hereford, Hay & Brecon Railway (later the Midland) met the Cambrian from Moat Lane. Six miles south west was Talyllyn Junction leading to Brecon or Dowlais on the Brecon & Merthyr Railway.

Apart from the local villagers no one in their right senses alighted at Three Cocks but it is not hard to imagine Edwardian gentry being met at the station in the cold half light of winter; beyond the booking office door stood the old horse cab with its musty dim interior smelling of hay and Bedford cord, with its roof reinforced and railed to carry the heavy luggage. In those days the Midland trains were smart in an immaculate livery of crimson lake – a very different and much purer colour than the maroon of later LMS years. It has been recorded officially that there was no difference in the colour but in practice there were clearly differences, possibly because of the preparation which gave the Midland colour far more depth. But even in the 1950s Three Cocks was a pleasant spot for the enthusiast to tarry awhile, one never quite knew what motive power might turn up, for a change had taken place and the old Hereford, Hay & Brecon was part of the Western Region. Sometimes the Hereford trains had L&Y 0-6-0s sent south on being replaced by more modern power, sometimes ex Midland Class 3 0-6-0s or even Great Western Dean Goods. The Cambrian line was the perquisite of Dean Goods and Cambrian 0-6-0s until the coming of the more modern standard small 2-6-0s.

The Hereford, Hay & Brecon Railway was originally a Midland inspired incursion to Welsh territory hopefully to Swansea, but it

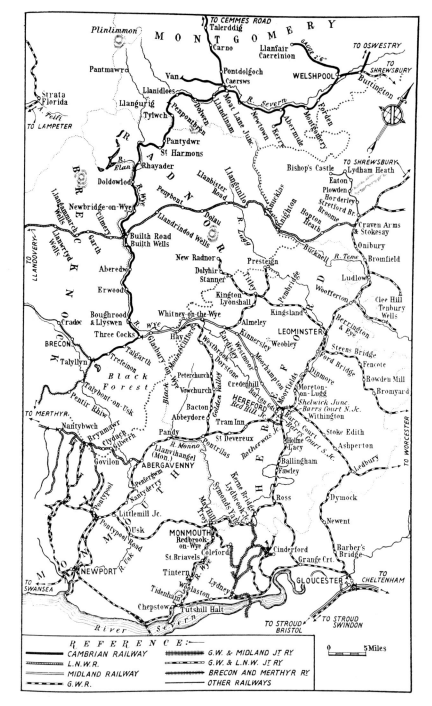

reckoned without the Great Western over whose metals it had secured running powers from Worcester. The Great Western not only refused the Midland access to its Barr's Court station at Hereford but blocked, with an engine and some wagons, the connecting spur which made through running possible, relegating the unfortunate Midland to its own station at Moorfields from which the only connection to the Great Western was via a junction at Barton involving a reversal. So the

Hereford, Hay & Brecon section became and remained a quiet backwater, its modest trains running with their complements of market-going farmers and their wives from the Welsh border; in later years Midland HH&B trains were grudgingly admitted to Barr's Court via a bay platform. Through trains to Swansea ran until 1 January 1933. There was even a through coach from Birmingham via Worcester, Malvern and Hereford until 1916.

THREE COCKS JUNCTION

(i) Cambrian 0-6-0 (Beyer Peacock 4-03 of the first of the large Belpaire goods) No 887 leaves for Brecon in July 1950. It carries an Oswestry (89A) plate but was probably sub shedded at Moat Lane. This class was soon to become redundant with the advent of new Class 2 2-6-0s and all engines were gone by 1954. Three Cocks was the junction for the old Hereford, Hay and Brecon line and the Cambrian from Moat Lane (on the main line to Aberystwyth).

(ii) Midland Class 3F 0-6-0 No 43491 of Hereford (85C) recently incorporated into the Western Region heads the 12.44pm Hereford to Brecon train in the summer of 1950, the last year before the introduction of ex Lancashire and Yorkshire 0-6-0s displaced from the North West.

Swing Bridge. The Severn Bridge (Severn & Wye Joint Railway) linking Sharpness (MR) with Lydney (S&W), on 1 November 1952. Built in 1879 it was 4,162ft long with 21 spans. In later days it was incorporated in a relief route when repairs were undertaken on the Severn Tunnel but carried heavy weight restrictions. Taken from Sharpness the photograph shows the signalbox which also controlled the swing bridge section across the Berkeley Canal – seen in the bottom foreground. The signal on the right controlled the movements of ships on the canal as they passed from Gloucester to the open sea.

Severn & Wye Junction. Lydney (S&WR) on 29 July 1950 with Wolverhampton built 0-6-0 pannier tank No 2080 of 85B (Lydney – sub shed to Gloucester) heading for Lydney Town – the truncated remains of the Severn & Wye passenger service – with a train from Berkeley Road. On the right is the locomotive shed; the stock is composed of two brake thirds. Lydney Town closed on 26 October 1960 because of the demise of the Severn Bridge.

Working the goods to Stranraer in the 1920s

Hardly anything seems to have been written about the work of the Drummond 0-6-0s, and to understand Drummond engines properly it is necessary to know the conditions of their advent in 1913. I fear that by 1912 the G&SW had become a somewhat pharisaical line, which went its own way and gave thanks that it was not as other railways. Of the working of other railways, the average Sou'-West man was then about as ignorant as he was of the habits of the Kamchatkans. I remember that we got a new goods guard who, it was darkly rumoured, had come from the NB. We gazed upon that poor soul with a wild surmise. I think we imagined he possibly had a tail. No, the Sou'-West, and Jimmy Manson – just gone out in a blaze of glory with those splendid superheater 4-6-0s, 128 and 129 – the Sou'-West, of 18¼in cylinders and Stirling steam reversers and steam sand and right-hand drive – that was the *World*, and no other could exist.

So crash into our Utopia came Peter Drummond – 'P.D.,' with his left-hand drive and his marine big-ends, his dry sand and his Drummond steam reversers, his Weir pumps and his tender heater – pah! Need it be wondered that there was opposition and resentment and that the 0-6-0s, as pioneers of the new order, got an indifferent reputation? Certainly they heated a lot, and compared to the nimble Manson 0-6-0s were probably clumsy and sluggish. It was not until the LMS, who had been quietly replacing marine with cottered big-ends, decreed that the loads be increased that drivers suddenly began to realise that the 'P.D.' 0-6-0s were very sound, powerful big engines, capable of a good day's hard work. By then they had largely been dispersed from main line express goods. Some were at Ayr for the Waterside minerals; some at Corkerhill (Glasgow) for secondary work on the main and coast roads. Probably the hardest work of their career was performed with Corkerhill men on the 1.00am goods, College (Glasgow) to Stranraer, returning the same evening on the 6.35pm Stranraer to College.

The 1.00am was inaugurated about 1924 and was the direct descendant of the 'Midnicht'. This train left Eglinton Street, Glasgow, in the late evening for Stranraer, and called at Falkland Junction about the Witching Hour for a pilot. This was a grand job for some of the young Ayr fire-eaters, for once over Maybole it was thunder-and-turf for Girvan in a desperate attempt to keep ahead of the train and keep these couplings tight through the dips. Glasgow and Stranraer men worked the train night about.

But whereas the Midnicht had contented itself with a train of 30 to 40 wagons, the 1.00am loaded up to 70, and that made all the difference. It wasn't the *hauling* of the load; it was the keeping of the couplings tight through the dips between Maybole and Girvan. If you reached the bottom of a dip with couplings hanging slack, then whenever you struck the upgrade you got a 'rug,' and a rug is a big whaling tearing jerk that just about puts you out through the front window, and ten to one you break a coupling or a drawbar. So night after night they were breaking-away on the 1.00am. There was an old miner at Bargany who used to walk to work along the railway. 'Boys,' he said, 'the line was busy this mornin', I steppit off t'let the goods go by, an then I steppit on again, an' I near got run doon by anither goods. It had nae engine on it,' he explained in parenthesis.

The golden rule was to come over Maybole as slowly as possible and gradually increase your engine's speed as the speed of the train increased. But with variations of crews on the Corkerhill train engines and the Ayr pilots, you would always get somebody who would come storming over Maybole at 35 miles an hour, and by the time you got to Kilkerran a couple of 5Xs couldn't have kept ahead of them. But they did their best. Jimmy Sewell used to roll up his sleeves and 'pump' the regulator of his big Drummond and shout 'They say you – shouldna open the – second valve on a – Drummond. By hokers if she – had *three* valves I'd hae them a' open!'

The guards did their bit too. Old Johnny Maule used to have a brake-stick with which he would screw up his brake-handle till the gear threatened to snap. Jock Geddes had a length of point-rodding, which he would stick on the brake-handle and tramp round like a sailor at a capstan. Then the van floors took fire from the heavy braking, and the man on the back end would sometimes reach Girvan of a morning uncertain if he'd been hired as a guard or a fire-brigade. It was gloriously exciting, but not all profitable. Then one morning came a bold unknown experimenter. He forced his will upon all, came nearly to a stand at Kilkerran, picked up his couplings from rest, and reached Girvan intact, with little time lost. Others followed suit and so, very simply, most of the 1.00am's troubles were cured. Not all – there are other snags besides Kilkerran, but a breakaway is now a very rare occurrence. How much better it is, but we regret we shall not see again those wild charges down Crosshill bank. – From an article by David L. Smith in *The Railway Magazine*.

3

A DAY IN THE LIFE OF A COUNTRY STATION

**Signalling of Trains
Conveying Special Horse or
Pigeon Traffic**
Where instructions are given in
the Special Train Notices for
trains conveying special horse or
pigeon traffic and composed of
coaching stock to be signalled by
the bell signal of 5 beats (given 3
pause 1 pause 1), such trains must
take precedence of all other trains
except express passenger trains,
breakdown van trains going to
clear the line, light engines going
to assist disabled trains, or fire
brigade trains.
*S&DJR Appendix to Working
Timetables*, 1933

*Pick Up Freight. A sight now
disappeared from the railway scene
is the stopping goods picking up and
setting down wagons at local stations
and sidings. LMS Ivatt Class 2
2-6-0 No 46482 of Tweedmouth
(52D) moves on to the wagons
collected from Tweedmouth
marshalling yard at Coldstream
station before running to Kelso on
1 June 1962. This was the 7.42am
working from Tweedmouth to Kelso
and back. Coldstream was on the
NER line from Tweedmouth to
Sprouston and was the junction for
the 1887 line southwards to
Alnwick. The NBR had a branch
from St Boswells on the Waverley
Route to Kelso; this line and the one
from Tweedmouth made an end on
junction between Kelso and
Sprouston.*

Most of them started coming to life early though slowly. Except where locomotives were stabled, the first man on duty was usually the early-turn signalman, perhaps arriving by bicycle to open up the box for the down freight, whose wagons would be ready for unloading at the large town at the branch's end by breakfast time, or switching in for the first passenger on shorter lines with less emphasis on freight. The first minutes naturally varied dramatically according to the time of year and weather. In winter oil lamps had to be lit, the embers of the fire left by the late turn man stirred to kindle sticks for the new blaze. Perhaps a dog to settle, a note to read from the lateman, with a request for a half hour's swop of duty, the kettle to put on, tea and shaving, fetching up coal and cleaning up the box to be fitted in . . . actual signalling was only a detail, though switching in the box and recording the opening moment on which the payment of overtime would be calculated was always first priority.

At many stations the signalman had to book passengers on the first passenger train, and to handle heavy parcels traffic arriving by it. Few branches had separate parcels or newspaper trains and from the 1920s the early-morning distribution of mail and especially newspapers was increasingly by road from the nearest main-line town, though other mail and weekly and monthly magazines went by rail. The first or second up train was often the busiest, bringing the stationmaster on duty (a separate booking clerk only at larger places) on Mondays when weekly seasons were sold and extra passengers, such as school children who boarded away from home, were carried.

Strange though it might sound, the normal rhythm of a country station's life only started after the first trains had passed on their way. Then attention could be concentrated on cleaning up, trimming and refuelling the signal oil lamps, answering the telephones, dealing with customers in the goods shed and yard and the parcels office – and that everlasting paperwork that was the bane of almost every country railwayman's career. Way-bills, timesheets, returns of ticket sales, letters to and from customers and district office (at most stations handwritten, the typewriter age being only grudgingly accepted even in the 1960s). Who needed trains? Of course they provided the links with the outside world that provided the country station's raison d'être, but what a nuisance they could be interrupting the work flow.

The stationmaster had to postpone his inspection of the junction box which, not being attached to a station, came under his jurisdiction. The porter realised he would not have time to finish his current piece of paperwork before wheeling out the parcels ready to go. The signalman who had a hundred and one genuine or spurious reasons to be away from his box had to leave the ladies' waiting-room lavatory half cleaned in order to get back to accept the train from the next station. At the busy, well-run country station, especially in the mornings, there was more time to stand easy and gossip when a train was a-coming than after it had gone and everyone returned to their jobs.

An interruption of a more permanent kind was the arrival of the day's main goods train. Even on branches with several daily freights each way, one was allocated time to do the main station work. The station truck would grind to a halt outside the parcels office and those heavier items consigned goods for cheapness would be thrown out. Some wagons might have to be detached or attached before the train ultimately went

Sheep Special. Kerry, the terminus of the short branch from Abermule on 23 September 1955. The engine, No 2538 an Oswestry engine (89A) is the last survivor of the famous Dean goods 0-6-0s and the only class used on the line for these Tuesday, Thursday and Saturday only trains; they were allowed forty-five minutes for the almost four mile run with a ruling grade out of Abermule of 1 in 75. With no other traffic the branch was worked by a wooden train staff and one engine in steam. It is indicative of the agricultural prosperity of the region that these three trains a week were still de rigeur even at this period. Passenger traffic ceased as long ago as 9 February 1931 which is hardly surprising as the station was a good mile from Kerry village. The layout shows a once busy line complete with its small shed. The Kerry branch closed to all traffic on 1 May 1956.

on its way, probably after the engine had taken a copious drink, and fifty-fifty had run round its train which would also have been overtaken by a passenger. But the core of the operation was shunting the yard, trundling endlessly up and down the headshunt as wagons were sorted. The goods manager, usually only a clerk, generally acted as conductor, perhaps holding things up while an extra wagon was loaded and labelled, directing the man with the shunting pole who dextrously coupled and uncoupled the chains. Who he was varied. At some stations a goods porter spent a couple of dangerous hours daily with his pole; at smaller places the guard or almost anyone might oblige even the stationmaster himself to keep his hand in, officially or otherwise. Even in a yard of five roads where only a score of wagons would normally be seen, the daily shunt could take an hour, every wagon in the yard and on the train being exactly in the preferred position.

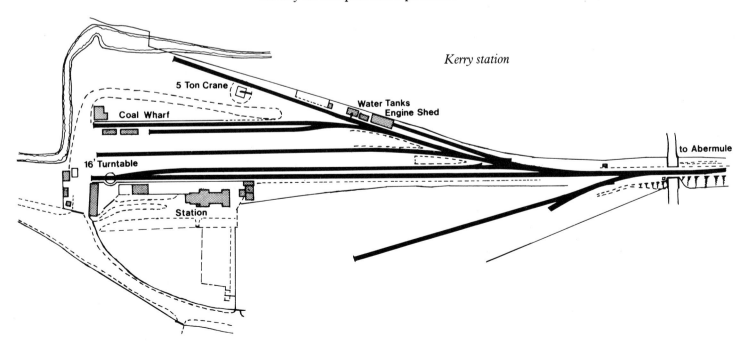

Kerry station

5 Ton Crane

Coal Wharf

Water Tanks
Engine Shed

16' Turntable

Station

to Abermule

In the same way that most drivers stopped their trains well down the platform, better ready for the exit, so most 'shore' railwaymen had the urge to get on. 'You're on top of it or it's on top of you' was the attitude. New recruits who wanted to delay cleaning the gents or applying more whitewash to the platform edge soon had to learn better. By noon most routine tasks, including the daily balancing of the books and return of cash in the pouch for district office had been accomplished. If district office had any occasion to telephone or even to send the rat catcher on his tour of inspection, it would most likely have happened by now. If a local big-wig thought of needing a special vehicle, or if the stationmaster felt he should order extra horse boxes or cattle trucks – or even a special train – for an upcoming agricultural event, that also would probably be done by noon or at least half past. Even the school trunks for the start of term a couple of days ahead would have arrived. The lengthman would have covered his section, perhaps two sections, one on foot the other by motorised trolley, which might be taken off the track at a hut equipped with intermediate token.

Lunch time had its distinct aura. Lucky were the stations where the train service respected a siesta. The height of many a stationmaster's day was his leisurely lunch at the station pub, where of course he was a big-

Cross Country Link. An ex LNWR Webb 2-4-2 5ft 6in radial tank No 6748 from Rhyl shed (7D) on loan to Denbigh, blows off in Ruthin station during May 1947, the last year of the LMS. It heads the 3.45pm train from Denbigh which has just arrived – the signal at the rear of the train is still off. This was an LNWR attempt to tap traffic from the Great Western's route from Ruabon to the Cambrian at Dolgelly – scarcely a paying proposition at its best. It is a very North Western scene, locomotive, coaches, station buildings and the tall double arm starting signal.

Farthest North. Thurso station and yard in June 1951. This photograph, taken at Britain's northernmost station shows a typical market town terminus – small covered passenger station with a single island platform, signalbox, goods and cattle loading platform, locomotive shed (coal wagons outside), turntable, and general freight sidings. The engine is an ex Highland Railway Small Ben class 4-4-0 No 54399 Ben Wyvis fitted with an ex Caledonian boiler and, sadly, a stovepipe chimney. It is later to take the 3.35pm passenger train (coaches just visible in the platform) to Georgemas Junction for connection with the Inverness to Wick service headed by an ex LMS Class 5 4-6-0.

Herefordshire Idyll. Steens Bridge station, the penultimate stop for trains running over the Bromyard branch from Worcester to Leominster situated on the LNWR/GWR North to West line. A GWR railcar waits for time with the 4.30pm ex Worcester shown in the timetable as '3rd class only, limited accommodation'. This was a fine example of a Great Western country station, basic but still providing passenger comforts – for example a coal fire in the waiting room in winter. With time on their hands between trains the staff took a pride in their station – they were not only gardeners but topiarists too. The section from Bromyard to Leominster closed on 19 September 1952 and that from Worcester to Bromyard on 7 September 1964. The photograph was taken in the summer of 1952.

wig, more important and sophisticated than all, since his better-educated rivals in village and small town hierarchy such as the schoolmaster, parson and doctor would be very unlikely to be there. At the signalbox, the early turn man departed with his dog's tail wagging, leaving all spick and span for the colleague he for ever met briefly at this time but none other. He might have started up the engine to pump water into the tower tank supplying the locomotive water columns, sent a couple of churns to the next station or junction signalbox without a supply, and even despatched a pint of cider and the morning paper to a remote colleague. All such things were normally morning tasks.

In the afternoon most trains – and there were fewer of them – generally did little business and caused less interruption. There might though be a couple of baskets of racing pigeons to release – clear of overhead wires and not if it were stormy – with the release time noted on the basket's label. Pigeons were often sent this way by fanciers for training flights, out by train, fly home, with the empty basket returning by train. If a down goods had a few trucks to drop off, they would be left in a position cleared by the morning shunt, or put into their final place by the next morning's. But it could of course be that the afternoon brought the first crossing of passenger trains. On most branch lines of any length, both platforms (or even both tracks where one of them did not serve a platform) were used together only a couple of times a day, signalboxes then thoroughly coming into their own as most levers were used within a few minutes of each other. Especially where the signalman also had to collect tickets and help take parcels over to the far platform, even these few minutes of intense activity were apt to be so disliked that truth about one train's position would be slightly warped in an effort to move the 'crossing' one box up or down the line. But some signalmen loved the furious activity because the passengers of both trains could

Cornish Shed. Small wheeled Great Western Prairie tank No 5557 of St Blazey shed (83E) resting at Moorswater on the Looe branch on 15 March 1960. The time is 12.40pm and the crew are having lunch in the van: at 1.15pm they climbed back to Liskeard. Just hidden by the van is the famous 'loo' on the Looe (River), which used the old firebox from the Liskeard & Caradon Railway locomotive, Caradon. *This is one of the Cornish branch lines to escape the axe; it is still open for passenger trains but has been closed for freight since 4 November 1963.*

Overtaxed

Two things that especially disturbed the equanimity of life on the country railway were the non-arrival of the signalman on early turn and traffic so dense that consultations had to be held to prevent every movement being blocked by the one before.

The Midland & South Western Junction from Cheltenham to Southampton suffered from both when heavily pressed with freight traffic in the second world war. A queue of southbound freights and an odd passenger were held up because the signalman at a wayside crossing station overslept one winter's morning when a motorcyclist despatched to the rescue was held up by ice.

But more serious was the delay when five trains on a layout of a simple loop and a short refuge siding got themselves so entangled that nothing could move until something else had. Many were the rumours of such stalemate. That stalemate could indeed happen was proved on an enthusiasts' excursion along a Cornish china clay branch, which involved dropping steeply downhill with a reversal at a dead end, Indian mountain style. Four times the train was broken into the available siding space, only for the guard to discover there was no way forward. Eventually, to catch a main line train, one of the enthusiasts had to jump into the road and hail a lift. 'Excuse me, my train up there is so late that I wonder if you could take me to St Austell station', he asked. The prominent Cornishman stopped did not know there was a clay line behind the bank and asked what on earth his would-be passenger meant about the train being delayed.

Many stations had occasional times when every inch of track was occupied and trains had to be split in two for stowage or tails backed down refuge sidings over *continued opposite*

witness how important a job they were doing ringing out bell codes, picking the correct levers and exchanging single-line staffs or tokens, and because two trains at once meant longer interludes.

While the goods office and drivers of the goods delivery lorries continued working, if at a reduced pace, on normal days the signalman now had time to garden or paint a bicycle while the stationmaster paid calls more for social than business reasons. But depending on the season and the local crops and the time of the up teatime passenger or parcels special, if there were one, the station might now have been the destination of a whole variety of empty vehicles ready to collect perishables for the cities. Such business was as seasonal as the running of fertiliser specials, but almost every station contributed something: fruit, mushrooms or early vegetables, flowers, day-old chicks, rabbits. Because what was picked one day was for sale the next, it had to be late afternoon or early evening traffic. It often meant hard, long work – but work that self-evidently led to the railway with its national wage scales seeming to be a more generous employer in country than in city. Sometimes there would be a queue of horse and motor vehicles waiting to deposit their produce, and every barrow would be loaded and out on the platform by the time the train with its empties came. Great was the relief when all was on board, and the last significant number of passengers for the day booked and away.

Now an idyllic peace would descend between trains. The goods office shut shop, and at most one other man (porter or stationmaster) would be on duty beside the signalman. Only occasionally would the telephone ring or someone call to collect a parcel. There might be a couple of trains down from the junction in sharp succession, one bringing home the children attending school or college in the nearest big town or city, the other a few passengers from London plus a few workers going home. Then very little until the last trains passed each way. These might include an up freight non-stop over the branch, or an empty stock or even an excursion train if the line served a tourist area, but their passage gave minimal work.

What memories of the last train! The station bus had long been parked for the night and anyone meeting someone (and you were someone if you arrived by the last train) had to drive, or more likely cycle or walk, perhaps being asked by the signalman into his box to keep warm and pass the time of night. Why was it always the last train that was late? One of many answers, of course, is that there were none to follow and so connections had to be maintained with late-running main-line expresses. Usually only a handful of passengers got off, hardly anyone on. Those arriving included the occasional person completing a long journey from the other half of Britain, and especially on Saturdays the fish-and-chippers and cinema goers. No old ladies needing help with their heavy baggage.

Token exchanged, tickets collected, the signalman gave 2 pause 1, train out of section, on the bell to his colleague next up the line followed by his 7-5-5 code indicating he was closing down. In a few minutes the

man the other side who had just acknowledged train entering section would be doing the same. The few minutes were used stowing away any parcels, locking up, extinguishing the platform lights, setting the road for the first train next day, sorting tickets, dousing the fire and putting the cycle clips on. Two pause one. Out from the cosy box which has regulated the passage of trains serving the countryside's most important trading post into the crisp air.

Of course it changed a lot from place to place and time to time. Summer Saturdays brought extra activity to large parts of the system, seasonal extras running to even small resorts and also on many inland branches that could be strung together to form alternative routes (indeed had probably originally been promoted as such) to relieve pressures especially at key junctions. Sunday school specials and livestock specials (sometimes loaded late into the evening after a particularly busy cattle or sheep fair) were once seen almost everywhere.

Milk sent by churns used to bring evening activity to thousands of stations, but from the 1920s the creation of centralised creameries supplied by road vehicles generally meant there were regular milk tanker movements or no milk went by train at all. It was indeed when the churns began leaving local farms by road, and the London papers came by road, albeit they had left London by train, that the days of the country station became numbered. The 1939–45 war prolonged things. Not only was it hard to get petrol, but coal retained a grip over agricultural and horticultural economies and everything else changed less rapidly in wartime. Hitler in effect put the clock back. Thus many branches that in continuing 1930s conditions would surely have lost at

Coaling Up. Hayling Island station on 3 May 1953 with ex LB&SCR 0-6-0 Terrier tank No 32677 of Fratton shed (71D). No sophisticated facilities here, just a sleeper platform and a couple of shovels. But the engine is clean and in lined-out black, complete with Salter spring safety valves. Note the pre-grouping signals. The Hayling Island branch closed to all traffic on 4 November 1963.

continued
hand-locked points to allow crossing. But it was again war time that brought the most prolonged exceptional pressures, though the record for congestion probably dates from the first and not the second world war – on the Highland line to the Far North serving the British fleet.

Military pressures often made themselves felt in Ireland, too, but here it has usually been special traffic of a more peaceable nature – people and horses going to races, and pilgrimage specials.

Camp Coach. There could scarcely be a better place for a railway camping coach than Gara Bridge – beautiful countryside, river bathing and fishing plus good local farm produce ensured that. The old Great Western Railway was a believer in this form of holiday, after all it not only made certain that the occupants travelled to this accommodation by rail but often provided a few perks for the staff as well. Certainly this party of schoolboys was enjoying itself in August 1959. The coach is No W9925W.

Light, Frail, and Bulky Packages
Packages of a light frail nature, or such as are bulky in proportion to their weight, such as Paste-board Boxes of Light Millinery or Feathers, Stuffed Birds and Animals in permanent cases, packed in boxes or other receptacles, Stags' Heads, Picture Frames, Marble Clocks, packed in cases, Light Furniture packed, Violins, Banjos, Guitars, Mandolins, and other similar Musical Instruments packed, Brass Musical Instruments unpacked, Photographic Cameras, Bottles of Medicine in packages, Hampers containing Bottles of Essence for use of Confectioners, packed and addressed 'Glass with Care,' Electric Light Lamps (ordinary small), Wood Patterns for Castings (unpacked), and Parcels containing Brittle Articles, such as Glass, China or Porcelain – are charged 50 per cent more at Company's Risk, and 25 per cent, more than the ordinary Parcels Rate when sent at Owner's Risk; and a Risk Note must be signed when the articles are carried at Owner's Risk.
GWR Parcels & Goods Arrangements, 1914

least their passenger service by the end of the 1940s in fact lived to enjoy their best services ever in the 1950s.

Country stations have always reflected the changing economy. For instance, they played their part in the great fuel crisis of 1947 when, with wagons run down by the war, and coastal shipping almost halted by storms, there was a national campaign to empty wagons, particularly coal trucks, as speedily as possible. Especially in the flatter part of Britain, American airmen and their aerodromes' traffics did not cease immediately with peace. Flatter countryside also produced sugar beet whose annual harvesting still rises to a furious crescendo in parts of Ireland, echoing other and more romantic seasonal traffics like the Kent hop-pickers, Somerset teasels and Fife raspberries that have gone along with nearly all Cornish brocoli, Devon strawberries and fish from ports large and small.

Nearly every branch line had at least one source of seasonal traffic even if it did not serve a mine, quarry, cement works or factory – as many of course did. The fascination of the country railway indeed lay in its diversity – the way it adapted itself to its unique piece of physical landscape and exploited whatever traffic source it could. Yet it was also fascinating because the unpredictable was played with a standard set of rules. You might not know why there was a special goods train, but you expected to understand when and how it ran. You expected mornings to see people busier than day ends, for Saturday evenings to produce extra business, for late trains that ran on Saturdays only in lean times to run every day at least in summer in better ones. You knew, of course, when the last school-children should be safely home, when to expect hops to be carried to the breweries, fishermen to switch coasts in Scotland. All these special movements had just as natural a place in the country station's daily routine as special happenings do in a school's. To be at the station before seven thirty in the morning meant you were able bodied but not intellectual. After seven thirty at night you were able bodied *and* intellectual, wage-earners not travelling then. And so on. If you were a signalman and did not clean your box, including mopping the floor and polishing the levers and brass, by eleven, you were a slut.

The smaller the station of course the more serene its life, the more time for gardening, but seldom that before lunch. The bigger, the greater the load and usually also the variety of traffics, but compartmentalisation of staff responsibilities. At a terminus or junction with heavy traffic, the signalmen kept to their boxes as rigidly as enginemen were separated from platform staff. The country engine depot had its own daily life. At very small depots with only one locomotive, two sets of men had to do everything from lighting her up hours before the first train, to clearing her out long after the lights had gone out in the station house. 'Her' was regularly swopped, once a week, so heavier maintenance could be done at a larger depot. A relief crew had to be sent out for holidays and sickness, but cases of nobody being available to take people to work were rarer than the signalbox failing to open; to be sure, even at a village depot there would be a knocking up arrangement with the police (or the company would provide a telephone). One-machine depots persisted at isolated points such as Princetown until the end, but where light-engine running was not so wasteful centralisation began to be preferred (as across the moor at Mortonhampstead whose branch engine was transferred to Newton Abbot).

Depots with two and three engines allowed a modicum of special-

Crossing Point. Gara Bridge station on the Great Western Railway branch from Brent to Kingsbridge in August 1959. The service was an adequate one of six down trains Monday to Friday with eleven on Saturdays and six up Monday to Friday with nine on Saturdays. Looking at the photograph nothing apart from the train livery and engine smokebox numberplate has changed since Great Western days, the large spotless signalbox (polished linoleum and shining levers with dusters for the signalman's hands) with its huge wheel for winding the road crossing gates, a stationmaster's house beyond the platforms and the passing of the daily pick up freight. At this time workings were in the hands of 45XX class 2-6-2 tanks as seen by No 5558 of Kingsbridge shed (sub to Newton Abbot 83A) and the later 96XX 0-6-0 pannier tanks. The branch closed on 16 September 1963 at the end of the summer timetable.

isation, there being a senior driver if not a shedmaster (all small depots came under a large one anyway, even if the control was remote) and a spare man, usually the youngster who lit the engines up one by one and did the cleaning. Getting *him* out on time and doing his vital work on which the regulation of a whole valley's social and economic life depended, rarely gave the problems one would suspect in later days when especially early Monday trains often lacked the promised catering because 'he didn't turn up'. The youngster was almost certainly son of one of the crews, looking forward to a life of engine-manning and knowing that others less fortunate to date would love his job. So there he would be, whistling away, a keen teenager booked on well ahead of his seniors, lighting up one engine and cleaning her, then another, the only rule he broke being that he learnt to move the machines to slightly more convenient positions. He of course coaled up, laboriously, and when the depot was emptied of locomotives, emptied the loco coal wagon, sometimes removed the last night's ashes to a permanent home and generally cleaned up.

Few country sheds had engines on them during the day, though the machines of visiting specials would come for coal and water and general attention, the visiting crew having to help themselves to stores. Since at least one machine at a depot allocated two, three or four was mainly used on local freight, the daily run-down began quite early, in many cases no later than teatime.

Terminus stations with their own engine sheds had a special character in which sound and smell played an important part. In winter, of course, getting the engine on the passenger trains in time to give a modicum of heat was important, only larger stations normally having carriage heating installed at the buffer stop. The country guard was another character, not as well paid as the stationmaster or driver, but especially in really remote areas usually a man of stature, again far better paid than most rural workers, enjoying his interesting, secure job. The well-being of the carriages was his responsibility.

Yorkshire Country Station. Wetherby on the North Eastern Railway cross country line from Leeds to Harrogate. This is the second station along the section – opened 1 July 1902. Like the Halesowen line in Worcestershire, although close to Victorian industry it is truly in the countryside. The stony garden is cared for, the wooden building newly painted and the footbridge well maintained for it is still only May 1953. Note the NER slotted post signal.

Where enginemen and guards were based, there was a busy freight-yard, parcels and booking office, one or more signalboxes, and the stationmaster of course found himself head of a tightly-knit community whose daily comings and goings were punctuated with time-honoured ritual, including gentlemanly greetings. Much self and communal help was provided, the engine driver dropping a supplementary lump or two of coal to the signalbox, turns being switched to help domestic circumstances, trains (especially goods) even being unofficially speeded up or retarded for the local common good. Not only were these men happier than their city and suburban counterparts, but the long hours they worked added to worldly wealth. It was still cheaper to have two sets of men with extensive overtime to fill a nineteen-hour day than to keep open round the clock. Added to that, especially on late turn, many men had anything up to two hours with nothing more to do than just be around.

So with the engine simmering gently away outside, staff of all kinds could congregate for tea in the parcels office, or if the engine was on shed the driver could tend his plot as the signalman might also be doing at the foot of the embankment near his box . . . but once more nobody relaxed until essential tasks had been completed and any kind of inspection could have been taken with equanimity.

With so much traffic at the beginning and end of the day, it was hard to shorten opening hours and where it happened did much damage to the takings. The last train in might (except on Saturdays) be lightly loaded, but its passengers would include those who had on their departure paid the highest fares. Cutting a round trip up to the junction and back during opening hours saved only coal. Where a useful service could be run beyond the junction, a main line 'filling in' turn sometimes helped the productivity. In other cases a middle-of-the-day gap between turns was tried, and some flexibility like the station-master doing two hours in the box between turns and a parcels porter taking the guard's role on the last trip. But at any time in their history, branch lines would have been condemned as wasteful (and the higher wage rates the more so) by economists. The Great Western showed what savings could be made by diesel railcars and some signalling was simplified, but not until the third decade of British Railways was there a concerted drive to hammer the costs of remaining lines.

By then the daily rhythm of custom had declined, almost dissipated. The village coal merchant whose arrival at work, his emptying of trucks and deliveries, all went to time-honoured patterns integrated with that of the rest of the staff at the station, now found himself the only person based there. He could only wave to the driver of the diesel multiple-unit stopping, perhaps even reversing, at what had become an unstaffed halt. Even his coal was delivered to his railside site by road.

The mint once picked every Friday, the flowers taken home for mother on Saturday, the rhubarb whose first succulent stalks had been so treasured, grow on forgetful of the fact that the signalman no longer arrives coughing on his bike at five thirty to let the down goods through.

Journey's End

Misther D— was a bachelor and something at a Dublin bank, of the premises of which he daily shook the dust from his feet at about 4.30pm by the clock, proceeding straightway to his club, where he remained for about two hours before taking the train home. His habits, customs, and time-table had become stereotyped; he always went by the same train and, except upon one celebrated occasion, had never been known to travel by any other. The exception . . . occurred when he omitted the club and put in an appearance at Westland Row station at about 4.30pm dressed in immaculate garb. He does not seem to have gone to sleep, and at Blackrock the astonished porter caught sight of him as the train came in; but the latter did not lose his presence of mind, for the carriage door was duly opened, the name of the station announced, and the occupant duly exhorted to alight. 'Oh! it's all right,' said the passenger, 'but I'm going on to Killiney.' 'Arrah now! Misther D—,' said the unbelieving porter persuasively but firmly, 'ye know ye've got to get out, and phwat will your sister be sayin' av ye don't go home?' 'But I assure you, 'pon my honour,' said the squeaky voice, 'it's perfectly correct; I'm going to a picnic at Killiney.' The porter was obdurate, and, after further persuasive efforts, called up the guard: 'Here's Misther D— on the wrong train, an' he says he's goin' to a picnic at Killiney.' 'Picnic!' retorted the guard with emphasis, 'it's a foine picnic he'll be going' to, an' we kaping the train all this blessed time. Shure! Misther D—, ye'll have to come out.' At this point the unfortunate passenger for Killiney was firmly grabbed by the two guardian angels and hustled unceremoniously on to the platform. – E. L. Ahrons in *The Railway Magazine*.

Isle of Wight Central. These scenes of Ventnor West station, Isle of Wight, show how little matters changed over a period of more than fifty years. The branch from Newport via Merstone Junction was rural and this was the lesser used of Ventnor's two stations – the Isle of Wight Railway's line via Sandown to Ryde being by far the busier. Ventnor West (Town until 1923) closed early in BR days, on 15 September 1952.

(i) Station layout showing tracks, platforms and buildings as seen in 1949 virtually unchanged from its opening on 1 June 1900. Only the former LCDR four-wheelers show the more recent Southern ownership.

(ii) Taken by the author's paternal grandfather just after opening, this photograph shows Stroudley ex LB&SCR Terrier tank No 75 Blackwall (IWCR No 9) sold in March 1899, an early disposal of a successful class. The coach is ex North London Railway.

(iii) Another Terrier with temporary BR livery as Isle of Wight section No 8 Freshwater, and with the words British Railways newly painted on the tank sides. This is a sad moment for it is Easter Monday 18 June 1949, the last day of A1X working on the branch. Better news is that the locomotive (ex LBSC 46 Newington/LSW 734/FYN 2/ SR W8/BR 32646) withdrawn in November 1963, is now actively preserved on the Isle of Wight Steam Railway.

(iv) Using the same stock in July 1949, LSWR Adams O2 class 0-4-4 tank No W36 Carisbrooke (the then standard class for Isle of Wight passenger services) takes water while waiting for the 9.40am departure.

The starting signal is exactly that depicted in the 1900 photograph. The driver and fireman are at their traditional tasks with the latter heaving the water column bag into the tank and watching for levels.

Clerk's Eye View

In 1939 aged sixteen, the writer joined the GW's Traffic Department as junior clerk, paid the princely sum of £45 per annum.

Thus it was that I received a letter from the divisional superintendent at Worcester instructing me to report at Pershore on Monday April 17. It enclosed a pass and told me that I must take out a Company's service season ticket to cover subsequent daily journeys.

That Monday morning I watched the 8.55am Worcester Shrub Hill leave for London, its Castle shining in all the splendour that was expected of an express engine in those pre-war days; and then with some fear and trepidation, I joined the 9.5 which followed from the bay platform and was the stopper for London calling first at Pershore.

Having been inspected by the station master, a little man with a severe military bearing made all the more impressive by the GWR pill-box hat, I was taken down the ramp, across the line leading into the dock, and much to my surprise was ushered into the goods office. I had always imagined that the 'goods' was a separate department and so it was on all Great Western stations of any size, but at all the smaller stations Traffic Department men did the lot.

Pershore was an excellent station to begin one's training. Clerks on the Great Western did not go on a course but learnt the job as they went along, and it was usual to start a junior clerk at Pershore each April when things were fairly quiet so that when the fruit season got under way, culminating with the plums in August, he could make himself fairly useful.

The system used was, I felt, very wasteful in clerical labour, but then clerks were cheap to employ in those days. The whole thing was geared to make sure the correct charges were raised and that nothing got away unentered, that is, without charges being made. No end of trouble was taken to collect even 6d and nothing was ever written off without a very good reason. I don't think the system had changed since before the Amalgamations of 1922, for exactly the same code numbers, 343 and 344, were used for the outwards and inwards goods books as in my grandfather's time some thirty years before in the Goods Department at Worcester. How stable things were in those days and how different from today.

Details of every consignment to be forwarded, whether a truck load or just a bundle of empty sacks, had to be entered on a consignment note which was filled in by the sender. When the item was loaded it was checked by the outside staff who then passed the note into the office. From this an invoice was made out which showed details of the sender, consignee, goods and weight, and finally the charges, either 'Paid' in which case the sending station was responsible for the collecting of money, or 'To Pay' in which case it was the responsibility of the receiving station. To raise this charge it had first to be decided to which of 21 classes the goods belonged, and although many clerks almost knew the book off by heart, it was quite often necessary to refer to the Railway Clearing House General Classification of Goods by Merchandise Train. Below is part of page 44 of the 1938 edition, and the book ran to over 400 pages.

	Class
Basket Trunks, nested	19
Basket Work, e.o.h.p. minimum 10cwts per truck	20
Baskets, Bass or Rush, in bundles	18
„ Coal (Collier's) rough	13
„ Dress – (as Trunks)	
„ Fruit, cardboard, with tinned iron handles, nested, in bundles, min. 10cwts per truck	18
„ Iron	16
„ Japanese, minimum 10cwts per truck – (as Baskets, e.o.h.p)	
„ Japanese, nested – (as Basket Trunks (nested))	
„ On Wheels or Castors NOTE – If not packed as damageable goods not properly protected by packing	19
„ Osier or Twig – (as Hampers, empty, e.o.h.p.)	
„ Spale, or Spale Swills, or Chip, in crates or in bundles not packed nor wrapped, minimum 10cwts per truck	18
„ Wooden, nested for plants, fruit or vegetables	18
„ Workmen's Tool – (as Bags, Workmen's Tool).	
„ E.o.h.p., minimum 10cwts per truck	20

(E.o.h.p. – Except otherwise herein provided)

It was then necessary to find the correct distance to the destination station and by means of a scale it was now possible to read off a rate per ton, but this was only a station to station rate and a further amount had to be added if cartage was involved at either or both ends. Having now established the correct rate per ton a ready reckoner was used to arrive at the appropriate charge. I always felt that the railways made a great mistake in treating cartage as a separate service. The customer was only interested in having his goods moved from A to B and the exact location of the nearest station and its distance from either A or B was quite immaterial. There was an added complication that there were many exceptional rates for larger quantities that passed regularly between particular places, and woe betide the clerk who charged the normal rate for say 1 ton, 15cwt. when it would be cheaper charged as a 2 ton-lot at the exceptional rate.

Daily and weekly totals of weight and money were made of all the traffic passing and the books were closed at the end of each month to enable returns to be made to Audit Section for all local traffic i.e. to and from other GW stations; and to the Railway Clearing House for all foreign traffic, i.e. to or from the other three groups, the Irish Railways, joint lines such as the CLC and such places as the Manchester Ship Canal Stations.

At Pershore the fruit traffic built up each summer to a peak of about 100 wagons a day. Deliveries were guaranteed in time for the early morning markets next day at Birmingham, Manchester, Liverpool and London, and special trains ran for the season like the 1.0pm Worcester–Banbury which conveyed traffic for the Great Central stations, Leicester, Nottingham, Mansfield and Sheffield. Some fruit went to destinations as far away as Sunderland, Newcastle-on-Tyne and Glasgow; and with such highly perishable traffic speed was essential if it were to arrive in good condition otherwise a claim would be received. There was a fair amount for Welsh destinations – Cardiff, Swansea, Llanelly, Carmarthen, Barmouth, Dolgelly and so on. One felt one was learning a foreign language when one had to invoice traffic to such places as Tonypandy and Trealaw for Llwynypia.

One soon became quite knowledgeable about the economy of the area. One saw how the fruit and vegetables produced by the local growers were distributed all over the country, how the supply of groceries arrived daily for the local shops, how the fishmonger received his daily supply of fish from Hull or Grimsby, and how the fertilizers, seeds and animal feeding stuffs arrived for the farmers of the area. – From an article by Harold Tupper in the *Great Western Society Magazine*.

4
RETRENCHMENT AND DESPAIR

While many lines enjoyed their most frequent services in the period immediately before closure, changes (partly because of dieselisation) were taking place increasingly frequently on both main and branch lines, resulting in generally poorer connections and at least temporary breaks in many time-honoured services taking people to work, shopping and hospital visits. Sometimes indeed it was the timetable planner's very desire to get the maximum mileage out of the new diesels that meant less fine tuning of services to the local community's needs and led to a simultaneous decline in the number of passengers carried.

There were, of course, many exceptions. In some cases branch line trains were sensibly extended along the main line to the nearest big centre (some from Workington and Keswick went through to Carlisle, for example), while in others BR cut their losses by withdrawing all but one daily service (as between Cheltenham and Swindon on the former Midland & South Western Junction). But generally more trains were run on country railways in the 1950s than when the railway's share of the traffic was greater in the 1920s and 1930s, and certainly more than in Victorian days of railway monopoly. Especially at the end of the 1950s and in the early 1960s, new diesel multiple-units and railbuses shuttled to and fro, often ridiculously empty. At the end, enthusiasts outnumbered regular passengers on many services, which was not surprising when no connections were provided at junctions. For enthusiasts aboard the railbus from Crieff rounding the curve into Gleneagles station, there was sometimes an unforgettable view of an A4 Pacific thundering through with a non-stopping Glasgow express while, to quote just one other example, the Kingsbridge train was due out of Brent a couple of minutes after a Plymouth-bound train had passed through.

There is really no polite way of saying it: for the most part BR was inept. The more you study the evidence, the stronger you come to believe this. That is not to say that many managers did not achieve excellent results locally, and officials could always quote examples of progressive action. But by and large money was thrown away on crazily-uneconomic services, and everything from motive power to signalling and station arrangements seemed calculated to ensure that ultimately there would be no alternative to total shutdown. In practice there was seldom a political motive such as that; just stubborn refusal to move with the times and cut the coat according to the cloth. Above all the railways still Victorian in essence had no real understanding of what competition was let alone how to answer it.

Conditional Appointment

Seven miles from Scarborough on the Whitby line, Hayburn Wyke had several claims to fame. In 1886, the total tickets issued from it yielded the North Eastern only £68 14s, a mere 78 passengers booking in January, and leaving the stationmaster in his chalet-like office on the single platform singularly lonely.

But as the posters pointed out, it was an East Coast beauty spot, with 'Romantic Bay and Scenery, Hotel in Beautiful Grounds,' and in high season hundreds, sometimes thousands of trippers arrived daily – though whether even in the days before road competition they would agree with the railway's claim of a 'frequent train service' (in summer there were eight each way, other times only four or five daily) is arguable.

The North Eastern did not think this was a suitable station for a bachelor to be master of. For when a clerk at Driffield sought promotion, he was told he would only get the job if he married. Legend has it, says J. Robin Lidster in his centenary volume on this picturesque line, that he was only given two weeks to find his wife, which he did successfully by advertising in a Driffield newspaper.

Census

Judging by the figures that appeared on the annual traffic census returns taken at many country stations, it is surprising that branch lines were not gold mines. News of the census spread as rapidly as did that of the arrival of an inspector from the Ministry of Food in the second world war. People who travelled only occasionally but valued the local service made a point of taking a trip, and others encouraged friends to stop off – especially breaking their journey and so revealing a 'traffic' that revenue from ticket sales would not.

Even outside census periods, a few people drummed up business for the country station as though it were a charity. Two elderly ladies travelled every Monday to Friday for months trying to persuade the Western Region to stop the Devonian from Bradford at Kingskerswell during the summer as well as winter.

Agonising to the keen country railwayman were regulations that allowed the junction station to sell cheaper tickets, or to sell them earlier, than he could. At some stations one man might bend the rules to ensure the revenue fell to him, while his colleague on the other turn would not.

Even less fortunate was the stationmaster keen to sell a long-distance ticket, but unable to do so because he 'didn't have the fare'. Fares to unusual destinations had to be requested from district office and usually took at least two days. 'I haven't a fare to Southampton or even Andover, but Mrs Hicks went to Marlborough last month so *please* let me book you there', pleaded the stationmaster at Eckington on the Midland line between Worcester and Cheltenham. But the passenger who had to change at Cheltenham insisted he would rebook there. 'What a disappointment', said the stationmaster.

Take the matter of unstaffed halts. The Great Western had pioneered them in the earlier years of the century with great benefit to itself and the public, more people often joining trains at them than at the nearest staffed station (usually a crossing place built more because of its geographical convenience to the engineers than its proximity to centres of population). But throughout the 1950s and well into the 1960s, the largest region, the London Midland, steadfastly refused to allow them. The public and the Central Transport Users' Consultative Committee pressed for them. But: 'The British Transport Commission, on the other hand, have put before us a paper criticising the policy of creating unstaffed halts, in which they contend that the only saving is in wages; that buildings, footbridges, and approach roads, still have to be maintained and lit; that only a limited number of tickets can be issued on trains even if the guards have time to issue them at all, which they can do only on corridor stock; that children will play on the platforms, may fall under trains, and damage windows and lighting installations; that there is sometimes destruction caused by deliberate hooliganism if the stations are left open and unattended.' That was in 1963. The only saving is in wages! A few years later the name Paytrain was invented for services, over East Anglian branches whose station became unstaffed, and eventually the practice was grudgingly adopted even on the London Midland Region.

It would be possible to quote a dozen more topics on which BR's original stance was overtaken by events. Idiotic waste was not just an occasional accident but everyday policy. Tracks really were relaid months before trains were withdrawn, stations painted at the very time of closure – a brand new heating stove for one waiting room being delivered on the very last day the station was open for traffic. Just how was such an appalling state of affairs allowed to develop, and how was it resolved?

The problem really began in the early days of railways, when it was not sufficiently appreciated just how the economics would vary between a trunk main line and a rural branch. As has already been said, in the British Isles, a railway tended to be a railway, many of the same standards adopted throughout the system: high platforms and elaborate station buildings and signalling in particular. We paid the price for being early and also for having an inelastic government approach, Light Railways being allowed too late and even then hemmed in with restrictions that did not apply in much of the rest of the world. Branch lines were therefore expensive to operate, and when road competition began seriously in around 1919, things were not helped by a universal adoption of a very traditional outlook. A railway was still a railway, which in practical terms meant it was inflexible and could not be expected to change with the times, even though after some classic disputes railwaymen had won a much higher standard of living and working conditions for themselves.

Some services had of course been withdrawn even before 1900, especially in inner city areas where tramcar competition was strong, and

Disaster. The Severn Bridge being demolished. In October 1960 an oil barge hit one of the piers, a second hit the first and caught fire. Five men died and two spans of the bridge crashed into the river. It was considered uneconomic to repair the damage.

Push and Pull Train. Great Western 0-4-2 tank No 1438 (once 4838) takes the 5.03pm Wrexham (Central) to Ellesmere service out of High Town Halt, Wrexham, on Easter Monday 18 April 1960. Although it was then in the London Midland Region of BR and the coach was painted in maroon, the locomotive is back in green once more showing that Swindon's influence has not been totally dissipated. The whole scene is still reminiscent of GWR days though illumination is provided by an oil storm lantern, protected by a wire cage and padlocked against theft.

Motor Notes
The use of motor traction for dealing with parcel collection and delivery is rapidly developing. In addition to the six motor vans which are now at work at Birkenhead and Birmingham, the Directors have authorised the purchase of three 'auto-carriers.' These may be described as motor tricycles fitted with a body capable of carrying a load up to 6cwt and working up to a maximum speed of 20 miles per hour. *GWR Magazine*, April 1910

Last day. Ettington station on the erstwhile Stratford on Avon & Midland Junction Railway on the final day of passenger service from Stratford (Old Town) to Blisworth, 7 April 1952. Freight trains continued to run until 3 February 1964. Latter day services were in the hands of ex Midland and LMS Class 3F and 4F 0-6-0s. No 44567 of Stratford shed (21D) heads a Stratford bound train. This was one of many late Victorian cross country routes intended as penetrating lines into other companies' territories.

between the wars a small but significant number of rural services closed. But for the war this process would undoubtedly have accelerated, though the receipts from heavy freight traffic in town and country alike prevented any immediate overall crisis. During the war most country stations had their services pruned but issued and collected record numbers of tickets; they had never been so profitable and were never to be so again.

Meantime, in association with the Road Traffic Act of 1930, the railways had lost their right to be direct operators of bus services (pioneered in many districts by the Great Western among others), but had become substantial shareholders in the 'territorial' bus companies. That generally meant there could be neither outright competition or sensible co-operation. There were honourable exceptions, the Southern Railway's timetable giving details of many bus connections to places off its own system in the West of England, but generally trains and buses ran along parallel routes ignoring each others' existence, usually carrying quite different types of traffic. People going to the nearest market town to shop, visit friends or enjoy an evening at the cinema, increasingly went by bus. The train retained people beginning and ending long-distance journeys, and many workers and schoolchildren taking advantage of cheap season-ticket rates.

The most extraordinary thing, in retrospect, is that nobody in authority seemed to realise that with the end of hostilities in 1945 things would never return to what they had been in 1939, when anyway the writing had already been on the wall. In retrospect? At least one young and impudent journalist bombarded his regional newspapers about the need to simplify branch-line working, suggesting that diesel railcars be introduced and that at some termini the complicated layout be reduced to a single track ending at a buffer stop. Nobody was ready to listen. After nationalisation, BR built its thousand steam locomotives as though it were operating in a time capsule.

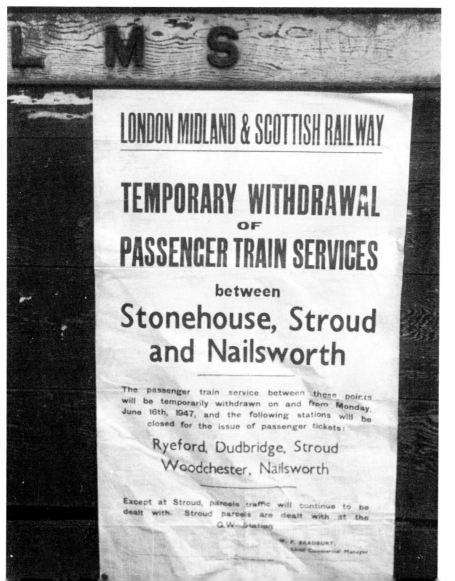

The End in Sight. A severe fuel crisis hit Great Britain and Ireland in 1947 and the railways were not slow in allowing this excuse to terminate some services which they regarded as being unrewarding. One such line was the ex Midland branch from Stonehouse and Stroud to Nailsworth in Gloucestershire, though the withdrawal of trains was only said to be 'temporary'; few believed this, and they were right. The last trains ran on Saturday 14 June – a single coach behind ex Midland class 3F 0-6-0 No 3754 of Gloucester Shed (22B). That in the photograph was the 4.45pm from Nailsworth. There were no mourners at the funeral, bar the photographer and one other enthusiast who shared the same car – petrol was rationed in those days.

Believe It or Not. The 'temporary' closure notice, issued by the LMS in respect of the Nailsworth branch.

LMS

LONDON MIDLAND & SCOTTISH RAILWAY

TEMPORARY WITHDRAWAL

OF

PASSENGER TRAIN SERVICES

between

Stonehouse, Stroud and Nailsworth

The passenger train service between these points will be temporarily withdrawn on and from Monday, June 16th, 1947, and the following stations will be closed for the issue of passenger tickets:

Ryeford, Dudbridge, Stroud Woodchester, Nailsworth

Except at Stroud, parcels traffic will continue to be dealt with. Stroud parcels are dealt with at the G.W. Station.

W. P. BRADBURY,
Chief Commercial Manager

The Divided Island

Since the setting up of the Border there had always been a certain amount of smuggling across it, but the unnatural conditions obtaining while the state of war existed in the North meant that certain commodities were in short supply up there, whereas others were difficult to get hold of in the South. It was a smuggler's paradise and one gets the impression that almost the entire population at one time or another was involved in illicit trading, not the least backward being employees of the GNR. Within a few days of each other cases were brought before the courts in February 1942, in the first of which a restaurant car attendant was fined £250 and imprisoned for two years for offences under the Defence Regulations, which included bringing into Northern Ireland two letters from Eire, while in the second two men were fined £750 at Dundalk with the alternative of six months inside. An onion smuggler hardly sounds a very romantic figure, but no doubt there was money to be made out of the business; indeed, two Dundalk men attempted to infiltrate five tons of the vegetable into the North by removing the wagons containing them from the main part of the train in which they were marshalled whilst the customs officers were examining it, and then slipped them back in again.

A rather different case concerned an entire restaurant crew of five who had regularly been bringing two loaves of white bread from Belfast to Dublin each day. It was pleaded on their behalf that quite often the restaurant car stocks ran out and the men gave their own bread to the customers. Whether the magistrate's heart was softened by this or whether he did not regard the crime as a particularly heinous one in any

continued opposite

Ironically, it was partly because of eased hire-purchase restrictions and the large sums being poured into the purchase of first cars that led to BR's first deficit, in 1956, a poor season at the resorts. Many country trains that had been wastefully run for decades (apart from the immediate war years) were now earning less than ten per cent of their keep in the fares and freight charges collected. Bus services were usually more frequent and cheaper, but soon even the buses would begin losing traffic as more and more country people owned cars and gave lifts to those who did not. Now the pattern developed of the trains on many lines only carrying specialist traffics which for one reason or another the roads could not take so well. People beginning and ending long-distance journeys continued to change at the junction; the journey to work and school was still frequently quicker as well as cheaper by train; half-day excursion fares continued to attract large crowds on a highly selective basis, such as to seaside resorts on Sunday and Bank Holiday afternoons; mothers with prams needed the extra space the train afforded; and railwaymen, retired railwaymen and railway enthusiasts stuck to the rails for obvious reasons.

On many routes it was clear that these specialist traffics could be accommodated far more cheaply with a reduced train service designed especially for them; that indeed it might be possible to encourage more business with fewer but better-timed trains, and that the reduction would bring economies in signalling and station arrangements as well as in the cost of the trains themselves. But almost uniformly throughout Britain nothing was done until the coming of the new diesels. A few more lines were closed, a few further services cut, a handful of attempts made to revitalise traffic with a more enterprising service; but generally it was stalemate, the same types of steam locomotives idling away the same hours between duties hauling the same unnecessarily-long rakes of coaches year by year. Any intelligent person could have calculated the waste, yet it came as an enormous shock to the Western Region when ultimately a more sophisticated cost accounting was introduced that no less than sixteen per cent of its total expenditure went on maintaining (not replacing and depreciating, but just repairing and maintaining) its quite unnecessarily large fleet of passenger coaches. Dieselisation generally provided the proof, two or three-car multiple-units replacing four, five and six-coach trains. Excluding the London service, the number of passenger-carrying vehicles plying in and out of Norwich Thorpe probably declined by more than two thirds on dieselisation, frequencies being if anything improved.

Diesels were often seen as a saviour. Generally they cost only about one quarter as much per mile as their steam predecessors, in 1963 terms that is about 4s (20p) a mile against 15s (75p). So dramatic did this appear that Sir Reginald Wilson, chairman of the Eastern Region, said: 'We shan't be able to close any railway until we have tried the DMUs.' And on many parts of the system, that is the philosophy that was followed. However, operating costs had become so utterly out of control that it was clear that diesels would not be ready in sufficient quantity soon enough, and doubtful if they alone would make enough difference on many routes. Operating costs had in part gone out of control since belatedly Britain was entering a technological era where high wage increases would in most industries (but decidedly not on the country railway) be partly offset by mechanisation. Labour-intensive industries were bound to be the worst affected. At the same time, government policy in the first fifteen years after the war was to keep transport costs down, Churchill in his one Government after BR's nationalisation personally preventing a round of fare increases. The gap between expenditure and income was becoming unbridgeable, at least with BR's inflexible management and backlog of sensible adjustments.

Closure proposals quickened from the mid 1950s, and in much of Britain the pruning shears had already been hard at work when Dr Beeching was appointed BR's chairman with the brief of making the railways profitable, even if that meant wholesale closures. The famous Beeching Plan, officially named *The Reshaping of British Railways*, was published in 1963. It was an ill-prepared document whose sole intention was to justify its pre-conceived conclusions. Thus it spoke of the point 'at which the withdrawal of services becomes financially justified,' with no attempt at questioning the bases of the costs. All its financial examples assumed that the same expensive Victorian methods of operation would continue, including full signalling and the retention of staffed stations. And even using this method of judgment, some of the figures were highly suspect; for example, the savings that were said to arise from the closure of lines were much higher per mile than those forecast in the average of closure proposals made immediately before the report's publication. Apart from a few sentences of rhetoric, no consideration was given to the possibility of even some lines fulfilling a different but still worthwhile role in the Britain of the 1960s, though as D. L. Mumby, reader in Economics and Organisation of Transport at Oxford University pointed out in the *Journal of Industrial Economics*, the statistical information included in the report itself could be used to show that in some cases fewer trains and higher fares could have made certain lines profitable in themselves, and still valuable as feeders to the main line. Instead, it was naïvely assumed that when a branch line closed, buses running on the parallel road would still feed traffic into the nearest railhead.

Such was the crisis that there had to be a Dr Beeching and a report recommending sweeping changes. But not this report, which did the railways great harm – including the fact that even such piecemeal changes and closures that were taking place ahead of its commission were halted during its preparation. It was especially at fault on the freight side. While it was correct to recommend the introduction of liner trains and the concentration on single-load trains wherever possible, its dismissal of the value of single-wagon traffic resulted in wholesale loss of business, part of which has been expensively regained only in much later years. Above all, it heralded a dogmatic era in railway management in which only those prepared to push the correct political angle were likely

continued
case is not recorded but the men were let off with small fines.

On one memorable day in July 1942, the 5pm train from Bundoran was so delayed while its occupants were searched that it was 4am before it pulled into Belfast. Around this time customs officials were particularly vigilant, and a search of a Dublin–Belfast express produced something from practically every occupant of the packed train, 800lb of butter, boxes of chocolates, saucepans, kettles, knives, forks, boots, shoes, vast quantities of every commodity scarce in the United Kingdom and plentiful in Eire. Goodness knows where some of the larger items were concealed; the usual places for small articles were in pouches and belts which the women hid beneath their skirts.

In the 1940s shiny red lipstick was all the rage, yet it was almost impossible to get hold of it in Northern Ireland. The build-up of troops in the Province provided unlimited possibilities of attachments to eligible young men, and the young women of the Six Counties were determined not to let the chance slip. Lipstick was easily obtainable in the South and rapidly became one of the most profitable items in the smuggler's repertoire. The dummy fire extinguisher in the Great Northern carriage which had been used to smuggle tea into Eire made its return journey packed with cosmetics, and one of the biggest hauls the customs men ever made was at Clones, when they discovered 430 packets of lipstick in a train bound for Belfast. – Michael Baker, *Irish Railways Since 1916*.

to gain promotion. This resulted in many managers putting forward the detailed evidence for closures and seeing the closures approved that they knew were against BR's true interests. 'It is a sad day they have agreed to this one,' said the district manager responsible for putting forward the plan to close the Taunton–Minehead line, for example.

The closure procedure was the subject of continued criticism and unease. BR formulated the details and submitted them to the regional Transport Users' Consultative Committee. Customers affected were invited to send any representation to the Committee by posters displayed at stations. Unimaginatively, they were headed 'Public Notice'. The rules were always weighted against protestors but, as procedures were tightened up at the time of the Beeching Report, it became clear that there was to be little attempt at anything but the most rough justice.

The sole consideration the TUCCs were supposed to undertake was whether the proposed withdrawal of a service would constitute hardship, and if so whether an alternative bus service could eliminate that. Mere inconvenience was not enough, though there was, of course, no definition as to where inconvenience ended and real hardship began. Objectors to BR's proposals were not allowed to question any of the information in the written brief, even though the inaccuracy might sometimes be startling. Nor was any discussion about the way in which a service had been, or might be, operated allowed. Time after time, throughout the country, protestors were ruled out of order as they tried to suggest that BR had (deliberately or otherwise) piled on the expenses and made no effort to trim costs to current needs. The council of a seaside resort was allowed to claim that the withdrawal of holiday trains would cause economic mayhem, but not to suggest that the dozen signalboxes might be reduced to two and the stations left unmanned.

Modern Times. A two-car diesel multiple-unit leaves Keswick bound for Workington in the winter of 1956/57. Steam has now been banished but modernisation is to no avail and the service to Workington has but months to go. Though warmer and more convenient for the crews and more bus-like for the passengers, these trains could not compete with road services. The dmu was then brand new. Note bars on drop light windows for working over the Maryport & Carlisle section which had restricted clearances. Through trains from Penrith to Workington ceased on 18 April 1966, though freight had gone by 1 June 1964. Keswick to Penrith closed on 6 March 1972.

Many such statements, naturally, were squeezed in, sometimes to the accompaniment of cheers from the crowds, but they were not allowed to sway the TUCC's verdict, and keen chairmen openly boasted that such evidence would not be noted. Newspapers such as the *Guardian* published leading articles about how undemocratic it all was. Almost irrespective of politics, local newspapers described the procedure as a farce. The greatest farce was that the proceedings were almost identical whether the subject was a truly redundant service that should have been closed years before, or a major one where closure might result in a negative saving in any social balance sheet. Value for money had nothing to do with it. Thus when the driver of an invalid carriage which he took into Exeter by train complained that the withdrawal of service at nearby Stoke Canon would result in real personal hardship, he successfully had a stay of execution for a period. That was identifiable hardship! But even though thousands might be seriously inconvenienced, most closure proposals were rubber stamped.

Sometimes the regional committee recommended retention, and occasionally (especially pre-Beeching) was brave enough to recommend

Last Days. One of the Great Western's primarily suburban 2-6-2 tanks No 5183 stands at Lustleigh with the 9.20am from Newton Abbot on 26 February 1959, a trivial duty for an engine of this class, just two coaches and a van. Lustleigh, on the Moretonhampstead branch closed to passengers on 2 March 1959. Although there were only a few days to go cheap fares were on offer – the day return fare to Newton Abbot was as low as 1s 10d (9p). Closure might be considered to have been premature as the TUCC recommended dieselisation as a trial. Before the second world war a camp coach was stationed here with a beautifully tended lawn and gardens.

Writing On The Wall

The directors of the Invergarry & Fort Augustus Railway have become tired of losing money by keeping the railway open. The railway, which is 24 miles long, was opened for traffic in July, 1903. The district traversed is a notable shooting area, with some crofting. When first opened the railway was worked by the Highland Railway, which has no physical connection with the line, but at the expiration of its agreement the Highland Railway was pleased to let the North British Railway have the opportunity of working the Invergarry and Fort Augustus Railway, and this agreement has now been terminated. Although neither the owning nor working Company gives it as the cause for the closing of the line, the view is generally held that much of the non-success of the railway is attributed to the growing use of the motor-car in the Highlands.

* * *

It is evident that motor car services, controlled by railways, will form an important feature in future railway traffic development, as they provide, in many cases, an effective means for competing with the train services of another railway when 'agreements' do not debar competition. How efficient such competition can be made will be appreciated when it is remembered that at many places it had been usual for the omnibus of a railway whose nearest station was several miles off to compete with the trains of the railway actually serving the place. If this were possible with the slow horse-hauled omnibus, how much more effective must be the competition of swift motor cars, carrying thirty or more passengers? How much wider the field of effective competition can be, may be judged from the circumstance that during the past *continued opposite*

that closure be postponed until a diesel unit could be tried. In such cases, the Central Transport Users Consultative Committee then had its say. To quote another Devon example, the South West committee recommended the retention of the branch to Moretonhampstead, at least until dieselisation. The Central committee allowed closure but said that the branch should be reopened at least experimentally once a diesel unit became available in the area. BR overlooked this, no reopening taking place, on the grounds that diesel units were only acquired for specific services and it would not be possible to acquire one on an experimental basis.

Only when there was no reasonable bus alternative did the TUCCs really have a say. Coniston retained its passenger trains for several months while the parallel road was improved to allow the Traffic Commissioners to approve the operation of a bus service. The Somerset & Dorset Railway out of Bath also survived for several months, albeit on an emergency run-down basis with only a skeleton local service, because the running of buses had not yet been licensed. These were hollow victories.

As already indicated, the actual nature of the replacement bus service was not inquired into. A bus was a public service that would prevent hardship, and that was that. So in very few cases were buses diverted or extended to the main-line railway station, and even most of the bus replacements that had to be provided from scratch at BR's cost merely ran to the usual bus station. Where buses did run to railway stations, moreover, there was no guarantee whatsoever that there would be a useful connection. BR and the local bus companies changed timetables on different dates, and for whole years or more the bus from the town that had lost its trains might and did arrive at the former junction station minutes after the express to London had left, hours before there was another. When the Princetown branch was closed in Devon, however, the bus was made to run down from Yelverton village to the railway station . . . which it continued doing for years after Yelverton also lost its trains. The media were full of such examples. BR merely regarded such ridicule as anti-railway, and shoulders were shrugged.

It was perhaps inevitable that with such wholesale closures there would be an embittered public. Some railway managers certainly felt that whatever they did, short of retaining the full loss-making system, they were on a hiding to nothing. Such views were strengthened by foolish opposition to small pieces of rationalisation such as concentrating traffic on one instead of two adjoining routes into the city, with perhaps the loss of only one sparsely-used suburban station. Many people, on the other hand, felt that a measure of justice and at least an attempt to be fair and to consider value for money would have influenced the thinking public and resulted in at least some more sensible decisions. BR officials would have been given a touch of public accountability, which would have led to more management activity in reducing costs. Seldom have managers of any kind been more shielded – behind a general barrier of 'whatever we do will be wrong'.

Many of the losses incurred by branch lines from the early 1950s until their closures were both astronomic and unnecessary. Again, in addition to piling up capital losses BR could not afford, it meant that so much had to be done at once that bitterness and wrong decisions were inevitable. In many areas, for example, staff should have been run down by natural wastage many years before Beeching's arrival. In turn, some branches should undoubtedly have been kept open longer to prevent the wholesale redundancies that have partly caused today's embittered railway industrial relations. Had they been run properly, with the minimum of staff, and only trains when there was a demand for them, some of the Beeching casualties would indeed still be usefully at work today – perhaps as many as one in ten. Part of the evidence for this is the livelier traffic levels on some of the branches that have survived, whether or not they were in the Beeching Plan for closure. Fewer trains running at times people need them, and a growth in the proportion of the population who occasionally make long-distance journeys, especially to London, have helped, though in other cases such as Exmouth (proposed for closure by

Dereliction: The remains of Moretonhampstead station in August 1967.

continued
summer the Great Western Railway had motor 'buses serving such distant places as Bettws-y-Coed from Corwen, a distance of 22 miles, despite the fact that Bettws-y-Coed is given an efficient train service by the LNWR. Many towns that are now lucrative 'preserves' of some one railway might easily be made to give up a fair part of their traffic to the motors of a rival railway, if the latter had a station within 20 miles. – *Rail & Travel Monthly*, December 1910.

St. Ives as a Spa

St. Ives as a Spa

The recent discovery of radio-active springs at Trenwith, St. Ives, is a matter of far-reaching importance, and is likely to have the effect in the not far-distant future of raising this delightful western resort to a place amongst the leading spas of England. The *Western Morning News*, in its report of the chairman's speech at the recent general meeting of the St. Ives Consolidated Mines, Ltd., says:

'The Board were advised that the water at the Trenwith mine was radio-active, and it was determined to investigate this and to ascertain, if possible, the extent of the radio-activity. The water had its source in the radio-active springs of the Trenwith mine. They were anxious some time ago to have the tests made, but this could not be done until the water of the St. Ives Consols had been isolated from the water of the neighbouring country. So soon as that had been effected Mr. Norman Whitehouse, the late assistant of Sir William Ramsay, inspected the company's property at Trenwith and examined a number of springs for radio-activity. He had reported that he found all the springs exhibited radio-activity to an abnormal extent, even when compared with other mineral waters, such as the Bath hot springs, which were themselves noted for their pro-nounced activity. Analysis showed that the water of Tren-with was twenty-six times as active as that of Harrogate and about seven times that of Bath. He considered these springs at Trenwith, on account of their strong radio-activity, to be a valuable asset of the company.
GWR Magazine, April 1910

Beeching) increased business has justified more frequent trains. On the other hand, some lines that still survive could easily have been dispensed with had there been proper bus replacement services.

Research for the Lake District Transport Inquiry and the North Devon Railway Inquiry, showed that when trains were withdrawn, generally only one in three passengers transferred even temporarily to the bus making roughly the same journey. This was not surprising when remembering that the trains were by then generally only carrying specialist traffics that did not find the bus convenient. But after a year, only a third of those who had started using the bus alternative were still doing so. Bus services thus reaped little advantage from a railway's closure, and indirectly often lost since more people were forced into car ownership. Very few of the bus services specifically started as train replacements lasted more than the mandatory three years, and at the end were often running with extremely sparse traffic.

There are many might-have-beens. Had only dieselisation started earlier, some money made available to modernise branch lines (especially level-crossing arrangements), the Paytrain accepted a decade earlier, replacement buses run in certain cases as true replacements giving priority to main-line connections; and so on. Railway enthusiasts realised that it was so obvious that common sense would not prevail that they tended to lose themselves in the nostalgia and especially the hardware of the country railway while it still ran – and after seeing one line decently 'buried' moved on to enjoy the next while they could. This of course led to the very words 'railway enthusiast' being anathema to BR's managers. 'I hope you are not an enthusiast,' was about the most insulting remark a manager could make. They were the days when not a puff of steam was allowed on BR property, and occasionally a stationmaster would refuse to issue you with a ticket unless you actually travelled and further kept down 'enthusiasm' by collecting your ticket when you alighted from the last train. Happily, though, most men on the job, as opposed to managers in their ivory towers, were keen to help, perhaps unscrewing a notice or other artefact off the wall since otherwise it would have gone to the scrapheap after closure. David Shepherd tells a wonderful tale of how he acquired spare parts for his steam locomotives now on the East Somerset Railway: *The Man Who Loves Giants*.

Not surprisingly, many lines carried more traffic in their last week of operation than they had done in the previous three or six months. The pattern was usually the same. A steadily increasing proportion of enthusiasts among the passengers during the last few weeks made the branch into an unnatural living museum, and in the last few days the usual quietness and very character of the line was often destroyed by the constant clicking of cameras. On the very last day, however, the local public came out in force, restoring a less artificial balance though producing the pressure in booking halls and gentlemen's lavatories that previously had only been experienced for the annual show or a rare visit by some famous person. The very young and the very old were always especially in evidence, the former often making their very first trip by

Spring in Cornwall. Bodmin General on 27 May 1961 with ex GWR 2-6-2 tank No 4552 shunting the yard with a train of china clay wagons. The sunshine has ensured a good flowering of rhododendrons. The picture clearly shows a scene now very much in the past, a full working Great Western country station, the single platform terminus, wooden topped signal box, water tower and small covered goods shed. Note the bull's eye oil lamp on the rail-built buffer stop and the loading gauge at the goods shed entrance.

Opposite above:
Cross Country Pick Up. For many years the road to Llandovery and on to Swansea was the preserve of ex LNWR Super D 0-8-0s with their characteristic beat of 'one TWO three four' as they took their trains under the Sugar Loaf mountain. By 16 August 1962 even these hardy old veterans were coming to the end of their lives and No 48895 may well have been the last of the class to run over the line. The scene here is at Builth Road.

Opposite below:
Farewell to the Wye Valley. Monmouth Troy station on the last day of service over the Ross–Monmouth and Monmouth–Chepstow lines of the erstwhile GWR. In the station is the Stephenson Locomotive Society's 'last train' special headed by 0-6-0 pannier tank No 6412. The headboard on the buffer beam reads 'Last Train Monmouth–Ross 4th Jan 1959'.

North Eastern Veteran. A Whitby to Malton train near Beckhole in the spring of 1956. The engine is ex NER 4-6-2 tank of LNER Class A8 while the leading coach, an NER brake third is still in teak livery.

train, while the latter sometimes recalled opening day eighty or more years previously.

Many extra tickets were sold, especially cheap ones to the next station or halt for which there had been little demand in the motor age, and any old issues dating from before nationalisation. Lucky enthusiasts might even obtain a luggage label of a pre-grouping company. The last daylight trains were especially well photographed, the final train of all carrying the largest number of passengers. Often this was a late Saturdays-only service, many 'funerals' going on well into the night, an occasional communication cord being pulled to delay departure until Sunday morning. The local railway or history society frequently hung a wreath on the front of the locomotive or DMU, and out came the chalk to record thanks to the railway while it was allowed to last and to relieve emotion as it died. Despite official discouragement, detonators were frequently placed on the track ahead, dogs barking and cats running for shelter as the train made its noisy departure, whistle of course held continuously down. Local businessmen often gave farewell parties aboard. And so off into the night, the slow pace with a heavy load resulting in time dragging even in these exciting conditions. You had to conclude that it was not surprising that some trains had not retained much patronage, though conversely some last trains ran faster than anyone has since been able to travel between places at either end, especially where the railway had a more direct route across a river.

Until the end, many branch line locomotives and coaches were stabled at the terminus, and then the question arose as to whether there would be a return working to the junction or main-line stabling point – and, if so, whether the public would be allowed to use it. 'It is advertised as empty and if you travel it will not be empty will it?' was the much-quoted retort of the guard at Helston when asked by enthusiasts if they could travel back to Penzance. Their spokesman had twice been assured by the district manager in Plymouth that the coaches would be left at Helston, only the locomotive returning. Nobody senior came to bid an official farewell, and to keep on the right side of the law, the enthusiasts waved the empty procession off into the night, BR losing a couple of hundred fares and yet more goodwill. On other occasions, managers co-operated to give the line the best possible (and also most commercial) burial party. Many enthusiasts recall all the details of the individual closures that taxed their Saturday night diaries twenty to thirty years ago.

Sometimes the Locomotive Club of Great Britain, Railway Correspondence & Travel Society or the Stephenson Locomotive Society, ran a special train for enthusiasts on the Sunday. Indeed, closure was announced as and from the Monday, the first day that there would have been trains normally, which meant that Sunday was anyway 'funeral' day for stations with a Sabbath service. Where freight traffic continued running after closure to passengers, there were often further opportunities for specials, sometimes by rakes of guard's vans (which also included routes that had never enjoyed a passenger service), sometimes

Opposite above:
Into the Far South West. Skibbereen station on the Cork, Bandon & South Coast Railway branch to Baltimore, 4 September 1954. The train behind CIE Class F2 2-4-2 tank No 432 is heading for the branch terminus while across the way the engines and stock of the 3ft gauge Schull & Skibbereen Light Railway await their fate.

Opposite below:
Narrow Gauge in County Kerry. Perhaps the most infamous of all the Irish narrow gauge lines was the 3ft gauge Tralee & Dingle Railway climbing up over the hills for thirty-three long miles and whose engines needed the faculties of Kerry goats. In the last years since the fuel 'emergency' of 1947 trains only ran once a month – on Dingle Fair days – the roads were then incapable of taking the cattle out: these were double headed, going out to Dingle on the Friday and returning to Tralee on the Saturday. In July 1950 the engines of an outward bound empty stock special take water at Anascaul before attempting the 1 in 30 grade to Lispole. This rare and historic colour photograph has been taken from a 16mm cine film.

Ungated Crossing. One of the many specials chartered to mark an imminent closure was this Stephenson Locomotive Society train from Birmingham to Cleobury Mortimer and Ditton Priors via Kidderminster and Bewdley. The motive power was one of the two remaining Dean goods 0-6-0s No 2516 (now preserved at Swindon) then, over the one time Cleobury Mortimer and Ditton Priors Light Railway the branch engine, 2021 class 0-6-0 pannier tank No 2144 of Kidderminster shed (85D). The Ditton Priors locomotive was fitted with a spark arrestor in the later years of the line's existence because of shunting operations within the Admiralty yard near the remote country terminus. The date of the special train was 21 May 1955 while the branch closed on 16 April 1965. The locomotive number and shed plates had been removed from the smokebox door and Great Western style figures painted on buffer beam.

End of the Beginning. Proud in its LB&SC colours – Stroudley's improved engine green – A1X class Terrier 0-6-0 (ex LB&SCR No 35/635 Morden) leaves Robertsbridge with a special 'last' train over the Kent & East Sussex line on 19 October 1958. The train is banked at the rear by yet another Terrier No 32678 (ex LB&SCR No 78/678 Knowle Isle of Wight W14 1929–37). This was a familiar scene, even in the pre Beeching era but other lines were not so lucky as after many vicissitudes and great determination the railway in part has been saved and restored by enthusiasts: based on Tenterden, it is still full of character. The engine in the photograph was not so fortunate; although dolled up in pre grouping livery, and used as Brighton works shunter, it was eventually sacrificed and broken up in 1963.

by DMU provided enterprisingly by BR itself. Though usually extremely enjoyable in themselves, such outings showed up how wasteful was the running of the country railway even in its last, dying stages, perhaps served by only two or three goods trains a week. In particular, track was maintained to a much higher standard than would have been thought economic in most of the rest of the world. There were cases of more maintenance men being employed per mile after the closure to passengers than before, and of level crossing keepers enjoying extra years of employment to open and close gates for the goods on alternate days. And when BR went back to the TUCC for authority to withdraw freight facilities, some of the very costs that had been claimed as going to be saved if passenger trains were withdrawn were re-presented – as in the case of the Coniston line.

It is hard not to be bitter. 'There is nothing wrong with railways, just the way they are being run,' was a sentiment shouted and shouted again. Most enthusiasts had their own list of lines and stations they thought should be closed – ironically including some stations that because of inertia BR still serve today. If only . . .

Shropshire Railtour. The now preserved GWR Dean Goods 0-6-0 No 2516 runs tender first over the Albert Edward bridge at Buildwas on a return journey from Longville. It headed a complicated tour, organised by the Stephenson Locomotive Society, over lines closed to passengers made on 23 April 1955. The journey began at Shrewsbury with the train running to Wellington, Buildwas, Longville, then to Madeley Junction, Wellington, Coalport, (return) and Minsterley.

Country Railway in modern times. A weed grown Achnashellach station on 22 September 1973 with a Kyle of Lochalsh train headed by diesel-electric locomotive No D5128. All signalling and the passing loop have been removed and the station is unstaffed. But the line is still open operated under radio block remotely controlled from Dingwall.

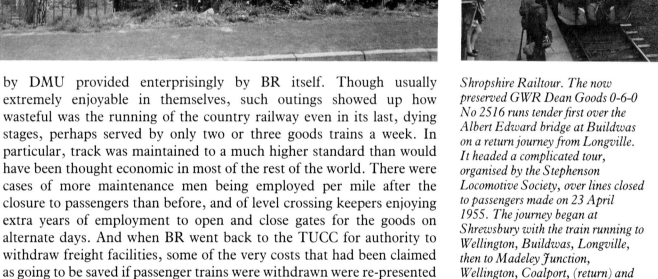

Ireland

Irish Single Wheeler. Great Southern Railways (ex Waterford & Tramore Railway) No 483 at Waterford on 7 July 1934. Built by Fairbairn in 1855 this 2-2-2WT was the last single driver to run in regular service in the British Isles. Overhauled as late as 1931, the engine was said to perform her task of trundling over the entirely isolated Waterford & Tramore section with considerable efficiency, burning only 16lb of coal per mile. And so it might have continued for many years to come if No 483 had not met with an accident, becoming derailed in a cutting on 24 August 1935. It had been hoped that she could be repaired and returned to traffic to perform her duties again, but it was not to be.

Sky Blue and Scarlet. Great Northern Railway (Ireland) U class 4-4-0 No 203 Armagh stands immaculate at Fintona Junction with an Omagh to Enniskillen train in August 1951. These lovely Beyer Peacock built engines were introduced as late as 1948; all were painted in sky blue with scarlet frames and coupling rods and were used on cross country services including that out to the Atlantic coast at Bundoran where the company owned a large and luxurious hotel. On the opposite side of the platform lay the tracks to Fintona worked to the end by a horse tram. Both lines closed on 30 September 1956 when many railways in the Six Counties were abandoned, leaving Dublin no option but to close any lines which crossed the border by mischance.

Anachronism. The famous horse tram, pride of the Great Northern Railway of Ireland, running from Fintona Town terminus to Fintona Junction on the Omagh to Enniskillen line. The hut to the left beyond the station's overall roof is the 'shed', that is the horse's stable. At the junction end there was a further 'shed' where the horse was placed temporarily to prevent it being frightened by the adjacent steam locomotives and bolting. Normal progress along the branch was at a slow trot down to the branch terminus and a much slower walk up the grade to the terminus – so slow indeed that a fast walker could get there first. It was no irrecoverable disaster to miss the tram.

Irish Terminus. Bantry, at the end of the main line of the one time Cork, Bandon & South Coast Railway showing the station, yard, turntable and water tower with ex CB&SCR 4-6-0 tank No 468 awaiting the next day's duty. The photograph was taken on a July Sunday in 1952 and the line closed to all traffic on 31 March 1961. The extra width of the 5ft 3in track against the British standard gauge of 4ft 8½in, is apparent on the siding to the left of the picture. It is almost a scene from a model railway.

85

Kerry Junction. Farranfore where the branch to Valentia Harbour (the farthest west in Europe) left the main line of the former Great Southern & Western Railway from Tralee to Mallow. In the platform, one July day in 1952, is the 4.20pm all stations to Valentia Harbour.

The train is made up of J15 class 0-6-0 No 126 and seven six-wheeled coaches of ancient vintage: some actually have lavatories – see the tanks on the roofs – although the second coach, a brake third, has a guard's birdcage lookout above the roof. It has come from Tralee,

shunted into the branch platform and is awaiting the 2.15pm from Mallow arriving at 4.06pm. Behind the leading coach are the chimneys for the coal fires (sometimes turf fires) of the two classes of passenger waiting rooms. The branch closed on 30 January 1960.

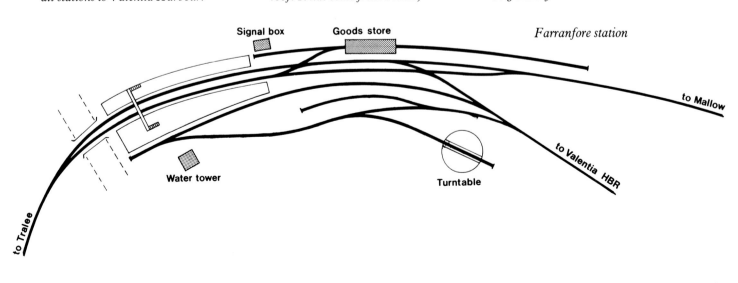

Signal box   Goods store

Farranfore station

to Mallow

Water tower

Turntable

to Valentia HBR

to Tralee

VALENCIA Co KERRY 4605 W.L.

Farthest West in Europe. A train of six wheeled coaches at Valentia Harbour station around 1905 with Great Southern & Western class J15 0-6-0 No 107 at its head, a scene including locomotive and coaching stock which would hardly change in the next 50 years. There is something of a similarity here between this engine and the London & North Western locomotives of the same period including the cast cabside numberplates. Valentia Island and South West Kerry were extremely remote even in the 1950s when the Irish language was very much a part of daily life; strangers were not always the most welcome visitors.

It was the virtual extinction of the narrow gauge in England and Wales which led many to make their railway pilgrimages to Ireland, and quite rightly so. But it would be a mistake to think that the Irish broad gauge had no individual character for this was very far from the case. Even the choice of the un-English gauge of 5ft 3in fits the pattern of individuality which makes the island's lines still attractive even though closures there have been as drastic if not more so than 'over the water'. The first Irish railways appear to have been constructed in an anarchical fashion in their choices of gauge, almost every one was different. Obviously this could not be allowed to continue and the matter was resolved in a very suitable way when Sir Charles Pasley, the Inspector General of Railways, who understood the Irish character, found a truly diplomatic solution. He added the various gauges together and divided the total by the number, result, 5ft 3in the now standard Irish gauge. A very useful additional carriage width for more portly passengers.

Because Ireland is a land of agriculture with any major industry in the north, there has always been a country atmosphere, stations are further apart, branches more

87

remote, people more friendly. Even in the 1950s with steam still going strong, most of the 587 locomotives (of 114 different classes) inherited by the Great Southern Railways in the Free State merger of 1925 were still working; some of them were fascinating curiosities, including a single wheeler on the Waterford & Tramore section. J. R. Bazin, the GSR's first CME is reported as saying 'I like historic locomotives but I wish I had less of them in day to day traffic'.

The visitor to Ireland just after the second world war found trains made up of a motley collection of stock with representatives from most of the old companies, but the great thing was that they were *clean*, putting Britain's railways of the period to shame. On the longer distance trains, most of them semi fasts by English standards and scheduled to stop at all stations, there were elderly clerestory vehicles with perhaps gas lighting alongside modern elliptical roofed steel sided coaches: on the branches you found yourself bumping along di-bong di-bong di-bong in ancient 'sax whalers' without spring seats and with old oil lamp pot-holders still in the roof, spotlessly clean outside and in.

Leaving aside the Belfast to Londonderry, Belfast to Dublin and Dublin to Cork routes, there was no Irish line which could not be thought of as unfrequented by-ways in England or even Wales and Scotland. It was pure joy to travel in a comfortable, well stocked dining car with licencing hours non-existent as always on a train, across the midland bogs towards the exciting far west of Connaught or Kerry, an air of adventure really, for the trains ran maybe only once or twice a day. L. T. C. Rolt, that great lover of the countryside and of the railway too once put it that the contrast between this comfort and the wildness of the country through which the train passed, made him think of a ship at sea.

There was so much to see. One day you stood on the platform at Fintona Junction when the Great Northern Railway 4-4-0 No 203 *Armagh* swept into the station with a train from Omagh. Her livery was immaculate in sky blue and scarlet, an elaborate coat of arms on the driving wheel splasher and brass nameplates flashing in the sun. Even more fascinating was that Fintona Junction met the branch to Fintona Town which was still worked by a horse tram, albeit a Great Northern Railway one and in the timetable. Then, the archaic Sligo, Leitrim & Northern Counties line wandering across the border between North and South, travelling in its clerestory roofed tri-composite coach, 1st, 2nd and 3rd class and, looking at the graveyard of old 0-6-4 tanks at Manorhamilton: how much further could you get away from the world of boring commerce? The variety, it seemed, was endless. Let us take one longer glimpse of broad-gauge Ireland. Farranfore, County Kerry. The long village straddles the main road from Killarney to Tralee as it falls to the wetlands of the River Maine, and comes to an abrupt stop at the level crossing over the end of the station loop. Here an imposing (for a country village)

brick-built station-cum-stationmaster's house presides over the up platform and a down island; of awnings there are none. On the far side of the island one of McDonnell's elderly J15 0-6-0s, black with tall built-up chimney and rudimentary cab, stands at the head of four equally elderly six-wheeled coaches, gas lit and painted in a deep shade of crimson lake. It is what is known in Kerry as a 'fine, soft day', which means that there is a thin drizzle in the air and the Slieve Mish mountains, seven miles away, are all but hidden in the mist. There is an air of expectancy on the platform, but as yet precious few passengers for the Valentia Harbour train. It may go to the furthest-west station in Europe, but there are no commuters and few shoppers to be carried on its 39½ mile run. It ekes out a precarious existence mainly from interchange traffic with the main line – tourists, relatives visiting from Britain and the United States, mails, provisions and a little livestock, for the main towns and villages, Castlemaine, Killorglin, Glenbeigh, Cahirciveen and the ferry to Valentia Island. Never mind that the scenery is spectacular as the line hugs the steep flanks of Dingle Bay beyond Mountain Stage and twists over the slender and sharply-curved Gleensk viaduct; the population is thinly scattered and the views butter few parsnips.

A distant whistle warns of the approach of the Dublin train, and driver and fireman emerge from the first compartment to rejoin their bleak footplate. The express runs in behind one of Coey's superheated 4-4-0s, with a motley array of corridor stock, including a clerestory-roofed diner with gas lighting. Doors open, passengers look around for the Valentia train, and lug heavy suitcases across the wet platform to its shelter. A countryman, hessian sack draped over shoulders for protection from the drizzle, makes for the rear van to collect a package from the guard while the porter is dealing with mailbags, some trunks, a bicycle and a pair of goats. A whistle, and with chunky beats and a momentary slip the 4-4-0s moves off over the level crossing towards Tralee and journey's end.

Doors open and bang in the branch coaches, and the handles are checked by the guard. The first-class compartments are kept locked until would-be occupants have established their bona fides. The signalman, having opened the crossing gates for the waiting road traffic, comes over to the engine with the single-line token in its hooped pouch. There is a final flurry of activity round the van, the guard consults his pocket watch on silver Albert, and waves his green flag. A screech from the J15's whistle, and with much steam from cylinder cocks and a breathy exhaust she pulls out of the platform as though towards Dublin before curving away and gently falling to the river levels, past little whitewashed farms and over crossings with minor roads. Even the trail of damp steam soon vanishes. The little train is on its way with its clutch of expectant passengers, headed for the far west and the Atlantic rollers.

5
ENGINES AND ENGINE SHEDS

Except perhaps for the Great Western, where a longstanding policy of standardisation ensured few surprises lurking deep inside its engine sheds, the country railway was home to an enrapturing selection of museum pieces which, like men of an older race hard pressed by an alien invader, had retreated to the more peaceful extremities of their homelands. True, once reaching the country junction life became all bustle and excitement for the short period when the main line train disgorged then enveloped its passengers. But back in the tiny one or two-road shed tranquillity reigned, time being related almost solely to the needs of livestock and the clock adorning the church tower. Many country branch lines never saw a modern locomotive during the whole of their existence.

High up in the Peak District of Derbyshire an ancient London & North Western 0-6-0 coal engine boiler once found itself as the power of a winding house used to haul wagons up an inclined plane while its contemporaries trundled the same vehicles along the flatter sections, one of these being a relative term as it included a 60 yard length of 1 in 14 near Hopton; this bare, treeless, stone-walled piece of railway boasted the steepest railway gradient in Britain to be worked by normal steam locomotives. It was an experience of a lifetime to travel on the footplate of one of the old four-wheeled L&NWR tenders drawn high above the valley floor up Sheep Pasture incline, then by the sole remaining 2-4-0 'Chopper' tank to Middleton Bottom, up the rope-worked section to Middleton Top and then, behind an elderly ex North London Railway 0-6-0 tank, to charge that 1 in 14 making the summit after much puffing and panting. Sometimes this needed more than one try. All for a modicum of stone traffic, with a by-product of carrying water to the hamlet of Longcliffe which was then wholly dependent on this source of supply. These engines, naturally, were the only survivors of their class remaining at work until they were ultimately replaced by standard austerity saddle tanks built for service in the second world war. Far from home, they worked out their lives on duties never envisaged by their designer or original owners.

Most of the companies built engines for specific duties which, because of increasing loads or replacement by later, more efficient classes, resulted in comparatively early withdrawal, leaving a few members to vegetate on country lines. Another one-time London suburban class to end its days in regular service far from its original haunts was the London & South Western Railway, Adams designed 4-4-2 tank. Because

Long Way Round
In the Summer service of 1924 a train appeared which certainly merits a mention. It was none other than a Carmarthen–Euston Express. This had the great distinction in my eyes of being booked non-stop to Llandilo and it proceeded as far as Shrewsbury independently of any connection from the Swansea line. As far as Llandovery it was hauled by one of our usual LNW 2-4-2 Tanks, but the real interest was in the coaches which, usually four or five, was a wonderful assortment of elderly vehicles from the main constituent companies, the LNW, L&Y, and Midland always being represented. Almost invariably the star turn was an LNW clerestory family saloon which must have graced many an express to the Highlands in mid-August at the turn of the century. I made several trips to Llandilo just to sample this vehicle and dearly wished I could have gone all the way to Euston in it. While the train no doubt did better business from the 'Central Wales Spas' I never saw a Carmarthen passenger wishing to travel on it to London and it frequently started on its journey devoid of any fare-paying passengers. The return working in the evening came down the Branch attached to one of the ordinary stopping trains – 6.10 ex-Llandilo. – G. J. Thomas, 'Carmarthen Memories', *SLS Journal*

Middleton Incline. The second (or third if one counts the original Sheep Pasture as two) inclined plane on the Cromford & High Peak line in Derbyshire. Both this section to Middleton Top and that from Cromford to Sheep Pasture were balanced rope operated workings with a steam winding engine controlling the movement of wagons which were hooked and spliced onto the rope by means of the chains shown in the foreground. Once an independent railway, the line was operated by the LNWR, LMS and finally, BR. Middleton incline was closed on 3 June 1963, the remainder lasting until April 1967.

Derbyshire Incline. Hopton bank on the Cromford & High Peak section on a cold 19 April 1949. This short stretch of 1 in 20-14 just short of Hopton Top was the steepest to be worked by normal adhesion on any piece of Britain's railways. For years a number of ex North London Railway 0-6-0 tanks were kept in service specially for the C&HP (ideal engines, powerful and with a very short wheelbase) until replaced by redundant J94 class Austerity saddle tanks in 1956 and 1957. Three loaded wagons were as much as a single engine could manage and this morning a pair made the trip – just – with a water tank (spare Webb tender) for the local village, four loaded wagons and a brake van. The leading engine, No 58862, still has LMS on its tanks and an original NLR chimney, the train engine, No 58856, is newly painted black with white British Railways lettering and numbers; it also has a Webb LNWR chimney. Both engines were stationed at Middleton Top sub shed to Rowsley (17D).

of a short coupled wheelbase and light axle load these engines were found to be eminently suitable for the sharply curved branch from Axminster, on the South Western's main line to Exeter, through the Dorset countryside to the lovely little port and resort of Lyme Regis, though, because of the relatively steep gradients, a couple of coaches were about all that the veterans could manage. On summer Saturdays, with through coaches to Waterloo, another of the class would be summoned from Exmouth Junction shed to double head the train.

A second L&SWR London suburban class of even earlier date long survived in Cornwall working mineral trains from Wenford Bridge to the country junction with the North Cornwall line at Wadebridge. This was the Beattie 2-4-0 well tank, again used for its short wheel-base. Wadebridge shed could also show off some other pleasing classes including Moguls and the handsome T9 class 4-4-0s once so aptly nicknamed 'Greyhounds' when in main line service.

But so it could go on, for the Southern Railway was kind to its old engines and, beyond the reaches of its Kent and Sussex electrification, one-time London Brighton & South Coast or South Eastern & Chatham

South Western Veteran. An Adams 4-4-2 tank of Class 0415 near Combpyne on the ex LSWR branch from Axminster to Lyme Regis in August 1959. The engine, No 30582, is one of three shedded at Exmouth Junction (72A) sub shed Lyme Regis, the class having been specially retained for use on this line for many years because of sharp curves. One, No 30583 (once used on the East Kent Light Railway), having been sold out of service by the LSWR and returned to the fold when repurchased by the Southern Railway in 1946, is now preserved and works on the Bluebell Railway in Sussex. The Lyme Regis branch closed to all traffic on 29 November 1965.

91

ancients, sometimes rheumy but never senile, inhabited the many pre-Beeching country lines.

Patriarchal engines also survived on branches of the LMS and LNER, the latter being almost as benevolent towards them as the Southern, particularly in East Anglia though the North East and Scotland had their fair share. The Eastern Counties, right into the 1950s contained some almost folklorean ancients including Great Eastern Holden J15 0-6-0s and the E4 2-4-0s, the last of their type to work in Britain. No matter what part of East Anglia one visited, there were byways and locomotives of character in abundance – Thetford to Swaffham and on to Dereham, Cambridge to Mildenhall, Wivenhoe to Brightlingsea, Cromer to North Walsham or Kelvedon to Tollesbury. On the North Eastern section similar engines plied their primogenial ways; J21 0-6-0s crossed the Pennines from Darlington via Barnard Castle (which also sported some 0-4-4 tanks) to Tebay and Penrith on the West Coast main line, stopping off perhaps at Kirkby Stephen on the way – the selection then seemed endless.

The LMS inherited so many senescent engines that it is almost unbelievable – it took some twenty years to sort them out. Those arose because the larger pre-grouping companies in the name of standardisation retained many of their older engines for much longer than normal, often replacing small classes of locomotives of younger years from the more minor constituents. Thus one found L&NWR engines dating from the 1890s and earlier as standard branch line classes, often until final closure. The same applied to Midland, Lancashire & Yorkshire and Caledonian

Some eight miles from Colchester one could find a short piece of light railway; it began at Kelvedon and ran to the somewhat hopeful little pier at Tollesbury on the Blackwater estuary in Essex. To its end the train service was run by ex Great Eastern Railway engines and in April 1949 the coaches were a pair of magnificently anachronistic vehicles from the Wisbech & Upwell Tramway – one an open end balcony coach – later broken up (though scheduled for preservation) by order of railway management 'modern thinkers' at Stratford works. Class J69 0-6-0 tank No 8636 in grimy LNER black waits in the late afternoon sun with the 5.45pm train to Tollesbury. Kelvedon was a sub shed to Colchester (30E). The line closed to all traffic on 7 May 1951.

Opposite above:
Working Home. A pair of LNWR 18in goods 0-6-0s leave Blencow station with a Penrith to Workington train in August 1949, an unusual sight even in those heady days. The pilot engine from Workington shed (12D) carries her new BR number 58396 in LMS style on the cab sides whilst the train engine (sadly unrecorded) still has a round topped firebox. Just as exciting is the leading coach which is an ex LNWR brake composite vehicle double ended for use as a slip coach.

Engine Head Lamps
Engines of S&D trains must carry head lamps as shown below:
Engines of passenger trains . . .
  A white light at the foot of the chimney and a white light over the left-hand buffer
Engines of freight trains . . .
  A white light at the foot of the chimney and a white light over the right-hand buffer
Light engines . . .
  A white light at the foot of the chimney.
The lamps must be carried in position day and night.
  When a train running on the S&D Joint Line is worked by two engines attached in front of the train, the second engine must not carry head lamps.
S&DJR Appendix to Working Timetables, 1933

Opposite below:
Cumbrian Mountain Local. With through coaches for the West Coast main line ex LNWR 18in goods 0-6-0 No 28589 has a good head of steam as it climbs up from Keswick to Threlkeld with the 9.38am to Penrith 8.35am ex Workington on 8 August 1950. In spite of being two and a half years into nationalisation, the engine still carries its LMS number.

engines and, in the pre second world war years, to many veteran Highland 4-4-0s. Examples are legion but the record for longevity must tend towards the L&NWR 'Cauliflower' or 18in goods 0-6-0s working the heavily-graded single-line branch, the one-time Cockermouth, Keswick & Penrith Railway, until replaced by the new standard LMS Class 2 2-6-0s designed by Ivatt, a CME son of a CME. Like the Southern and LNER, most LMS country branches were worked by these old pre-grouping 0-6-0s and varying forms of tank engines, mostly 2-4-2, 0-6-2 or 0-4-4 types. But unlike the other Big Four railways, the LMS built two quite new classes for branch-line work in its last years, the 2-6-0 mentioned earlier, and a 2-6-2 tank. These and other modified versions were continued well into British Railways days.

Although the Great Western was by far the most standardised of the four groups, its country branches usually being worked by 0-6-0s, small wheeled 2-6-2Ts, or various forms of 0-6-0 pannier, or 0-4-2 tanks, there were some oddities even thirty years or so beyond amalgamation. Back in 1947, trying to catch up on some of the more remote country branches before possible closure, you came across a few byways where an atmosphere of the past lingered on most stubbornly. One such example was the old Tanat Valley branch of the erstwhile Cambrian Railways running from Oswestry to Llangynog, where the little train rattled along its switchback single line, headed by an ex Liskeard & Looe 2-4-0 tank named *Lady Margaret* sent, like an old horse, to end her days shuttling up and down the Welsh countryside, seeming very much at home as well she might, being of Celtic stock. Sadly, soon after this visit Swindon passed sentence of death on this old lady, and she was replaced for the rest of the line's short life by two Cambrian 2-4-0 tanks and then by standard 0-4-2 tanks.

But country railways were not always comparatively short branch lines; many were once-important cross-country links or extensions into undeveloped parts, opening up the land to city markets or market towns, and perhaps later bringing the city dweller to the sea. Here the motive power was quite different. Bigger and stronger, it entered the landscape and held the stage.

The westernmost of the great cross countryside links and in some respects the most interesting, certainly in locomotive working, was the Somerset & Dorset Joint Railway, once part of the London & South Western and Midland, later the Southern and LMS. In British Railways time it came under the Western and Southern Regions which killed it off, sending trains to Bournemouth via Reading instead of Bath. During the days of joint operation the Midland (later the LMS) provided the locomotive power and in answer to the demands of the heavy gradients introduced a series of special 2-8-0 freight engines which, with the solitary exception of the 0-10-0 Lickey Banker, were the largest and most powerful locomotives ever built at Derby under Midland auspices. Passenger trains were worked by Class 2P 4-4-0s creating dreadful motive power problems with heavy summer expresses. Later LMS bridge strengthening allowed the use of Stanier Class 5 4-6-0s while the

Cambrian Branch. The Tanat Valley train in from Llangynog to Oswestry approaches Llynclys Junction on 22 April 1946. The engine is GWR No 1197, one of three 2-4-0 Sharp Stewart tanks built for the Cambrian Railways in 1866; the leading coaches are Great Western four wheelers. Engines and stock both worked out their lives on this branch which was closed to passengers on 15 January 1951 and freight on 1 July 1952. The engine is very Great Westernised with new cab, brass safety valve cover, copper capped chimney, running plate, tool box, and cast number plates. Of the three engines No 1192 was withdrawn in 1929 but both Nos 1196 and 1197 lasted until April 1948, each topping a million miles in traffic.

Opposite:
Summer Saturday motive power. When pressed, Bath shed rostered its unique Somerset & Dorset Joint Railway 2-8-0s to work the heavy passenger traffic over the Mendips to Evercreech and Bournemouth. These drew the faithful (in the 1950s only numbered on the fingers of two hands) from far and wide but without doubt the S&D photographer of all time has been the resolute Ivo Peters who knew each crew and almost every engine personally. On the return trip LMS-built Class 2P 4-4-0 No 40697 (shed 71G Bath) and S&D 2-8-0 No 53800 (the first of the class also of Bath shed) set off from Evercreech Junction northbound; ahead of them lies the 8½ mile climb, much of it 1 in 50, up to Masbury summit, 811ft above sea level. With the diversion of traffic via Reading and the Southern Region lines, the whole of this cross country route was closed on 7 March 1966 with all freight re routed after 29 November 1965. Main line expresses including The Pines Express were diverted from 10 September 1962.

1950s saw Bulleid's lighter Pacifics and even BR Standard Class 9F 2-10-0s. To travel over this twisting and hilly route, laboriously climbing the 1 in 50 gradient from Bath Junction to the summit at the northern portal of Coombe Down Tunnel was an experience in itself, the line climbing on a sweeping semi-circular curve, leaving the city far below. This was followed by an exhilarating sprint down the bank to Midford where double track began and along the undulating and tortuous section to Radstock where any fast running ended, for here began the seven mile ascent of the Mendips with long sections at 1 in 50 until the final summit between Binegar and Masbury, and an even steeper descent to Evercreech Junction. Certainly there were few lines in England where heavy expresses were operated with such despatch over so hard a road. It was here that the faithful came during those last sad years to record steam at its best with double-headed trains, each engine working almost in extremis with thundering exhausts as they climbed the banks.

Wales and Scotland, too, had their long cross-country railways, mostly single line where, at not so little country junctions, other tracks meandered off into the valleys serving the mountain folk. Here too came the mixed traffic engines, the Great Western 43XX class Moguls, the Manors and the double framed Dukedog 4-4-0s – hybrids of the earlier Duke and Bulldog classes, making for the Cambrian coast where the lighter 0-6-0s and 2-6-2 tanks took over. The little sheds at Moat Lane (junction for the Mid Wales line to Brecon) Machynlleth, Aberystwyth and Porthmadoc harboured ex Cambrian Railways' 0-6-0s even into the 1950s.

The train still takes the traveller through some of Scotland's most spectacular countryside from Perth to Inverness through mountain passes, historic towns and villages, Pitlochry, Dalwhinnie and Aviemore to Inverness the Highland capital. From here there are two choices of country railway, on over Britain's most northerly tracks to Thurso and Wick via the remote Georgemas Junction or west to the Atlantic waters of Loch Carron and Kyle of Lochalsh, the locomotive aimed straight at the massive mysterious Isle of Skye. Then there is the West Highland line to Mallaig via Fort William. This, perhaps, is the finest of them all and certainly one of the country's most memorable railway journeys.

Each route originally claimed its own native motive power. North of Perth the Highland Railway moved its trains with a variety of 4-4-0s and one well-famed 4-6-0, the Jones Goods – the first locomotive of this wheel arrangement in our islands: later came the other 4-6-0s the Castles and the Clans and, in LMS days, the ubiquitous Stanier Class 5 4-6-0s nicknamed the 'Hikers' which, as with the Somerset & Dorset line, transformed the motive-power scene until the end of steam in the 1960s.

The West Highland was served by those beautifully-proportioned Glen class inside cylinder 4-4-0s and they remained supreme, generally hunting in couples until the coming of the LNER. The latter introduced

An Ivy-Clad Tunnel Entrance
In 1839 three tunnels were being constructed between Bristol and Bath, but, owing to a very wet winter, a portion of the hillside at the west end slipped and so made the construction of an intended retaining wall unnecessary. Struck by the resemblance of the unfinished masonry to a ruinous medieval gateway, Brunel decided to leave it as it stood and ordered ivy to be planted to increase its picturesque effect. This was done, and it remained in this unique state until 1900, when a severely practical engineer had the ivy removed and the tunnel front completed in the modern style.
GWR Magazine

varying classes of 2-6-0 starting with the ex Great Northern K2s named after Lochs, then the specially-constructed K4s exampled by the *Great Marquess*, and last the K1: but even this range of sturdy power did not keep out the Stanier Class 5 and the B1 on the coming of BR. There were fascinating combinations from time to time, two Glens, a Glen and a Loch, two Lochs, a Loch and a K1, and last two Class 5s, the ultimate West Highland steam power.

Until the second world war the head end was often a Glen and a Loch though the *Northern Belle* cruise train used Glens almost exclusively. After the second world war there was no longer a *Northern Belle* but one could still get to Mallaig in luxury taking the overnight sleeper from Kings Cross via Glasgow Queen Street; by mid morning the train was at Fort William and by early afternoon Mallaig. Sadly, except for times of locomotive shortage, the Glens had gone, though trains were still worked by engines in tandem as the norm. By the end of steam these were usually ex LMS or BR Class 5s, though K2s and K1s turned up with reasonable regularity except for the very last days. But on 8 and 9 May 1959, the clock went back by twenty years and the West Highland was graced once more by a pair of Glens in regular service picking up the overnight sleeper from London at Queen Street and making the return trip to Fort William each day. They were Nos 62471 *Glen Falloch* and

Green Glen. Crianlarich Junction sometime around 1926 with an ex North British Railway Glen class 4-4-0 No 9408 Glen Sloy *heading a Fort William bound train and taking water from the stone based tank. The North British bracket signal is in the off position for the main line; to its left is the connecting spur to the ex Caledonian tracks to Oban, now the only route as the line via Callander was closed on 1 November 1965 after a landslide. A photograph of this engine on Fort William shed on the same date shows it was carrying a curved destination board 'Fort William' on the smokebox front, North British style.*

62496 *Glen Loy* in lined-out BR black; with seven coaches behind them they scampered up and down the banks, never looking over their shoulders. For those two days the trains were under the lenses of BBC TV and the footplate scrutiny of that recorder of railway legends, an ex NBR driver, Norman McKillop. Writing of the class he recalled the time he was in the cab of the then new 2-8-2 *Cock O' The North* with a test train of over 600 tons on the Edinburgh–Aberdeen road. They were waiting at Thornton Junction when a local driver gave the new 'Cock' a once over. After he had satisfied his curiosity, McKillop asked 'Do you like her Sandy?' 'Ach, no,' said Sandy, 'Ye'd do better wi a guid Glen!'.

At 5.45am each morning the guard's whistle blew as the train stood under Glasgow's glass-roofed Queen Street station and the train set off up the 1 in 45 through the tunnels to Cowlairs. Then along the Clyde to Craigendoran Junction with another steep gradient out of the chalet styled station, deep eaved and roofed with shingles imported from Switzerland. Dawn breaks early in May and the low sun glistened on the polished black engines as the train climbed beyond Garelochhead to Glen Douglas, the track on a ledge spectacularly overhanging Loch Long and the motor road below. From Ardlui it was a hammering slogging climb for 15 miles up Glen Falloch and through Crianlarich (the junction with the old Caledonian to Oban) to the Horseshoe Curve, the hills beyond

---

B.R. 32713

BRITISH TRANSPORT COMMISSION
BRITISH RAILWAYS

Motive Power Dept. *Scottish* Region.

11th May 19*59*

Weather *General; Moderate wind, & Rails Good.*

REPORT OF INSPECTOR *James Cunningham* ON THE RUNNING OF THE

5.45 a.m. Passenger ~~Freight~~ train from *Glasgow (Queen St.H.L.)* to *Fort William*

on *8th May* 19*59*

PASSENGER— Classification *A* Actual tons *270* Regulation tons *316 Tons (Double Headed.)*

FREIGHT— Classification ___ Actual & Equivalent Wagons ___ Regulation Load ___

(1) Driver *Wm Robertson & D. Thomson* Fireman *N. Hamilton & A. Cameron* Depot *Eastfield & Fort William*

(2) Driver *Jas Prior, P. McDonald* Fireman *R. Sinnari & J. Cameron* Depot *" " "*

(1) Loco No. *62496 (Glen Loy)* Type & M.P. Class *3 P. (D.34)* Depot *Eastfield*

(2) Loco No. *62471 (Glen Falloch)* Type & M.P. Class *3 P. (A.34)* Depot *St Margarets*

STATIONS	BOOKED TIMES Arr.	BOOKED TIMES Dep.	ACTUAL TIMES Arr.	ACTUAL TIMES Dep.	MINUTES Lost	MINUTES Recovered	CAUSE
	Am	Am	Am	Am			
Glasgow (Queen St.H.L.)		5.45		5.45			
Cowlairs Box		(5.52)		(5.52)			
Knightswood North		(5.58)		(6.02)	2½"		'Adverse Signals. Passl.park.
Milngavie Jct.		(5.59)		(6.12)			
Dalmuir Park		(6.3)		(6.52)			
Dumbarton East		(6.10)		(6.13)	¼"		Loco.
" Central	6.11	6.12	6.14	6.15			
Dalreoch Jct.		(6.13)		(6.16)			
Craigendoran Jct.		(6.24)		(6.27)			
Helensburgh Upper	6.31	6.33	6.34				
Garelochhead	6.46	6.48	6.49				
Glen Douglas		(7.1)		(7.4)			
Arrochar & Tarbet		7.11	7.13	7.14			
Ardlui	7.26	7.31	7.29	7.34			
Crianlarich Upper	7.51	7.59	7.54	8.8.	6"		Station & Loco Duties.
Tyndrum		8.12	8.21	8.22	1"		Loco Engine No. 62496 –
Bridge of Orchy		8.27	8.38	8.39	2"		" {Right leg end running
Gorton		8.46	8.59	9.0	2"		" {Very warm attention.
(continued)							& Photograph work

Remarks :— (—) "Passing" time

Signature_____

B.R. 32713

BRITISH TRANSPORT COMMISSION
BRITISH RAILWAYS

Motive Power Dept. *Scottish* Region.

19

Weather

REPORT OF INSPECTOR ___ ON THE RUNNING OF THE

5.45 a.m. Passenger Freight train from *Glasgow (Queen St.H.L.)* to *Fort William (continued)*

on *8th May* 19*59*

PASSENGER— Classification *A* Actual tons ___ Regulation tons ___

FREIGHT— Classification ___ Actual & Equivalent Wagons ___ Regulation Load ___

(1) Driver ___ Fireman ___ Depot ___

(2) Driver ___ Fireman ___ Depot ___

(1) Loco No. ___ Type & M.P. Class ___ Depot ___

(2) Loco No. ___ Type & M.P. Class ___ Depot ___

STATIONS	BOOKED TIMES Arr.	BOOKED TIMES Dep.	ACTUAL TIMES Arr.	ACTUAL TIMES Dep.	MINUTES Lost	MINUTES Recovered	CAUSE
Gorton							
	Am	Am	Am	Am			
Rannoch		8.58	9.11	9.12			
Corrour		9.14	9.27	9.28			
Tulloch	9.34	9.36	9.47	9.49		1"	Loco
Roy Bridge		9.47	9.57	9.58		2"	
Spean Bridge	9.52	9.56	10.2	10.7	1"	1"	1" Change - over.
Mallaig Jct.		(10.9)		(10.20)			
Fort-William	10.12		10.23				

Remarks :— *Time Lost by Adverse Signals 2½ minutes* }
Loco & Station Duties 12½ " } *Total Time Lost = 15 minutes*
" " Regained = 4 "
11 minutes late arrival.

Signature *James Cunningham*

Tank Engine Shed. Oxenholme (11D) on the North Western main line in the mid 1930s. Like Tebay, Oxenholme existed to house banking engines needed for the severe grades in the area, although it also held a number for the Windermere branch, at that time Whale 4-4-2 tanks. It was something of an experience to see the Windermere portion of the Lakes Express headed by these primarily suburban locomotives of Edwardian vintage. The photograph shows No 6784 (right) and an unknown member of the same class just on the shed – note the lamp on the head of the bunker. One of the bankers – a Fowler 2-6-4 tank – is being inspected with some head scratching. Although on the main line Oxenholme could scarcely be more of a country junction with everything, bar the Fowler engines, dating back to pre grouping days, locomotives, wagons, shed building, station and signalbox.

Parcels Addressed 'To Be Left Till Called For'
Parcels addressed 'To be left till called for,' if not applied for and removed from the Station to which they are booked either on the day of receipt or on the day following, an extra charge of 2d. per Parcel will be made to the Consignee; in the case of Parcels not applied for within the week, an additional charge of 2d. per week will be charged. For example – if a Parcel is received at a Station on a Monday, and is not called for until the next Wednesday, it is liable to a charge of 2d.; if not called for until Thursday, to a charge of 2d. extra, or 4d., the second 2d. freeing the warehouse rent up to the following Wednesday. Fractions of a week will be counted as a whole week.
GWR Parcels & Goods Arrangements, 1914

giving some of the finest views of the line. At Tyndrum they poured castor oil into a warm big end bearing on No 62471. The leading engine *Glen Loy* was running like a sewing machine. Down then to Bridge of Orchy with water in the boiler gauge glasses out of sight at the top one minute, and down to within an inch of the bottom the next, to cross the bleak Rannoch Moor up to Corrour, the highest point – still 20 miles away. Only the West Highland line crosses the wilderness of Rannoch where the builders floated the track on a bed of brushwood to keep it from sinking. At Cruach, just short of the summit, the train, with rocks forming sounding boards, pounded its way through Britain's only snow shed where in the first winter after the opening of the line there were drifts up to 25ft in depth and some travellers nearly starved to death. By Spean Bridge all was calm once more and just before 10.15 they rolled into Fort William where rows of seagulls resting on the railings at the side of the stone embankment contemplated, with angry eyes, the approach of the oncoming train before languidly taking off for safer perches.

Over the two days both veteran engines ran over 500 miles at the head of a regular service train some 50 years after their introduction with only a few minutes lost and a slightly warm big end; a fitting tribute to a fine class.

Home for all these engines was 'the shed' which dated from the earliest days of railways, coal, water and repair facilities at regular points being essential for the efficient running of the system. Each company produced its own designs (usually those of its chief mechanical engineer) but overall these depots fell into two categories, the roundhouse or the straight shed. The former was used by a few railways in larger towns or important junctions having a central turntable with radiating tracks, each with its own pit, the latter, generally the more common, with one or more parallel tracks. The buildings contained stores, offices and small workshop facilities while outside there were coal stages and water cranes or towers depending on the size of shed as to their numbers. Locomotives were sent to the main shed in the area direct from the works and each was marked with a code denoting that depot, differing railways using differing codes. For example, Oswestry on the Great Western would carry the letters OSW on the front locomotive frame while Abergavenny on the LMS was indicated by an oval cast iron plate numbered 4D carried on the bottom of each locomotive smokebox door.

Some depots were also equipped as intermediate workshops; these were often in country market towns such as Newton Abbot, Worcester, Carnforth or Inverness – almost always they were also important junctions when the shed could act as a main depot for the surrounding area, Newton Abbot, for example serving the Torquay, Mortonhampstead and Exe Valley lines as well as providing banking engines or pilots for the notorious South Devon inclines en route to Plymouth. Some other country sheds served mainly as stabling posts on a main line for bankers, Tebay for the climb over Shap, Bromsgrove for the infamous Lickey Incline, or Blair Atholl for Druimuachdar being a few examples.

At the end of the country branch lay some of the more appealing and very personal sheds, places where a locomotive might rest year upon year used only by perhaps two sets of men living locally. These could be found in abundance in the great days of the country railway some of the most picturesque, built in local stone in the West Country or the Cotswolds, timber in wooded country, and some just corrugated iron semi shacks – but all with a quiet solitude where engines retired every night to sleep undisturbed.

But it was the spasmodic bustle of the country junction which portrayed so much of the railway's life, like a market town semi slumbering during periods of relative inertia. Its shed and the men working within its compass did not necessarily lead quiet lives. John Powell, who worked his way through the system from an apprenticeship at Derby Locomotive Works, taking on posts as divisional maintenance engineer and assistant district motive power superintendent on the way to a senior position at British Railways Board, relates a day in the life of one such imaginary but typical country junction shed in the mid 1930s.

101

Working of Engines over the Severn Bridge

Trains running over the Severn Bridge must not be worked by more than one engine in front. Two engines coupled together must not, under any circumstances, be run over the bridge.

The following are the only engines that may be allowed to pass over the Severn Bridge:

Great Western Engines – 2-4-0 Class – Nos. 810, 3202, 3203, 3503, 3506, 3507 and 3516.

0-6-0 Class – Nos. 116, 132, 146, 331, 333, 334, 350, 358, 363, 395, 601, 607, 678, 693, 804, 875, 934, 937, 940, 942, 945, 1015, 1089, 1111, 1203, 1215, 2301 to 2360, 2381 to 2490, 2511 to 2580.

0-6-0 (tank) 2021 to 2160.

In the event of the failure of an engine at either end of the bridge and it is necessary for such engine to be taken to the opposite end, or if an engine fail on the bridge, arrangements must be made for the engine to be worked specially, and four wagons must be placed between the assisting engine and the disabled engine. A competent man must in all cases ride upon the disabled engine.

The following are the only L. M. & S. engines that may be allowed to pass over the Severn Bridge:

L. M. & S. Freight Engines – No. 1 Class bearing numbers between 2399 and 2867. No. 2 Class bearing numbers between 2900 and 3129.

Note – Engines of other classes bearing numbers as above must not be allowed to pass over the Bridge.

L. M. & S. Passenger Engines – Must not be allowed to pass over the Bridge.

GWR Service Timetable 1925

At 7.45am on a summer Friday the running shed foreman (RSF) looks down on the railway scene in the valley bottom as he cycles down Station Road, his bowler hat firmly on his head. The station, its three platforms partly covered by glass awnings, holds only the branch passenger train in the outside road, its 4-4-0 simmering quietly, waiting for the main line connection. Beyond the station by some 300 yards and connected by an ash pathway is his four-road dead-end shed at the end of its modest yard and, as yet, unaffected by any modernisation scheme. The elevated coal stage topped by a cast iron water tank lies adjacent to the ashpit, on which he can see one of the depot's 2-6-0 mixed traffic engines off the night through freight getting the fire cleaned. Beyond it is the 60ft turntable, manually operated. Adjacent to the main line, there is a small goods yard concerned mainly with the branch traffic, with outward coal and inward limestone, which is usually quite heavy. From it comes the sound of sharp exhaust beats and clashing buffers as an 0-6-0 tank sorts the wagons into trains. There is a sudden screech heralding the passage of the morning business express, city bound. It is a picture which has greeted him every morning for several years, even to one of his 0-6-0s sitting in the bank engine siding waiting its next spell of hard work.

The RSF muses on his modest domain as he approaches and gets off his bicycle; there is no other shed within 20 miles, save only his own little outstation on the branch, where a single 2-4-2 tank runs the motor-train from the small rural junction shed some three quarters of the way down the longish branch. There are 19 engines in his charge, ranging from three big 2-6-0s and three 0-8-0s for the main line freight, a pair of elderly 4-4-0s for the branch passengers, three 2-6-2 tanks for the main line stopping passenger trains some 0-6-0s for banking and pickup freight, and a pair of shunting tanks. These require 49 sets of enginemen, plus another two sets and a passed cleaner at the branch sub shed. Eight fitting staff plus a small group of shedmen, cleaners and clerks complete his men. Finally, there are the two running foremen, working afternoons and nights, week and week about; he himself covers the foreman's duties on the day turn. For good measure there are two venerable tool vans, one a six-wheeler of uncertain ancestry, for the breakdown work.

In his dingy office, its bay window looking out over the preparation pits at the yard end of the shed (which is still gas lit), the night shift foreman is waiting with the log book. All turns are covered, though there is one late start off shed, due to the driver booking attention to sanders while preparing his engine; *he* could find something wrong on a brand new one. One fireman has been late booking on for his 05.20 turn; 'Overslept'. This is the second time in a month, and the Riot Act will require to be read. Coal supplies are adequate, both Grade 2 and 3. Two engines have been stopped for washout and 'X' examination, but they should be available tonight. They need to be for the three weekend extras especially as the diagrams only arrived yesterday afternoon. Are they covered? Yes, with two crews from the spare link and one cancelled job in No 1 Goods link. 'OK Jack, away to your bed.'

The leading fitter puts his head round the door with the repairs list and the two washouts. 'Will the 4-4-0 be ready tonight?' Answer: 'It should be as there is a new steam brake cylinder coming by passenger train at mid-day'. Word has come to send the 0-6-0 to works next Tuesday so the coal must be off her before then. There is also the 'Shopping Proposal' for the 0-8-0 today: they may well refuse to take her at 44000 miles, but it can be laid on a bit thick, maybe that will melt any stony hearts! Is the branch engine covered for daily exam? This is in hand, and the fitter has been asked to look at the firebox while he is there – the arch is on its last legs and there are several tubes leaking. A replacement may have to be found for tonight.

The RSF takes a quick look round the shed and yard. In the enginemen's lobby the Engine Arrangement board is marked up to teatime, with nothing abnormal. A brief glance at the Roster Sheets, especially the alterations for tomorrow in red ink for the coverage of the specials. In the messroom the big cast iron kettle steams gently on the black grate, and the fireman of the morning branch freight is swinging two mashing cans as he makes his way out to his engine. On the repair road, water sloshes around as the tuber finishes cooling down the second washout; he has got a tin shield hitched on to the coupling rod to keep the stream of water away from the trailing crankpin. One light is almost

Lone Survivor. One of the serious reasons for travelling around with a camera in the immediate post-war days was the constant hope of catching a last glimpse of a thoroughbred which once raced past the countryside at the head of an express train now out to grass and possibly awaiting the scrap yard's call. Generally, these engines had retreated to particular depots with the LNWR Precursors and Georges centred on Chester, Llandudno Junction and Bangor. The last superheated Precursor No 25297 Sirocco was at Llandudno Junction (7A) in 1947 but it was a great surprise to find the engine on a Blaenau Festiniog branch train at Bettwys-y-Coed on 17 June, especially as this (2.15pm from the Junction) terminated there necessitating a tender first working on the outward journey. Perhaps something had failed.

103

Working Of Engines
THE SEVERN BRIDGE

The following engines only are permitted to pass over the Severn Bridge:

WESTERN REGION ENGINES

Class 2301 (0-6-0) tender, (non-condensing type) bearing numbers 2322 to 2356, 2382 to 2484, and 2513 to 2579.

Class 2021 (0-6-0) tank.

Class 4300 (2-6-0) tender. Subject to the strict observance of all Service Restrictions.

Class 7400 (0-6-0) tank.

Class 1400 (0-4-2) tank.

LONDON, MIDLAND REGION ENGINES

CLASS 1P. (2-4-2) TANK (L.N.W. 5FT 6IN).

CLASS 2P. (2-6-2) TANK (STANDARD).

CLASS 2F. (0-6-2) TANK (L.N.W., S.T.C.).

CLASS 2F. (2-6-0) TENDER (STANDARD).

CLASS 2F. (0-6-0) TENDER (L.N.W. SMALL COAL).

CLASS 2F. (0-6-0) TENDER (L.N.W. 18IN).

CLASS 2F. (0-6-0) TENDER (MIDLAND) BEARING NUMBERS 2987 TO 3127, 3695 AND 22900 TO 22984.

ALL ENGINES IN 'YELLOW' CLASSIFICATION.

TRAINS RUNNING OVER THE SEVERN BRIDGE MUST NOT BE WORKED BY MORE THAN ONE ENGINE IN FRONT. TWO ENGINES COUPLED TOGETHER MUST NOT IN ANY CIRCUMSTANCES BE RUN OVER THE BRIDGE.

WR Service Timetable 1951

out at the bottom of No 2 road; probably water in the gas pipe – must get that looked at. The sand furnace is also OK, but the wagon is almost empty. No wonder, it has been sitting there a fortnight. The stores seems in order but it might be wise to make spot-checks on some of the stock cards on Monday: tools are in short supply. A word with the coalman, who is having a breather and cup of tea before the next arrival empties half his tubs. The ashpit surrounds are a bit messy – the fireman of the 2-6-0 seems to have had a lot of clinker to paddle out of the firebox after his night run. Probably the result of the poor coal they loaded on to the tender at the other end.

Back to the office to report to the concentration depot ready for the morning Divisional conference. They will be ready to take the 0-8-0 that is due for Valve & Piston Examination on Tuesday. The foreman checks that they have sent the cylinder and valve sizes. Now the Union LDC secretary's head appears round the door. They discuss the rosters to be made out before the summer timetable comes in. He is a young passed fireman with lots of ambition who reminds his boss that Driver Wheeler is retiring next month so there will be one short on the foreman's relief panel.

Having got rid of him, the RSF can get down to answering the odd letter in between the phone calls and enginemen's queries. There is a driver to intercept as he books off duty; five minutes lost in running between A and B with a freight on Monday night. The culprit dredges his memory and says that would be the night they got stopped at C Station North while the bobby put an engine across the road in front of them. Was *that* even reported? Now is the time to retreat into the office for sandwiches and a mug of tea.

Outside the bay window, an 0-6-0 is being prepared, and there is a pillar of black smoke rising to the sky as the fireman builds his fire. The foreman goes out to remonstrate with him; he is a passed cleaner relieving, but that is not the way the firing instructor taught him. The afternoon foreman comes in and the handover takes place; discussion is interrupted by the phone as the head shunter in the yard reports two wagons derailed one pair of wheels each and buffer-locked by a rough shunt, blocking two roads almost at the yard throat and bottling up the first evening freight. They get the shunt engine across for the tool vans and collect the back shift fitter and his mate, plus one of the Grade 3 fitters who has just finished reblocking one of the washout engines, then it is a walk over to the yard to see what will be involved. The work is a straightforward job with rerailing ramps and packing, but the buffer-locking makes it that bit more difficult; some bosses call it wasteful if you burn through a 3-link coupling to get the job done faster. However, the Grade 3 fitter puts his torch to it and it parts with a mild bang. Packing in the four-foot, jack under the wooden headstock to clear the buffer heads, position the packing and rerailing ramps, a gentle pull to topple the wagon off the jack, and it rolls back on to the rails as easy as pie. Reposition and pull on the second offender. Then it is a case of loading up the tackle and getting out of the way as fast as possible. It takes half an hour to get the vans off the shed, an hour clearing the wagons, and as the RSF walks back to his office the pay clerk is arranging his pay tins at the outer office window ready for clocking-off time.

A word with the leading fitter; the washouts are finished, the brake cylinder on the 4-4-0 is up and almost ready, so both can be released for firing up. 'Willie reckons the branch tank will last out till tomorrow night. Oh, and while you were playing games across in the yard, we had word that the 0-6-0 stopped with loose tender tyres has been called in works next week for a General.' He passes through the General Office, where there is a query about the mileage of that 0-8-0 for valve and piston exam. There is some late mileage advice for when she was away last week, which will bring her to about 36500 when she goes in. So be it;

Day's Work Done. Driver and fireman walk from their ex LMS Black Five to book off. Once a driver had his 'own' engine allocated to him giving the footplate crew personal interest as happened for example in France almost to the end of steam. The only chance of this happening in Britain during the final years was perhaps with a few top link express turns or with a country branch engine which could remain at the same shed in between heavy repairs.

Caledonian Branch Terminus. Ballachulish in May 1949 with Oban (then 31C) 0-4-4 tank No 55163 on the branch train. Note the slightly unusual position of the shed plate on the top half of the smokebox door and the station staff snoozing on the platform seat complete with Highland Terrier. With only three Monday to Friday and four Saturday trains a day plus a small freight yard, it was a pleasant life.

perhaps the Divisional mechanical inspector will not be too hard on his next visit.

The foreman takes a final look at his desk; only two letters to sign and it is clear, and he can call it a day. A last look at the big framed pictures of pre-grouping locomotives on the wall, and he puts on his cycle clips and picks up his sandwich tin. He tells the shift foreman that he will not be at home but will only have popped down to the White Hart for an hour. He swings his leg over the saddle of his bike and pedals out of the gate. It has been nothing out of the ordinary, this Friday, but he will be glad to get into his armchair and listen to the radio – if he is allowed to.

Meanwhile, at the sub-shed, the new day starts as the senior driver signs on in the grubby time book at 6.30. It sits on a small shelf-desk in a corner of the little room attached to the single-road shed which does duty as enginemen's lobby, stores and messroom. Around it sits a whitewood table with bench seat, bags of dry sand sent from the parent shed, 40-gallon drums of cylinder and axlebox oil on stillages, and a kettle on a gas ring, while a few permanent and dusty notices grace a wall board. He is greeted by the sleepy-eyed night shift passed cleaner, who has spent his time coaling the 2-4-2 tank by hand direct from a wagon, cleaning out the pit and loading ashes to another wagon, and keeping the engine fire banked and water level safe, as well as giving the visible parts of the engine a wipe over.

A quick report on the circuit phone to the parent shed, and he and his fireman can start preparing the engine for the early turn: four return trips up the single-line branch to the little terminus in the foothills. Fill up the oil bottles and long feeder, then outside to position the engine over the pit for oiling round, keeping a weather eye open for any abnormalities. Meanwhile the fireman has the bag in for water while starting to make his fire up and testing both injectors. A whistle to old Percy the signalman and they take the engine along to the bay platform to couple (not forgetting the extra vacuum control pipe and the bell jumper wires) to the two elderly non-corridors which will be their train.

It is a boring job pottering up and down the branch, stopping at the one intermediate station. Up to the terminus they work engine and chimney first, since this is against the grade and it is better with both men on the engine. Coming down, the driver retires to the driving position at the front of the second coach, opening and closing the engine regulator by his vacuum control, while the fireman operates the reverser but leaves the regulator wide open; at least that is what the instructions say. In practice the one passed fireman drives the engine completely, merely working to the bell signals. The 7.30am up and the 4.55pm down are the only fairly busy trains, for they take the quarrymen to work and home again. Otherwise there are not a lot of passenger pickings, either local or off connecting trains. Time at the junction between trains for a meal, the booking office fire heats many a pie and mashing can.

The back shift provides the enginemen with the only break in this routine. The 3.10pm up gets extra time at the intermediate station to deal with the two loaded Express Dairy tanks from the milk depot. After stopping at the platform, he draws into the creamery siding to attach the tanks. At the junction, instead of using the bay platform, he is routed importantly into the down platform, then goes forward and in due time propels the tanks, city bound, on to the rear of the waiting passenger up train. Across into the dock, and he attaches two empty tanks in the rear, where they add to his load all the way to the terminus. Here there is a burst of activity as the whole caravan goes off into the small yard and is reformed with much huffing and puffing to get the tanks at the rear for the down journey, so that they can be propelled in through the creamery gate.

So two elderly drivers with their youngish mates hold down the working of a country branch. What made them apply for this job to finish out their time, in the almost certain knowledge that their seniority would get it for them? The regular hours and absence of lodging turns, giving them the time to put in on their allotments? The untaxing nature of the work? The joys of the country scene? The fact of being largely their own masters, without interference, trusted to do a good job? Service to the little communities? Probably a little of all of these, a more relaxed life than it would be at the parent shed up the line. And if they had been introduced to a young man of twenty, Richard Beeching, then studying for his degree, it would not have meant a thing.

The Highland At War

Forres shed in the winter of 1943–44 housed a somewhat motley collection of locomotives. The Highland was represented by *Loch Tay* (14385) and *Ben Slioch* (14406). The former usually made the daily goods trip over the Burghead and Hopeman branch. She would totter off to Elgin about 9am, return later to Alves, whence she ambled gently over the sand-swept rails to Burghead. Following some desultory shunting at that little harbour, which usually included the collection of a van or two of fish for London, she would propel a few wagons of coal along to Hopeman. *Ben Slioch* was frequently retained for banking duties up to Dava Summit. In the spring of 1944 some large scale manoeuvres, in preparation for 'D-Day,' were carried out on the Moray Firth. Fort George was the main base for these operations, and many train-loads of tanks were brought up from the south. When operations were completed the tanks were worked south again. Loaded on 'Warwells,' and headed by a couple of '8Fs,' these 750-ton trains were assisted by the aged 'Ben' up to Dava.

Within the cramped confines of Forres Yard a couple of ex-Caledonian 0-6-0 tanks struggled manfully with the heavy war-time traffic. They were 16299 and 16301.

One of the pair spent the whole day shunting in the yard. The other made a trip to Nairn in the morning to shunt the yard there and attend the freight needs of the Fort George branch. In the early afternoon she would return with Nairn's contribution to the south-bound and east-bound through freights. This usually included a heavy tonnage of timber from Brodie.

W. McGowan Gradon
SLS Journal, May 1952

Examples of Locomotive Allocations At Selected Depots
LMS DEPOTS.   November 1946

4A **Shrewsbury.**   83 engines

1F	0-6-0T	MR	1
4MT	2-6-4T	parallel blr.	4
3F	0-6-0	MR	10
5MT	4-6-0	taper blr.	12
1P	2-4-2T	LNW	2
—	0-4-0T	Sentinel	1
1F	0-6-2T	LNW	7
8F	2-8-0	taper blr.	11
7F	0-8-0	LNW 'G2'	15
3F	0-6-0	L&Y Class 27	8
0F	0-4-0ST	L&Y	1
2F	0-6-0	LNW coal	5
2F	0-6-0	LNW 18″	6

5F **Uttoxeter.**   8 engines

3MT	2-6-2T	taper blr.	3
4MT	2-6-4T	parallel blr.	3
4MT	2-6-4T	taper blr.	1
4F	0-6-0	std.	1

7B **Bangor.**   34 engines

3MT	2-6-2T	taper blr.	5
2P	4-4-0	MR and std.	2
4P	4-4-0	std. compound	1
5MT	2-6-0	taper blr.	3
4F	0-6-0	std.	2
1P	2-4-2T	LNW	7
2F	0-6-2T	LNW coal	12
3F	0-6-0	L&Y Class F19	2

12G **Dumfries.**   45 engines

3MT	2-6-2T	taper blr.	1
2P	4-4-0	std.	5
4P	4-4-0	std. compound	6
5MT	2-6-0	parallel blr.	4
1P	2-4-2T	LNW	3
2F	0-6-0	CR 'Jumbo'	18
3F	0-6-0	CR 812 class	8

20G **Hellifield.**   30 engines

3MT	2-6-2T	taper blr.	1
2P	4-4-0	MR	3
4P	4-4-0	MR & std. compd.	4
1P	0-4-4T	MR	1
5MT	2-6-0	parallel blr.	1
2F	0-6-0	MR	1
3F	0-6-0	MR	8
4F	0-6-0	MR and std.	5
8F	2-8-0	taper blr.	3
2P	2-4-2T	L&Y class K2	3

22C **Bath.**   43 engines

3MT	2-6-2T	taper blr.	2
2P	4-4-0	MR and std.	5
1P	0-4-4T	MR	3
3F	0-6-0	MR	1
4F	0-6-0	MR, S&D and std.	10
5MT	4-6-0	taper blr.	3
—	0-4-0T	Sentinel S&D	1
3F	0-6-0T	S&D and std.	6
0F	0-4-0ST	L&Y dock	1
7F	2-8-0	S&D	11

26E **Bacup.**   16 engines

3MT	2-6-2T	taper blr.	6
2P	4-4-0	std.	1
2P	2-4-2T	L&Y class K2	2
3P	2-4-2T	L&Y class K3	2
3F	0-6-0	L&Y class F19	5

32B **Aviemore.**   11 engines

5MT	4-6-0	taper blr.	1
2P	4-4-0	CR Dunalastair 3	2
2P	4-4-0	HR Loch	1
2P	4-4-0	HR Small Ben	2
3P	4-4-0	CR Dun'stair 3 reb	1
3P	4-6-0	HR Castle	1
2P	0-4-4T	CR	1
3F	0-6-0	HR 'Barney'	2

LNER DEPOTS.   January 1947

Leicester (Belgrave Road).   13 engines

B17	4-6-0	Sandringham	2
C4/4	4-4-2	GN	2
J1	0-6-0	GN	2
J2	0-6-0	GN	6
J69	0-6-0T	GE	1

Louth.   12 engines

D3	4-4-0	GN	1
J11	0-6-0	GC	2
C12	4-4-2T	GC	8
N5/2	0-6-2T	GC	1

Malton.   14 engines

F4	2-4-2T	GE	1
G5	0-4-4T	NE	6
J24	0-6-0	NE	5
Y1	0-4-0T	Sentinel	2

Melton Constable.   29 engines

C12	4-4-2T	GC	1
D2	4-4-0	GN	7
D15	4-4-0	GE	2
D16/3	4-4-0	GE rebuild	5
F3	2-4-2T	GE	3
F4	2-4-2T	GE	1
J15	0-6-0	GE	1
J17	0-6-0	GE	7
J69	0-6-0T	GE	1
J93	0-6-0T	M&GN	1

Northallerton.   12 engines

D20/1	4-4-0	NE	3
G5	0-4-4T	NE	2
J24	0-6-0	NE	4
J71	0-6-0T	NE	1
N10	0-6-2T	NE	1
Y3	0-4-0T	Sentinel	1

Wrexham.   20 engines

C13	4-4-2T	GC	5
J10/4	0-6-0	GC	3

J10/6	0-6-0	GC	1
J60	0-6-0T	LD&EC	4
J62	0-6-0ST	GC	2
N5/2	0-6-2T	GC	2
Y3	0-4-0T	Sentinel	3

Fort William. 14 engines

J36	0-6-0	NB	5
K2/2	2-6-0	GN Loch	7
K4	2-6-0		2

GWR Depots.   June 1947

DID   Didcot.   48 engines

1701	0-6-0PT		2
—	2-4-0	M&SWJ	1
2251	0-6-0		8
2301	0-6-0		1
27xx	0-6-0PT		1
33xx	4-4-0	Bulldog	5
43xx	2-6-0		9
49xx	4-6-0	Hall	4
57xx	0-6-0PT		9
72xx	2-8-2T		4
90xx	4-4-0	'Dukedog'	3
WD	2-8-0		1

WEY   Weymouth.   26 engines and 1 railcar

1366	0-6-0ST		3
14xx	0-4-2T		3
1501	0-6-0PT		1
29xx	4-6-0	Saint	2
43xx	2-6-0		8
45xx	2-6-2T		2
49xx	4-6-0	Hall	4
57xx	0-6-0PT		2
74xx	0-6-0PT		1
Diesel Railcar			1

TR   Truro.   22 engines

10xx	4-6-0	County	1
1501	0-6-0PT		1
1701	0-6-0PT		1
43xx	2-6-0		1
45xx	2-6-2T		12
49xx	4-6-0	Hall	4
57xx	0-6-0PT		1
74xx	0-6-0PT		1

LTS   Llantrisant.   16 engines and 1 railcar

—	0-6-2T	Barry Railway	1
14xx	0-4-2T		1
35xx	2-4-0T		1
42xx	2-8-0T		2
57xx	0-6-0PT		11
Diesel Railcar			2

WTD   Whitland.   22 engines

1901	0-6-0PT		7
2251	0-6-0		1
45xx	2-6-2T		10
57xx	0-6-0PT		1
74xx	0-6-0PT		1

81xx	2-6-2T		2

WLN   Wellington.   21 engines

2021	0-6-0PT		1
33xx	4-4-0	Bulldog	1
43xx	2-6-0		2
44xx	2-6-2T		5
51xx	2-6-2T		5
57xx	0-6-0PT		7

LYD   Lydney.   20 engines

14xx	0-4-2T		2
2021	0-6-0PT		17
2301	0-6-0		1

BCN   Brecon.   11 engines

14xx	0-4-2T		1
2301	0-6-0		6
57xx	0-6-0PT		4

SR Depots.   1947

AFD   Ashford.   62 engines

N15	4-6-0	King Arthur	6
N	2-6-0		6
C	0-6-0	SE&C	7
D	4-4-0	SE&C	3
D1	0-4-2T	LBSC	1
D3	0-4-4T	LBSC	5
H	0-4-4T	SE&C	13
J	0-6-4T	SE&C	5
L	4-4-0	SE&C	8
O1	0-6-0	SE&C	4
R1	0-6-0T	SE&C	4

STL   St. Leonards.   24 engines

V	4-4-0	Schools	9
C	0-6-0	SE&C	2
D	4-4-0	SE&C	3
D3	0-4-4T	LBSC	4
L	4-4-0	SE&C	3
O1	0-6-0	SE&C	1
R1	0-6-0T	SE&C	2

EBN   Eastbourne.   24 engines

B4X	4-4-0	LB&SC	1
C2X	0-6-0	LB&SC	1
D1	0-4-2T	LB&SC	10
D3	0-4-4T	LB&SC	3
E1/R	0-6-2T	LB&SC reb.	1
E4	0-6-2T	LB&SC	1
E5	0-6-2T	LB&SC	5
I1X	4-4-2T	LB&SC	2

3B   Three Bridges.   31 engines

C2X	0-6-0	LB&SC	8
C3	0-6-0	LB&SC	1
E4	0-6-2T	LB&SC	8
E5	0-6-2T	LB&SC	6
I1X	4-4-2T	LB&SC	2
I3	4-4-2T	LB&SC	6

DOR   Dorchester.   11 engines

G6	0-6-0T	LSWR	1
K10	4-4-0	LSWR	2

L11	4-4-0	LSWR	1	WC	4-6-2	West Country	16
O2	0-4-4T	LSWR	5	Z	0-8-0T		1
T9	4-4-0	LSWR	1	E1/R	0-6-2T	LB&SC reb.	4
700	0-6-0	LSWR	1	K10	4-4-0	LSWR	5
EXJ	**Exmouth Junction.**	131 engines		L11	4-4-0	LSWR	8
MN	4-6-2	Merchant Navy	5	M7	0-4-4T	LSWR	26
N	2-6-0		26	O2	0-4-4T	LSWR	7
N15	4-6-0	King Arthur	6	S11	4-4-0	LSWR	4
Q1	0-6-0		1	T9	4-4-0	LSWR	11
S15	4-6-0		6	0395	0-6-0	LSWR	1
U	2-6-0		3	0415	4-4-2T	LSWR	1

Bangor Motive Power Depot. The junction shed described in this chapter is based loosely on Bangor, though the real depot had a six road building, not four. Otherwise there are considerable similarities; Bangor provided power for some main line freights and occasional stopping trains, it was also responsible for two sub sheds at Caernarvon and Amlwch as well as serving the long branch to the junction with the Cambrian Railways line at Afon Wen. The branches to Nantlle and Llanberis (closed in later years), Bethesda and Red Wharf Bay, off the Amlwch line in Anglesey were serviced direct.

On the formation of the LMS, the shed held thirty-five locomotives with around a dozen at out stations, two of these were at Amlwch, the rest at Caernarvon. There were still thirty-

one locomotives stationed at Bangor on nationalisation including as many as eleven from the LNWR. The shed code was 7B.

The allocation in 1945 was as follows: 72/3, 133/4/7 (LMS Stanier 2-6-2 tank) 495,675 (LMS Class 2P 4-4-0) 1093 (LMS Compound 4-4-0) 2948/51/84 (LMS Stanier 2-6-0), 4305, 4445, (LMS Class 4F 0-6-0) 6643/5/69/81, 6710/3/55 (LNWR 5ft 6in 2-4-2 tank) 7705/21 7808/12 (LNWR 0-6-2 coal tank) 12176, 12230 (L&YR Class 2F 0-6-0) 27604/19/54 (LNWR 0-6-2 coal tank) 28392, 28404, 28513/53, 28618 (LNWR 18in 'Cauliflower' 0-6-0). The shed closed on 14 January 1965.

Junction Shed. Ex LNWR 5ft 6in radial 2-4-2 tank as LMS No 6681 takes water at Bangor on Whit Monday 1947; fitted for push and pull working, this was the Amlwch branch engine. The standard railway ritual is being observed, the driver at the standpipe controls, while the fireman climbs up to put the bag in the water tank and watch the level – or more often, the overflow. In 1947, Bangor shed (7B) still had a sprinkling of LNWR locomotives, in the form of 0-6-2 coal tanks, 5ft 6in 2-4-2 tanks, a Watford 0-6-2 tank and that weekend superheated Precursor 4-4-0 No 25297 Sirocco, the last of the class.

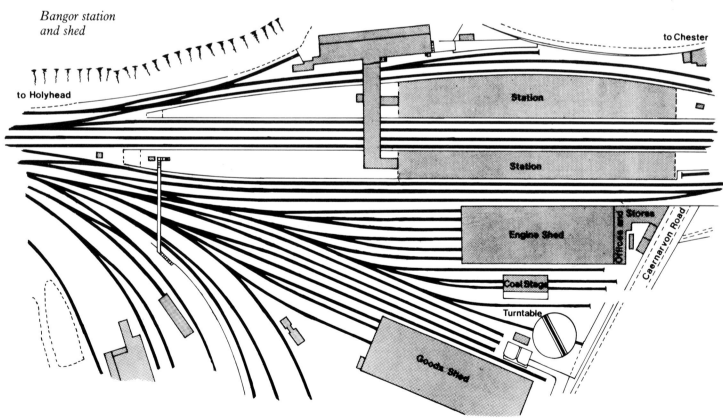

*Bangor station
and shed*

to Holyhead

to Chester

Station

Station

Engine Shed

Offices and Stores

Caernarvon Road

Coal Stage

Turntable

Goods Shed

Branch Terminus. Coalport station, terminus of the LNWR single line branch from Wellington, Shropshire. The engine is a Webb 5ft 6in radial 2-4-2 tank No 6601 of Shrewsbury shed (4A) and is the branch locomotive for the week; it will return to the main depot for boiler washouts and minor examinations. The branch shed (combined engine and carriage) is to the left of and behind the second coach with the water tower and small turntable beyond. The whole is simple in the extreme, stationmaster's house, oil lamps, paled fencing and no signalbox – only ground frame on the platform.

To the right is a very small goods yard – note the loading gauge, just past the bridge. The date is the summer of 1948. Passenger services ceased on 2 June 1952 though freight still ran until 5 December 1960.

Coalport Shed. This depot is taken as an example of an end of branch sub shed which at one time housed as many as seven locomotives. In later years, a more normal number was probably two or three. These were LNWR 0-6-2 coal tanks, 2-4-2 5ft 6in radial tanks and 18in 'Cauliflower' 0-6-0s, all of which were in use on passenger trains at nationalisation, though the tank engines were the norm. One point of interest is that the building was a combined locomotive and carriage shed. On transfer to the Western Region in 1948 Coalport technically became a sub shed of Wellington but ex LMS engines were used to the end, the final class being Fowler 2-6-2 tanks. After passenger services ceased on 31 May 1952, the shed closed and the men were transferred to Wellington.

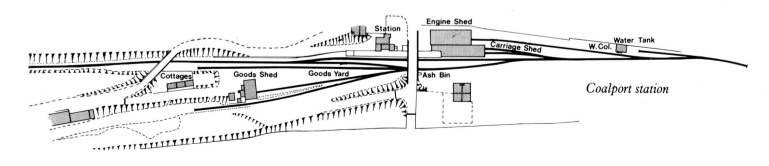

Coalport station

Manx Beauty. Beyer Peacock (1524/1875) built 2-4-0 tank No 6 Peveril blows off outside Peel shed in 1954. All engines on this anachronistic 3ft 0in gauge railway were Beyer Peacock built displaying typical maker's features of their period, inclined cylinders, polished brass dome covers with Salter safety valves and copper capped chimneys. Sadly, the Isle of Man Railway is no longer a common carrier but the section from Douglas to Port Erin is still open for tourists.

Overleaf:
Railway in Wight. One of the classes of engine to become standard on the Isle of Wight system was the ex LSWR class O2 0-4-4 tank. Even in BR days these engines carried names and in the spring of 1955, No W24 Calbourne (since preserved) is seen here near Ryde with a train for Cowes. During the winter service this section to Smallbrook Junction was worked as two single lines.

Speyside Pickup. An ex Great North of Scotland Railway 4-4-0 of LNER Class D40, No 62262, makes her gentle way down the Speyside branch from Craigellachie to Boat of Garten and approaches Grantown in August 1954. Only two years before, the engine would have been spotless, a condition and tradition applying to all locomotives on the GNoS line: even now she is adequately clean.

Sunday Rest Day. Fort William shed (63D) on 2 August 1953 still very much as it would have been twenty years back with ex North British engines and Gresley's K2 2-6-0s, named and carrying improved cabs for the West Highland line. It was Bank Holiday Sunday with a special working that weekend bringing what was by that time a great rarity – a Glen in the form of No 62482 Glen Mamie (behind the cab of J36 class 0-6-0 No 65300). The K2s include No 61781 Loch Morar. To the left is K4 2-6-0 No 61996 Lord of the Isles specially built for the West Highland line in 1937. The Glen returned to Glasgow next morning, coupled in behind Thompson K1 class 2-6-0 No 62012.

The Country Carriage

The country railway carriage came in all sorts of shapes, sizes and styles. For much of the last century carriages on branch and secondary services on main lines and cross country routes were mostly four-wheelers, little different from those on the faster main line trains. From the 1870s main line trains had progressed to six-wheelers and gradually by the end of the century to bogie vehicles. Corridors and restaurant cars added to express trains meant that longer distance express services were equipped with newer generations of carriages and so began the practice of passing on hand-me-downs of the older non-corridor carriages to the branches and cross country local services which with succeeding generations of stock continued until the coming of the diesel age from the 1950s.

Country trains were largely formed of non-corridor carriages although not exclusively so. By the 1930s a wide variety of stock could be found on country services from the antique former main line types to the newer non-corridor types similar to those built for inner city suburban use. The Great Western, of all the four group companies between the wars, built more new stock specifically for country trains than the others, with some two-coach non-corridor sets of compartment stock, with guard's and luggage accommodation, mostly third class compartments and just one solitary first class compartment in each coach. Better known were the open saloon auto trailers built in quantity for push-pull branch and local country services to be operated by pannier tanks or the familiar 0-4-2 tanks.

Another type perpetuated by the other three group companies for longer cross country journeys was the non-gangwayed lavatory carriage. The principle of a carriage with a toilet compartment tucked in between passenger compartments and accessible from only those adjoining

dated back to the 1870s for main line use, but with the advent of restaurant cars through corridors were added to coaches for express duty. But the non-gangwayed lavatory carriage was ideal for intermediate journeys where the lack of refreshment facilities meant that through corridors were not needed. Passengers with the greatest need – a family with children on a longer journey for example – had to be adept at knowing their carriage designs since only a few compartments were served and it was not always obvious from outside. The LNER managed things much better for in the 1920s and 1930s it built large numbers of lavatory composites and lavatory thirds with internal corridors so that all compartments were served. The lack of through gangways meant that they were unsuited for inclusion on restaurant car trains but that did not stop the operators from using them on long distance express services and on cross country excursions.

But despite growing standardisation some antique gems survived for many years after the grouping and indeed in a few cases after nationalisation. Open end balcony coaches with saloon interiors, originally supplied to small local railways, turned up on a number of branches and light railways – the Weston, Cleveland & Portishead, the Lambourn Valley, the Leek & Manifold Valley and the Garstang & Knott End for example, the latter seen below after transfer to the Wanlochhead branch in 1931. The last six wheelers in passenger service on BR were former Great Eastern main line coaches found on the Haughley and Laxfield branch (see page 93).

This venerable Highland four-wheel first class carriage, bottom, was built in 1873 for main line work but ended up on the Aberfeldy branch in the years before the first world war, seen here sandwiched between a later Highland luggage brake and two third class carriages.

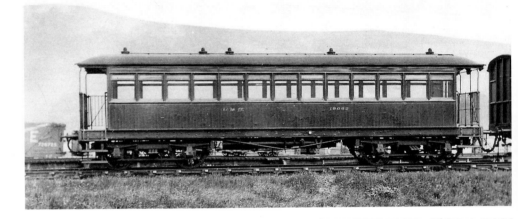

Like a number of other railways the Great North of Scotland tried rail motors built in 1905 and like other railways they were not a success. This is the carriage portion of a GNS rail motor rebuilt as a third class saloon.

A brake composite specially built by the GWR for the two-coach B sets for use on branch and cross country stopping trains in the late 1920s and early 1930s.

Three examples of the non-gangwayed lavatory carriage. The Caledonian example was ideal for through coach working with two first and four third class compartments linked by corridors to central toilets, and with a guard's and luggage compartment. The LNER semi-corridor or full corridor non-gangwayed coaches were widely used in East Anglia and the Midlands on cross country services. This is the corridor side of a lavatory third. The South Eastern & Chatham Railway built numerous three-coach non-corridor set trains for its cross country services right across Kent, Surrey, and into Berkshire. As built they had first, second, and third class, with toilets in two coaches serving a few of the compartments. This is the former centre first and second class composite, including a first class saloon with armchairs, luxury indeed on the country train.

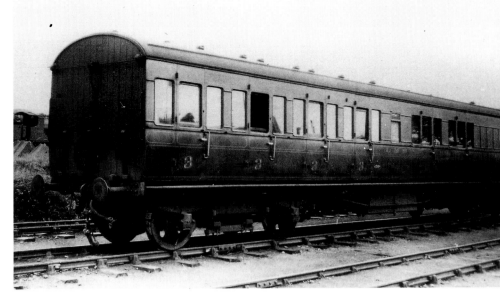

6
INDEPENDENTS
AND ODDITIES

If one travels the road to mid Wales from Craven Arms to Newtown over the Marchlands to Clun, with its stump of a castle, to the right lie the villages of Lydham Heath and Bishop's Castle and, on closer inspection a few, very few, artifacts in the form of crumbling bridge abutments of what was once the Bishop's Castle Railway.

Of all British standard gauge lines the Bishop's Castle was, almost certainly, the closest rival to the well known though sometimes infamous, Colonel Stephens collection of minor lines scattered around England and Wales. In some ways it surpassed them all, for the latter at least had some ups and downs; the Bishop's Castle had no ups at all: it was bankrupt in its opening year and worked its seventy years out under a receiver. Unlike the Colonel Stephens railways, it did not recognise the internal combustion engine except for an ancient Berliot bus, which lived in an old carriage body in the yard at Bishop's Castle and was used as a substitute for the train in times of absolute crisis; these had to be absolute as the railway lived in crises all its life, almost all of a financial nature. Indeed, one of its first locomotives was seized for debt.

There is the story that when one of the railway's creditors died, his executors put the bailiffs in. These gentlemen, aware of the snail-like nature of the concern, waited until the train had gone up to Bishop's Castle, took out a rail length and sat down to await its return. Sadly, the bailiffs had not realised just how snail-like the railway was, and how many friends it had; cold and despondent by nightfall, they allowed themselves to be lured away to the nearest pub. Willing hands replaced the rail and under cover of darkness the train of cash-producing freight returned to Craven Arms. To cap the matter, some sympathisers purchased the locomotive in hock and leased it back to the railway.

But there is little doubt that of all the light railways in Britain, those under the charge of the redoubtable Colonel Holman Frederick Stephens were the best known and remembered. Apart from his sojourn with the narrow-gauge Festiniog Railway in Wales, which is a story unto itself, this stalwart champion of the Light railway ruled five standard gauge lines from his office in Tonbridge. These were the Shropshire & Montgomeryshire, the Weston, Clevedon & Portishead (of unfortunate initials), the West Sussex, the Kent & East Sussex, and the East Kent railways, all of which could be judged as being on the border line of poverty even before the first world war. After that they were only kept going by cheeseparing, including the provision of second-hand equipment of a bewildering assortment drawn from all parts of the country.

Near Miss
My last journey on the GVT was made one summer not many years before the line closed and was marked by one of those minor contretemps which sometimes added a spice of excitement to narrow-gauge travel. At Pontfadog it became evident that our driver had expected to cross a Chirk-bound train on the loop there, but after a wait of some minutes we eventually proceeded on our leisurely way. Suddenly, however, our train came to as abrupt a stop as its limited braking power could achieve. Alighting to investigate, we discovered that, on rounding a sharp curve, our crew had suddenly been confronted by the stationary Baldwin, lurking concealed behind the high hedgerow. One wagon of her goods train had become derailed and had turned on its side, partially decanting its load of granite into the hedge. By the combined efforts of the two train crews, the passengers and some sympathetic passers-by along the road, the errant wagon was righted, re-railed and its cargo shovelled back. The Baldwin and its train then re-treated before us to Glynceiriog. – L. T. C. Rolt, *Lines of Character.*

Train of the Marches. A mixed train leaving Bishop's Castle in the last days of the Bishop's Castle Railway, the summer of 1934. This bankrupt and decrepit line was built as early as 1866 to join the LNWR/GWR joint line at Craven Arms with the prospect of extending westwards into Wales though only reaching the villages of Lydham Heath and Bishop's Castle. The engine is a Kitson (1860) built 0-6-0 carrying the name Carlisle *and the coach a very ancient London & South Western six wheeler. The railway expired on 20 April 1935.*

Over this empire, the Colonel presided like a deity over a kind of railway purgatory, where old and decrepit locomotives awaited his judgement in the limbo of dark sheds and grass grown yards. An engine which to the casual observer seemed doomed to oblivion would suddenly re-appear on another line, resplendent in new livery, possibly even carrying a name. The Colonel had a personal interest in Greek and Roman mythology and these names were sometimes applied to successive engines re-incarnated on the same line, or even to different contemporary locomotives on his several railways. Of these, *Hesperus* was the most popular, the name serving on each of the lines except the East Kent, until like her schooner namesake the last carrier of that famous legend came to final wreck.

L. T. C. Rolt, in *Lines of Character*, gives a charming vignette of one of the Colonel's railways – the Shropshire & Montgomeryshire, telling of happy days spent on the line: 'With its two through platforms and branch bay, Kinnerley Junction was by far the most imposing station on

the system and boasted quite an impressive array of signals controlled from a frame of thirteen levers which was protected from the weather by a corrugated iron shelter. Here presided as station master my friend Mr Funnel, plump, genial and rubicund. He was also captain of the village cricket team, employing a runner when he went to the wicket because of his high blood pressure. Fortunately the proceedings at Kinnerley Station were not calculated to endanger his health by any call for violent exertion. In my recollection only the up platform was used for passenger trains, the down platform and bay being usually filled either with goods wagons or coaching stock in various stages of decay. When Mr Funnel heard a down train from Shrewsbury approaching (the Fords announced their coming as soon as they left the next station at Edgerley) he would indicate by a desultory motion of a flag that it was expected on the up side. This obviated much unnecessary effort in pulling off signals and crossing from one platform to another.'

The Shropshire & Montgomeryshire Light Railway, to give its proper

Colonel Stephens Railbus. Llanymynech station, the junction of the Cambrian and Shropshire & Montgomeryshire Railways with an S&M railcar in the platform. These machines, known to the local inhabitants as 'the rattlers' consisted of two Model T Ford buses back to back with the driver of the leading unit clasping a steering wheel (see photograph). Their hollow steel wheels made such a noise that in the quiet Shropshire countryside they could be heard at a range of at least a mile and a half.

123

title, had a last but intensive burst of activity: it was taken over by the Army at the beginning of the second world war and used to supply a new ordnance depot in the area. Imagine the shock of ex main-line railway officers detailed to take over and run this decrepit and grass-grown system, where the last *Hesperus* was still notionally intact! Even the Army failed (after considerable determination) to make her move again.

The LMS lent some aged ex LNWR coal engines of 1880s origin to replace those of the same class, almost as derelict as *Hesperus*, which actually went to Crewe for an overhaul and lasted – even running troop trains over a relaid track – until the early years of peace. Other imports were ex Great Western Dean Goods 0-6-0s, some of them stalwart survivors from first world war army service. As always, these were firm favourites. Having lived with the antique LNW coal engines the staff could not have been more pleased if they had been sent 'Castles'.

Colonel Stephens was appointed civil engineer & locomotive superintendent to the once prosperous but then ailing Festiniog Railway in 1923, two years later becoming chairman and managing director of that company and the even more sickly, indeed mortally ill, Welsh Highland Railway. Thereafter the management of the two lines was supervised from his head office at Tonbridge. He tackled the job with his usual energy and enthusiasm at a salary of £400 per annum. From time to time he made flying visits from Kent, but more often sent his assistant W. H. Austen.

The Colonel had little sympathy for the Cymric race, and as year followed year correspondence with the Festiniog offices at Portmadoc, usually vitriolic, but often scintillating, became increasingly prolific. Fortunately, a great deal of this correspondence remains safely among the archives as the letter reproduced below, written by Stephens to Austen when the latter was in Wales clearly shows. It illustrates the degree of cynicism with which the Colonel viewed the staff and methods of this famous narrow-gauge railway, as he surveyed the scene from the comfort of his rooms down south. On the occasions that he made a journey to the Cambrian Coast Colonel Stephens would tend to drop in unannounced to see how things were going, but the canny Welsh soon put their defensive plans into action and developed personal warning signals passed on from man to man.

12.6.1926

Dear W.H.A.,

I think you have done very well. I'm sorry re weather. The people on the F.R. are quite different to our people, as you have found out by now. I found it out long ago. They can't help it, it's their nature. We have got to put up with it whilst we have the job.

Re-trucks – what strikes me is the sudden drop. They could not have finished all the "slightly damaged" in one certain week!! Tell them to pick a few light repairs to bring the numbers up. There is some game on probably, a scheme, between them to stop shortening hands as work draws to a close. Re weeds and grass. Can

Welshpool Market. Beyer Peacock built 0-6-0 tank No 822 (originally named The Earl *but now minus nameplates which were in store. Even in the 1950s vandalism and theft was a possible risk) stands outside its shed after shunting the yard one February morning in 1952. The sheeted wagons in the foreground will have been loaded at the transfer sidings adjacent to the standard gauge station: coal was the line's staple traffic with some farm produce working to Welshpool especially on market Mondays. Locally known as the farmer's line, the Welshpool & Llanfair was (and still is in preservation) a 2ft 6in gauge railway. It closed to normal traffic on 5 November 1956 when the price of coal rose to customers in Llanfair village.*

you get this mown to rail level and after it is dry, or partly so, set fire to.

The crossing where the engine came off at Dinas probably has loose V bolts, a lot of them have. Griffiths does not seem to look after them and have them screwed up. Can you look at this and get it done. I want all the old signal quadrants (the things used in place of levers) collected and sent to Boston Lodge for scrap, also broken chairs.

I have told Williams to put all the shirkers in Boston Lodge on 4 days a week short time starting Monday = 32 hours a week each. The wages bill must be reduced.

Yours faithfully,
H. Stephens

P.S. Bad weather here, a big gale yesterday.

Now it is hard to imagine those days of the Colonel Stephens railways; they represented the very tip of the iceberg of railway monopoly existing in the times when the motor car was a rich man's toy and commercial road traffic (until the last years) almost non existent. By the 1930s

flexible natured buses had begun seriously to replace the slow and rambling country lines, where mixed trains often stopped to shunt at stations far from the villages or hamlets they purported to serve. One by one the light and narrow-gauge railways passed from the scene, leaving a gap of human spirit that no main line railway could afford to emulate. In particular, the Colonel Stephens railways in the south east corner of England were rural links running through prosperous but lightly-populated areas, serving village folk who joined their trains at tiny stations or sleeper-built halts, each of which was operated by another member of the local community. Driver, fireman, guard or porter, each knew his passengers and each of them knew him.

On Sunday 11 March 1956 *The Observer* carried an evocative photograph of a railway scene taken deep in the mists of Welsh winter against a background of overhanging trees and drifting steam. Underneath, the caption read: 'The Welshpool & Llanfair Valley Railway is about to be closed down, together with some other branch lines beloved by the small communities they serve and by collectors of railway lore'. It was over a decade since the end of the second world war, the age of austerity was dying. With petrol no longer rationed, and cash in workers' pockets, the road and the car began a fast and relentless takeover, any narrow gauge lines were now destined for scrap or preservation. Their place as country railways could only remain as tourist attractions.

Because it carried coal to Llanfair more cheaply than the road, and with a lively Monday sheep market at Welshpool this 2ft 6in gauge line was one of the last survivors, certainly the last to carry freight for any major railway, on nationalisation the Great Western handing it on to British Railways. The rarity and delight was that this was the farmers' line. From Welshpool station yard the trains crossed the town's main street on the level and then, losing themselves among the back yards, almost swept the laundry from the lines on washdays, to emerge through a housing estate before beating up the long, wicked gradient from Raven Square along the valley of the River Banwy to its rural terminus. Even in the mid 1950s the atmosphere of the country railway was total, pictures remaining in the mind include that market scene on Mondays when, on a fine winter's day *The Earl* or *Countess* shunted the yard, steam rising from the Great Western type safety valves to hang still in the crisp morning air. It was always a wonderful mixture of noises, the auctioneer at his rostrum, the cattle, pigs and sheep in competition, and the clanging of couplings as the narrow gauge engine made up its train, the fireman at the controls, while the driver joined the guard for a brew inside the tiny brake van.

Although the body was later rescued from its coffin by preservationists the wake was quite a party, considering the W&L had done nothing but carry farmers' freight inconspicuously for the last twenty five years. It took the form of a special last train organised by the Midland Area of the Stephenson Locomotive Society. Musical accompaniment was provided by foreigners from nearly twenty miles away, the Newtown Prize Silver Band, who struck up with *Pomp & Circumstance* followed by the *Dead*

Clean Those Carriages!

Col Stephen's military style of remote control never went down well on the Festiniog. This extract from correspondence that drifted on over several years between him and the man on the job at Portmadoc perhaps shows why:

10 Aug 1925. Why are the windows of the 1st class compartment allowed to be open during heavy rain; letting the windows down for air does not mean letting them down for rain to beat in . . . You seem to have some perfectly stupid people to deal with or people who are not properly looked after.

Your first train for passengers purposes is 8.00am. Surely you can get a woman to come on at about 5.30am to 6.00am for a few days to have two hours scrubbing . . . Now will you take this as a direct order to get this work done and let us have no more trouble.

26 Aug. Re your letter of 25th inst, the carriage cleaning is being done by coalman T. Morgan and the porter at Portmadoc. All the carriages were scrubbed out in May this year, do you wish for them to be scrubbed out again'.

27 Aug. Yes, I want the carriages scrubbed out again; surely my letter of the 25th inst, stated this. Why give me the trouble of writing another letter.

8 Aug 1927. Have you a woman carriage cleaner? if so what does she do?

10 Aug. We have no woman carriage cleaner on either the FR or WHR.

12 Aug. Why have you no woman carriage cleaner? Can you get one? Can you use the Perfectol carriage cleaner?

15 Aug. The only time we had a woman carriage cleaner was when on your instructions the carriages were washed inside. We can use the Perfectol carriage cleaner.
continued overleaf

continued

[The guard remarks on his journal for 8.00am on Saturday, 'passengers refusing to go into 3rd class compartments, too dirty, had to put them in 1st class.]'

16 Aug. Take on a woman carriage cleaner temporarily on the best terms that you can arrange.

19 Aug. I am unable to get a woman carriage cleaner . . . there is a young man about here, a sailor by trade, and he is unable to get work, who I could put on to clean the carriages.

20 Aug. You had better take on the young sailor you mention on half time to start with. You should pay him at the rate of 40/- per week so that he will draw £1 per week as he is on half time.

13 Dec. How are you off for Perfectol for carriage cleaning please?

15 Dec. We have a supply of Perfectol. I am sorry that when this is used it takes the paint off the carriages, especially the yellow paint.

28 Dec. If the Perfectol is used properly it will not fetch the paint off. It shows you are using it too strong.

20 Jan 1928. Letter from a Capt L. Davies to Colonel Stephens 'I herewith return free pass which you granted me last year and I beg to acknowledge pass for this year . . . I used it once last year . . . I should mention that after leaving the carriage I looked more like a sweep than a first class passenger'.

March, though the centre of attention was the elegantly polished and still active corpse.

Then came the Great Chase as the train was followed by a motorcade of enthusiasts, and a bus containing the Silver Prize Band, still blowing hard, which all but collided with the train at Raven Square crossing. Every hedge, every gate, every field and tree seemed to contain a photographer as *The Earl* slogged up the hill and rounded the reverse curves. Amidst the autumnal red, brown and green of the Montgomeryshire countryside they breasted the first summit and the caterpillar-like train dropped over the other side with a clicketty-clicketty-clicketty. Llanfair was eventually entered with shrieking whistles and the journey was over.

While Wales abounded with narrow gauge oddities – all fiercely independent and mostly serving the slate quarries of the western mountains, in England it was a different story, for here, in a countryside densely populated and relatively flat, the particular advantages of the narrow gauge rarely applied, but there were two which came under the rather leaky umbrellas of the LMS and Southern Railway at Grouping. Each was individualistic, neither had a chance in the more modern world, and they closed within a year of each other, in 1934 and 1935. Strangely, both were also latecomers to the scene having been given belated encouragement by the Light Railways Act at a time when the first stuttering motor cars were already beginning to whiten the hedgerows.

The more northerly of the two, the Leek & Manifold Valley Light Railway ran from almost nowhere to nowhere else! Waterhouses, which was at the end of a branch line from Leek in Staffordshire, really put in for the carriage of stone, and Hulme End, roughly en route to Buxton, which it never reached. Its eight miles of 2ft 6in gauge track ran along the beautiful Manifold Valley, and is happily now a footpath. Its only real claim to fame was that it attempted to overcome the change of gauge problem at Waterhouses by means of low-loading transporter wagons. Special end-on sidings were built with the narrow gauge line at a lower level, enabling a standard ten-ton wagon or later under LMS ownership, modern glass lined milk tanks en route to London, to move from line to line. The original thinking, but much too late, was good, the prospectus stating that this facility would give farmers and miners along the route a standard-gauge railway for all practical purposes. Just what induced the North Stafford Railway to have anything at all to do with this scheme it is difficult to decide, though it is possible that the company could have felt there was a chance of robbing the London & North Western of any traffic there might be, and that was precious little. In the event the LNWR may well have been pleased to donate them their Cromford & High Peak line.

The second of these two English lines was quite another story. This was a 1ft 11½in gauge railway, the Lynton & Barnstaple, a much bigger enterprise winding 19½ miles through the steep Devon coombes on the fringes of Exmoor, Almost certainly inspired by the success of the Welsh

narrow-gauge railways then in their high days, the L&B served a considerable local need at the time of its construction, and on reflection, it could perhaps have been still with us, albeit as some form of preserved line, had it not been for two grave disadvantages which handicapped it from its inception. These involved its twisting length, due to lack of sensible negotiation with certain landowners, and the extremely unfortunate siting of the terminus at Lynton some 250ft above the town – and much too far away. Strangely, the latter was due to one of the railway's promoters, Sir George Newnes who, despite his enthusiasm for the project decreed that the railway might be heard but not seen among the beauties of Lynton. For these aesthetic scruples the railway paid dearly in its later years in extremis, for while the smart little trains became an attractive feature for tourists (even the Southern Railway cared for them in this respect) they were ignominiously excluded from the place they purported to serve.

As with other rural lines, trains were often mixed and in later days this was not a help. Once, the driver of an 'up' mixed, having detached his coaches at Chelfham station platform, to perform a shunting operation, absentmindedly continued to Barnstaple without them. His reaction when asked by the Town station staff what he had done with his train, and of his passengers when he returned to retrieve them may best be left to the imagination.

Summer traffic could be heavy, with excursions running in connection

Barnstaple Farewell. The Southern Railway's only narrow gauge line, the 2ft gauge Lynton & Barnstaple closed to all traffic on Saturday 29 September 1935, a tragedy of huge proportions, when one considers today's world of preservation and tourist railways. The last train was a public excursion hauled very appropriately by the railway's first and last engines, both Manning Wardle 2-6-2 tanks, Nos 759 Yeo and 188 Lew seen here just before setting out from Barnstaple junction.

129

End of the Dundalk, Newry & Greenore

The sad day came when public trains ran for the last time on the Dundalk, Newry & Greenore Railway. The evening of 31 December 1951 brought an intermittent blizzard so fierce that there were doubts whether the bus service which was to replace the trains would be able to get through, but thousands of people nevertheless turned out to see the end, and hundreds of tickets were bought as souvenirs. The blaze of bonfires, the explosion of detonators, the singing of Auld Lang Syne, and the music of bands from Newry and Dundalk heralded the belated passage of the last trains to Greenore. *The Irish Press* recorded that the last train from Dundalk (Driver Barney Dullaghan, Guard P. J. Rafferty, and Fireman Hugh Rafferty, with GNR(I) locomotive No 93) 'took twice its normal 50 minutes from Dundalk with boisterous passengers pulling the communication cord at intervals . . . Among the spectators was 97-years-old Paddy McShane, who started as a checker when the line began in 1873'. The train from Newry was driven by Edward Boyle and the guard was Thomas Carroll, who had 51 years' service with the DN & G Dr Finegan also rode on the engine. This train had on board 400 passengers, the Newry Town Band, and a goat. Initially at any rate the goat was a reluctant participant, having apparently been forcibly abducted by some of the 'mourners' from the lineside plot on which it had been peaceably meditating. But, having been shanghaied, the goat – one likes to think he or she was a direct descendant of the McKivron species which had figured so prominently in the earlier history of the undertaking – entered with zest into the spirit of the affair, *continued opposite*

with standard-gauge trains from as far away as Ilfracombe, Plymouth, Taunton and Yeovil, and publicity was never overlooked entirely by the Southern Railway, but despite these efforts the L&B found itself side by side with other country lines, a victim of road transport, and there could be little real hope of continuance. The railway remained a favourite with holidaymakers for the few short weeks of the season, but that could not be enough. Closure came at the end of the summer timetable, 1935.

As usual there had been meetings and protests, but the Southern Railway was adamant in the interests of its shareholders. There was a surge of hope at the eleventh hour when the clerk to Lynton Council received an anonymous telephone call suggesting that under the Act of 1895 the company was obliged to operate the line in perpetuity. There were two clauses relating to Woody Bay station which 'the company shall construct and for ever efficiently maintain' and the other that 'the line shall be constructed and maintained as a two foot gauge line'. The clerk to Lynton council was authorised to consult counsel and the outcome of this was a suggested course of action which, if the council lost would cost them about £500. A special meeting of the ratepayers was called to authorise the risk of this sum, but a mandate was refused by a narrow majority. Thus Lynton put its money where its mouth was, and one of Britain's most delightful country railways mostly went for scrap. But had it been a different outcome, although the last train had actually run, the railway may well have received an extension to its lifetime similar to that of the ex LBSCR Bluebell line in Sussex, when a similar objection was actually lodged necessitating the seeking of Parliamentary powers for closure by British Railways.

The last L&B train ran on Saturday 29 September 1935. This was a public excursion hauled, very appropriately, by the line's first and last engines, the Manning Wardle built 2-6-2 tanks Nos 759 *Yeo* and 188 *Lew*. *Yeo* had been used to haul the first passenger train only thirty seven years back. To start with the weather was fine, and hundreds of people turned up to travel and witness the last rites. Some among the crowd had come to say farewell to a loved friend, for there were many who regarded the railway as such, indeed, a number had seen the railway opened. Others came as enthusiasts for a last pilgrimage, but for all, the distinction of travelling on the final train was an excuse for having a day out. The double-headed train moved out of Barnstaple Town into the sunshine with whistles sounding defiantly, while more people crowded onto North Walk to watch the departure. Everywhere on the route old friends stood to watch *Yeo* and *Lew* on the last train – at one point in a field a farmer held up a horseshoe. The steep cuttings were already coloured with the bronze of autumn as the green engines and coaches threaded their way through the north Devon countryside. Over the high viaduct to Chelfham to take water, each engine in turn, then through deep rock cuttings and over more serpentine curves and steep climbs to Blackmoor before descending to Parracombe for more water. The last sections to Woody Bay and Lynton lay through heather-covered moorland hills commanding superb views before the drop down to

Lynton with its island platform terminal, where the train was met with ceremony by the chairman of the Council supported by yet another large crowd.

Soon the sadness began to take over, and after the last flicker of green from the guard's oil handlamp, the train moved slowly out into the darkness to the tune of *Auld Lang Syne* from Lynton town band, the engines whistles shrieking in chorus. Far down the train that chorus continued to ring for the band insisted on travelling up the steep climb to Blackmoor, as did the Council chairman. Almost fittingly it now began to drizzle with rain and the scene became dismal in the extreme. As station after station was left behind for the last time, detonators exploded under the wheels; as many who had come for miles from villages and hamlets stood in silent farewell.

As they neared journey's end there was some anxiety on the two footplates, for the prolonged whistling had taken toll of steam and water was getting low in the tanks. Just after 9.40pm they came home to Barnstaple, crawling round the curves within sight of the now windswept River Taw. Here was a crowd of almost a thousand people who had begun to gather as early as 9 o'clock outside the Town station in readiness to say goodbye.

The shortage of fuel and other travel restrictions during the second world war kept many of these unusual and delightful country lines alive – many preserved today could well have gone by the mid 1940s had it not been for this otherwise dreadful catastrophe. Some lingered on into the early 1950s, when seemingly out of the blue a new era began and the first railway in the world to be rescued was the tired and almost derelict Talyllyn Railway in Wales, acquired by preservationists in 1951. But that is another story, a re-emergence of the Great Days of the Country Railway, but under a very different guise. Here, much depends on a new generation, the younger volunteer, his wages the exhilaration of a moving steam engine. Herein lies a possible weakness in the Preservation theme for, like the independent lines of old, there is generally insufficient income to pay for both an adequate permanent staff, and proper replacement of capital items. Fortunately the new era works and works well, as can be seen by many of the resuscitated country branch and narrow-gauge lines. Independent and oddities they may be, but each provides positive practical leisure activities for those involved as well as an attractive day out to the public at large. But it is inevitably self-conscious preservation; very few passengers actually use trains about their daily business, and the guard's vans lack the miscellaneous cargoes of yesteryear.

It was in Ireland that the narrow gauge lasted longest as common carrier, and very unconsciously so, since even in the 1950s when the last lines were at work it was quite an adventure and cost for British enthusiasts to reach their remote locations. Unlike Britain, Ireland had two standard gauges, the broad 5ft 3in of the main lines, and the 3ft of the narrow-gauge systems that dotted especially the south and west of the country, though once you could leave Larne by a narrow-gauge

continued
and on arrival at Greenore charged headlong from a first class compartment to lead a rush of custom into the hotel. So the working life of the Dundalk, Newry & Greenore Railway concluded on the same spot where it had begun so auspiciously with flags, bands and speeches 78 years before, but this time no steamer waited at the pier; the *Slieve League* had made the last sailing from Greenore to Holyhead two days before. Chalked on the back of Guard Carroll's brake van were the words whose meaning no farewell festivities could efface: 'The End'.
D. S. M. Barrie in the *Dundalk, Newry & Greenore Railway*

Human Error
The danger of a head-on crash round a blind curve at full speed ever haunted the country signalman and engine driver, and indeed with a human error can never be totally eliminated. Classic head on crashes were especially part of the history of the Cambrian and Somerset & Dorset. Not putting the single-line token or staff in the instrument and getting permission to take it out afresh, not checking that the right one was handed over for the next section: these were the cardinal errors on the branch but happened only rarely. The signalman who prematurely pulled a point lever and the driver who let trucks bounce precariously over catch points: they were unpopular but did not lose their jobs or reputations.

131

Car Hire At Stations

Passengers desiring to be conveyed by Car to outlying villages and places distant from Railway Stations should apply to the undermentioned:

Station	Name, Address and Telephone No. of Car Proprietor
Aberdovey	.. E. Emyr Evans, 'Station Garage,' Aberdovey. Aberdovey 41.
Bovey	.... Moir & Davie, Central Garage, Bovey. Bovey Tracey 10.
Bovey	.... Aggetts' Dartmoor Garage, Bovey. Bovery Tracey 32.
Camborne	.. Messrs. Williamson's Garage, Church Street, Camborne. Camborne 56.
Cullompton	.. Cullompton Garage Co., High Street, Cullompton. Cullompton 27.
Devizes	.... Mr. H. W. Harris, 18 Long Street, Devizes. Devizes 213.
Devizes	.... Mr. C. R. Sudweeks, White Lion Hotel, Devizes. Devizes 291.
Dolgelley	.... Mr. J. O. Edwards, Merioneth Motor Company. Dolgelley 2.
Dunster	.... Mr. C. Ell, The Garage, Dunster. Dunster 237.
Fowey	.... Mr. W. A. Baseley, North Corner Garage, Fowey. Fowey 85.
Goring & Streatley	Mr. James Franklin, The Garage, Goring-on-Thames. Goring 37.
Hagley	.... B. Cutler, Garage, Worcester Road, Hagley. Hagley 610.
Handborough	.. *O. A. Slatter, Witney Road Garage, Long Handborough, nr. Oxford. Freeland 5.
Helston	.... Mr. W. Jory, Meneage Street, Helston. Helston 45.
Kingsbridge	.. Quay Garage Co., Ltd., Kingsbridge. Kingsbridge 23.
Kingsbridge	.. E. Y. Cranch Rosemount Garage, Salcombe. Salcombe 51.
Milford Haven	.. W. Thomas & Sons, Lord Nelson Garage, Milford Haven. Milford Haven 109.
Pangbourne	.. Mr. H. E. Talmage, Reading Road. Pangbourne 13.
Perranporth	.. Messrs. A. & J. E. Tregonning, Perranporth. Perranporth 31.
Princetown	.. T. C. Petherick & Co., Dartmoor Garage, Princetown. Princetown 14.
St. Agnes	.... Dales Garage, St. Agnes. St. Agnes 2.
St. Ives	.... Mr. Warren, West Pier Garage, St. Ives. St. Ives 139.
St. Ives	.... W. Guppy & Sons, Talland Garage. St. Ives 245.
Starcross	.... E. G. Coombes, Alexandra Garage, Starcross. Starcross 32.
Tavistock	.... Mr. John Backwell, Bedford Hotel Garage and Stables. Tavistock 34.
Tetbury	.... Mr. R. Street, The Garage, Long Street, Tetbury. Tetbury 16.
Whitland	.... Messrs. J. Griffith & Son, Central Garage, Whitland. Whitland 6.
Winchester	.. Chisnell's Garages, adjoining G.W.R. Station. Winchester 68.

*Trains can also be met at Oxford, Eynsham or Witney.

GWR Timetable 1936

corridor boat train. The gauge, however, was about all they had in common, since most of the self-contained concerns were grossly undercapitalised from the start – despite government support for the 'congested districts'. Congestion was not of the kind the word would imply across the Irish Sea; a congested district was one whose population, however sparse, could not be sustained by the inadequate soil and natural resources.

Some of the systems ran beside the road, sort of hybrids between railway and tramway. Several, such as the Tralee & Dingle, had branch lines of their own; and one, on the outskirts of Cork, with tourist and residential traffic in mind, even boasted a section of double track. Virtually none were ever profitable, and eked out miserable existences, usually making do with inadequate horse-power and inadequate everything else. Every line had its different locomotive types, and in make-do maintenance depots miles from civilisation there was no tradition in mechanical matters, patching-up varied greatly in quality. In a relaxed countryside, especially after lunch, a driver was known not to miss parts that had fallen off, one happily packing the gland on the same side the slide bar had dropped off. As though that were not enough, some of the systems were victim of raids and even murder of their staff during the Troubles.

One or two lines had some vestige of specialised traffic, the Cavan & Leitrim, where many locomotives spent their last days, serving one of Ireland's few mines; coal traffic helped keep it going until 1959. It had, of course, long lost its independence and ended its days as part of the nationalised CIE, though earlier the Great Southern had brought mechanical relief to many of the small systems coming into its ownership. At least engines could now be sent for major overhaul at a proper locomotive works. But most routes, like the Tralee & Dingle, depended utterly on what local business was on offer, and even the occasional visitor coming ashore for the first time from the Blasket Islands (and wondering if he were already in Tralee when the train had only got to the first of many stopping places) providing a welcome addition to the revenue. But as in much of the rest of Ireland, the railway really came to life on fair days and, well after the system had been generally closed, it stirred back to life as a pair of double-headed specials squeaked and squealed their way across the undulating countryside.

The Cavan & Leitrim was among the final trio the least visited because it was in central, non-tourist Ireland. The second was the West Clare, from Ennis to the coast, along it where the force of the wind sometimes brought traffic to a standstill, and after a triangular junction at Moyasta, by separate routes on to two small resorts, Kilkee and Kilrush. For years they depended on the visitors brought by the trains, whose irregular running became legendary following the company's unsuccessful libel case against Percy French, of music-hall fame, who was not so inaccurate in his comic diatribe. Even in CIE's days the roads were so bad that the system was dieselised; regularly more trains left Ennis by the narrow gauge for the Atlantic Ocean than ran down the main line to Limerick.

Here was a curious mixture of old and new. Along the route, when the diesel car was shunted into a siding to allow the daily freight passage along the running track, a bare-footed beggar boy would jump in and demand sixpence.

The last of the narrow gauge systems was in many ways the greatest, the County Donegal Railways, note the plural. Like a variety of other minor concerns that found themselves straddling the new political border after Dublin was given independence, it was not nationalised. It in fact had odd owners. The Midland (the English Midland Railway, that is) whose influence got just about everywhere in these islands, already owned the Northern Counties Committee system including the northerly main line from Belfast to Londonderry, and was interested in further acquisitions. The Great Northern Railway (Ireland) became alarmed, the result being that they bought the Donegal jointly. After 1948, that of course meant that BR via the LMS was half owner of the system, most of whose tracks and traffics were in what was by then an alien country, albeit much of the business was routed across the border via Strabane.

In its last decades, the County Donegal was fortunate in having two

Irish Railbus. The Sligo, Leitrim & Northern Counties Railway railbus No 2a (purchased second-hand from the GNR as a road bus in 1938 and converted at Manorhamilton) making a very slippery ascent of Glenfarne bank on 22 June 1955. The photographer was travelling from Enniskillen to Manorhamilton and progress was so slow that he was able to walk up the embankment ahead of the 'train', photograph it and get back in again. The conductor/guard was ahead putting dirt and ballast on the track to make adhesion more likely! The driver, a melancholy man of some 60 years, still wore his steam engine uniform of overalls and grease cap like some coachmen of old forced to give up his proud place on the box for the driving seat of a horseless carriage.

133

Where Is *Quintus*?
I was driving from Lulworth to Corfe Castle and, on reaching the top of Povington Hill, I had stopped to admire the magnificent view.

Suddenly, my attention was caught by a thin plume of steam rising from the valley not a mile away. Hurriedly I focused my field glasses on it. The steam was coming from a small saddletank which, even as I looked, started to move, and was soon lost to sight behind some trees. I pulled out my Ordnance Survey map; there, sure enough, was marked the track of a tramway.

The map showed that the road I was on crossed the line near Grange Gate, so without more ado I set off. To attempt to drive at any speed would have been dangerous, for the road was very narrow, and after a short distance it started to descend very steeply down the thickly-wooded hillside. A rough track led off the road through the wood and, as we approached this spot, we slowed to a walking pace, and then promptly came to a stop – for there, standing in a clearing, and simmering gently, stood the small engine that I had first seen from the hilltop.

What a picture it made resting so serenely in such beautiful surroundings. The saddle-tank was dappled by shafts of sunlight that pierced the thick foliage of the trees; brass and copper work gleamed and twinkled. From the tall chimney a thin grey smoke curled gently upwards through the trees. The engine was *Quintus*, built in 1914 by Manning Wardle & Company. I had a most interesting and enjoyable talk with its driver, who obviously took much pride in his charge, for although the paintwork was getting a little worn, *Quintus* had been cleaned until it shone. In fact, I never saw *Quintus*, or any other locomotive
continued opposite

fine managers, and what they achieved against heavy odds is often quoted by railway historians as an example of what a combination of drive and common sense might have brought about elsewhere. It was also fortunate in that the GN(I) welcomed pioneering with railcars, the Donegal being the first to use the internal combustion engine, helped by the GN's Dundalk works. Improvision, changing with the circumstances, making the best of what traffic opportunities there were – even if that meant carrying parties of Orangemen in the former Ballymena & Larne corridor boat train that was the name of the game. The population was sparse, the standard of living low, the routes were long (at its peak the system totalled 124 miles and included five termini), gradients were fierce, Dublin with which this part of Eire had most in common was remote (through traffic having mainly to be routed via Northern Ireland), and for many years the Donegal received far more than its fair share of attention in the Troubles. But its service was exemplary – though common sense did not stretch to co-operating with the other Donegal 3ft system, the Londonderry & Lough Swilly.

Several times daily three diesels met at the neat, fully-signalled Donegal station, while maintenance at headquarters at Stranorlar was good. Even in the 1950s, so few visitors arrived from England that a pass was willingly given 'To all stations and back' and to ride on one of the powerful steam engines (which included 4-6-4 tanks) prepared for a freight up through the Barnesmore Gap, the exhaust's echo being heard for miles around. The load included everything the countryside required: pieces of farm equipment, new kitchen sinks along with other building materials, petrol and oil in mini-size but modern tank wagons, groceries and of course Guinness. Consignments from Dublin travelled through the Six Counties in sealed containers to avoid double customs examination.

The usual extra trains were run during the Christmas period in 1959, services being withdrawn at the year's end, though a few steam freights continued briefly while roads were improved. No section of countryside in the British Isles was so well served as this, especially taking into account that there was virtually no originating mineral or industrial traffic.

Through the British Isles, at one time you would find the most individualistic of railways serving self-contained industries; papermills, sawmills, quarries, breweries, they all had their own locomotives, trucks, tracks and sidings. The rolling stock of several survive on today's preserved lines, but before finishing this chapter it is worth noting that one very country industrial system, as different from anything else as you could imagine, still survives – and that using the narrow gauge in Ireland. The peat board, Bord na Mona, currently maintains a network of some 700 miles, ever changing as some peat bogs are worked out and others developed. About 300 locomotives and 5,000 items of rolling stock (including passenger coaches for workers) are used. The story of oddities is not yet quite finished.

Furzebrook Railway. Until the mid 1950s, steam could be found hard at work not only on public railways but also in the service of country industries, particularly quarries, where ageing engines trundled their loads of stone or clay to factory or big brother. One of the most delightful was the 2ft 8in gauge system belonging to quarry owners Pike Bros & Fayle, the Furzebrook. This used a heterogeneous collection of ancient engines for its motive power all of which carried Latin names representing numbers. Quintus is seen here in August 1954 heading for the woods near Creech Grange en route to the weathering beds with a load of clay. Although seemingly Victorian Quintus was built by Manning Wardle & Co of Leeds as late as 1914, works number 1854.

continued

working on this line, except in a clean state. After this first meeting, it was not long before I got to know the line really well, and from then on hardly a year passed without my paying it a visit.

Then, last summer, the news came that the Furzebrook line was to be closed, and its services replaced by lorries. My heart was heavy as I telephoned the owners to ask permission to pay a final visit and, as usual, my request was readily granted. My idea was to photograph *Quintus* in colour in the woods, and I drove straight to Creech Heath where I was surprised to find *Tertius* being driven by Mr. Gover, who usually drove *Quintus*. *Tertius* is a sprightly 0-6-0 saddle-tank, built in 1880 by Manning Wardle & Company, but of rather ungainly appearance since it was rebuilt, particularly when compared with *Quintus*.

'Where is *Quintus*?' I asked Mr. Gover. He looked at me as if surprised that I should have asked such a question, and with sinking heart I noticed his downcast expression. 'She broke her back axle a little while ago.' He spoke with a quiet voice, and then, pointing down the hill, continued 'She is lying down there to the right – I don't think she is to be repaired.' I walked straight down to where *Quintus* lay in a short siding with its back end propped up. After weeks in the open, the paintwork had become dull and shabby and the steelwork, once so bright, was now covered in rust. For a moment or so I gazed at *Quintus*, and then turned, and went back to the car to drive home. Why had I gone to look? I wish so much that I had not done so, for now I can never recall the picture of *Quintus* resting quietly in the woods without it being clouded by the remembrance of seeing it lying derelict and broken. – Ivo Peters in *The Railway Magazine*, 1957.

135

Country engines

One of the joys of the country railway was its motive power. Often engines which had retreated from more mundane work or even express duties became rare examples of a class kept for special branch line duties; Beattie's 2-4-0 well tanks went to Wadebridge in Cornwall, Stroudley's Terrier 0-6-0 tanks to Hayling Island, Highland Small Bens to Strathpeffer and Thurso, even more wonderfully LNWR Jumbos, the famous Precedents, the success story of the main line in late Victorian times, ended their days on the Cockermouth, Keswick & Penrith line. On the other hand there were the country workhorses, mostly 0-6-0 tender engines or small tank engines of large numbered classes, the latter replaced on local work by more modern 2-6-2 or 2-6-4 designs. Examples of these are legion but there were some which seemed ever present, indeed sometimes by the eyes of those looking for more ancient warriors, too ever present. The Great Western's small wheeled Prairie tanks monopolised many of the South Wales valleys, LNWR 2-4-2 and 0-6-2 coal tanks could be seen on most branches on the system and Great Eastern J15 class 0-6-0s of 1883 vintage appeared on East Anglian branch lines seeming sometimes to spite the enthusiast looking for the last survivor of the British 2-4-0, the E4. LSWR M7 0-4-4 tanks, once in and out of Waterloo in huge numbers worked branches from Hampshire to Cornwall while the O2 class of the same wheel arrangement took over the whole of the Isle of Wight system.

The 0-6-0s had always been branch and mixed traffic engines; two classes which reigned supreme for many years were particular favourites, the LNWR 18in goods 0-6-0s nicknamed 'Cauliflowers' because of the coat of arms which adorned their splashers in pre grouping days and the famous well loved Great Western Dean goods. Each of these two classes could be found anywhere on their respective section or system. The Cauliflowers and Deans were both simple late Victorian designs, efficient and well liked by crews and maintenance staff for their reliability even if there were some not so muffled curses by those who had to get their heads into the inside motion from time to time.

There are long standing stories and myths surrounding such veterans, one relating to the 18in goods is that of a driver's claim to have passed Carlisle No 13 signal box in 16½min from a Penrith start. This would have involved speeds of over 80mph and even an exaggeration of two minutes in the time would have involved some very fast running. The late J. N. Maskelyne was more specific, he mentions a run behind a Cauliflower No 34 and a Jumbo No 2179 *Avon* with the 62¾ miles between Carlisle and Carnforth covered in 66min start to stop. A run through the Cumberland countryside faster than that of the Coronation Scot schedule. One imagines that the driver of the 18in goods deputed his fireman to feel if the big ends were hot on arrival! One thing is for sure, the footplate of a speeding Cauliflower must have been an exciting place.

The Dean goods, along with the 'Great Westernised' ex Cambrian Railways' 'Big Goods' 0-6-0s worked all over the central part of Wales. Along the coast they ran day in and day out from Pwllheli to Barmouth Junction over the great trestle bridge and on down the lovely Dovey estuary to Machynlleth, and over the hills from Moat Lane junction to Brecon. The Dean goods could be found anywhere from Moreton-in-Marsh to Newbury or Carmarthen to Kerry. What is more, so successful were they that the War Department commandeered them in two world wars when they served as far away as North Africa: some even served in *both* wars. A few even went as far as China at the end of the second world war. Thankfully one, No 2516, has been retained and rests appropriately in the Swindon museum.

Cross Country push pull. An ex LSWR M7 class 0-4-4 tank (Horsham 75D) runs through West Heath Common, Rogate, with the 2.40pm Petersfield to Midhurst train on 1 July 1950. The engine, No 30021, is auto fitted enabling the driver to control the train from a special compartment in the end vehicle. It carries Southern head code No 5, in the form of a single white disc; this is a route indicator, a system not used by the other Big Four railways or BR Regions.

Last Days of a Veteran. The 11.50am Workington to Penrith train headed by ex LNWR 18in goods 0-6-0 No 58396 of Workington shed (12D) passes Bassenthwaite Lake on 5 August 1950 en route for Keswick. Strangely, the engine carries no shed allocation plate on the smokebox door.

Dean Goods. Moat Lane, where the ex Cambrian main line met the Mid Wales branch to Three Cocks and Brecon; it was worked until the coming of the BR Standard 2-6-0s by either Dean goods or Cambrian 0-6-0s. These trains met the Central Wales line (ex LNWR) from Craven Arms to Llandovery and Swansea at Builth Road (Low Level). In 1947 the motive power was Dean goods No 2468 of Brecon shed; this and the stock are in final GWR livery. No one has yet thought of placing the headlamp code on the locomotive.

Cambrian Shed. Oswestry on 11 May 1949 with three 0-6-0s outside, two 2251 class Collett engines and a Cambrian 'Big Goods'. The latter is No 873 ex No 42 (Beyer Peacock 1919). Oswestry works was still in operation at the time servicing most of the engines off the one time Cambrian system.

7

COUNTRY JUNCTIONS

From Truro to Inverness, Carmarthen to Norwich, market town junction stations had a great deal in common – and most of it is now but memory. Local trains outnumbered expresses, the fireman jumping off his engine before it stopped to remove the headlight and jump on the track, shouting to his mate to 'ease up' to help get it uncoupled. The majority of passengers were travelling at most a score of miles, and many of them had never had occasion to board any of the grand expresses sharing the same platforms. The busiest hour for arrivals was from around 8.15am, when children, shop assistants and office workers, and usually a fair sprinkling of railwaymen, poured off a succession of strictly country trains. Always with such local services, the last passengers had disappeared out of sight before the unloading of parcels was even into its swing. The porter in charge would anyway give priority to closing doors and windows, especially in cold weather, looking out for a discarded paper or magazine. There was a constant moving around of carriages, horseboxes, cattle wagons, liquid-gas supply vehicles and many more, attaching and detaching going on almost throughout the day, while on the platforms themselves luggage trolleys were in constant motion and cleaners popping in and out of the trains being turned round. From below came the familiar sound of the wheel tapper at work.

Take a station like Taunton, serving Somerset's capital. Today you are bound to think of it as a main-line affair, still junction between two important routes. But for most of its life the majority of activity was devoted to strictly rural matters. All-stations stoppers arrived and terminated from seven routes: Exeter, Barnstaple, Minehead, Weston-super-Mare, Castle Cary, Yeovil and Chard. Even the trains that shared the tracks of the crack Great Western expresses were not in the least 'main line', in their speeds, loads – and least of all the conversations and dialect of the passengers. Nor did they have much in common with each other, the affairs of the marsh country served by Athelney where most of the living came from willow growing and basket making and those of the farmers of the Exmoor foothills up from Dulverton, or the richer dairy-farming country around Chard, seeming as worlds apart as those indicated by the destination boards of trains bound for Paddington or Manchester (London Road).

While the expresses might have carried a certain air, that was not to make the locals inferior. The station was basically theirs, and long before the first Paddington or North express arrived, the auto-car from Castle Cary, the three-coach set from Yeovil and the two-coach non-corridor set

Opposite below:
Boat Train. On summer Saturdays in the 1950s rail traffic to the Isle of Wight ports was always heavy with extra trains in abundance. The branch from Lymington Pier to Lymington and on to Brockenhurst saw some of these workings with their fascinating, if sometimes elderly, combination of locomotives and stock. Here in 1953 an ex LSWR T9 class 4-4-0 plus LSWR coaches heads a London bound train; it is seen approaching Lymington Junction, Brockenhurst – the outer home signal is just visible in the background. The locomotive carries Bournemouth line headcode – a down train would have shown a special code to indicate that it was for Lymington. The T9 working was due to weight restrictions on the branch. Note the large eight wheel bogie tender for use over the South Western company's old main line – there were no water troughs.

139

Buckinghamshire Junction. Princes Risborough, towards the western end of the Great Western & Great Central Joint line from Northolt to Ashendon Junction, was a good place to watch trains. Mighty Kings and Castles would sometimes stop here, 28XX 2-8-0s rattled through with long trains of freight and branch engines simmered in the platforms while they passed. Sadly, in the 1950s, the Great Central line no longer saw Director class 4-4-0s but as a consolation Gresley's Pacifics joined Collett's Kings in a headlong dash after thundering their way thankfully beyond Saunderton summit. On 31 May 1951 GWR railcar No W16 waits with the 5.45pm service to Thame. Behind it is one of the newer 0-6-0 pannier tanks No 4691 plus an auto coach forming the 5.48pm for the Watlington branch. It should be a push and pull service but as 4691 was not auto fitted, it had to run round at each end of the journey.

from Chard took their time on the main line – more convenient for the unloading of parcels than the bay. Many of these trains had no real connections to make, their timings having changed little for many years (though the Castle Cary service was still regarded as relatively 'new', a by-product of the 'cut-off' opened in 1906) and been ordained as it were between the Great Western Railway, local demand and God. The locals coming up through Norton Fitzwarren and along the quadrupled track for their last two miles were different in that a small but significant proportion of their passengers were on their way really up country. So during much of the day full use was made of the upside bay at the Exeter end, in order to allow tighter connections. After cleaning, the trains were then worked over to the downside, and when passengers arrived from far away they would find the Barnstaple and Minehead trains, their 'Moguls' usually simmering beside each other, in the two departure bays. One would leave main line immediately behind the express and the other go relief to Norton Fitzwarren. Most of their passengers undoubtedly felt more at home once they were underway beyond the junction, on their own route, where every field and hay barn was familiar.

And though they held their own at the junction, and drivers from country sheds found no difficulty in coping with the multitude of tracks and signals, it has to be admitted that branch-line trains always looked more natural where they really belonged. Or was it just imagination? Or the noise and dirt of the junctions? You forget just how dirty busy stations used to be, what a hardship the traveller from the pure Dartmoor air of Lustleigh found even the relatively industrial atmosphere of Newton Abbot with its power station and railway works and depot hard by the ever-busy station.

Though it was such large junctions, bringing passengers and goods to market and making exchanges with expresses, that gave the country train at least part of its raison d'etre, the more romantic junctions were those away from major centres of population. They came in many shapes and sizes, but were generally not so large as to be perpetually busy, and thus like the true country station had periods of sharp activity between lulls, though the activity could be varied and sustained at times. Their staff would mainly have been unwilling to work at a Taunton, Norwich or Inverness. At the real country junction, you had time to recover and reflect on the traffic you were handling. Imagine yourself working at Dingwall in November 1932, for example, on the Far North line on a darkening winter's afternoon.

The summer tourists have long departed, and the service has been curtailed from September to suit. There are only two daily trains now from Inverness to Wick, plus one as far as Helmsdale and three for Tain, with matching return workings. The Kyle line is thin indeed, with only one through Inverness train in each direction, and one down and two up mixes between Dingwall and the Kyle, the balancing down working being exclusively freight, as are a pair of workings on the Far North. So the station at this county town of Ross-shire at the end of Cromarty Firth and lying in the shadow of Ben Wyvis, has some lengthy quiet spells, only relieved by the little Strathpeffer train shuttling back and forth a generous ten times a day.

Further North. Helmsdale Station on the wild Sutherland/Caithness border with an ex LMS Black Five 4-6-0 heading an Inverness to Wick train taking water one October morning in 1951. In the up platform an ex Caledonian Railway Pickersgill 4-4-0 on the pick up goods waits by the wooden signalbox for clearance to recommence shunting its vans after the passenger train's departure. The porter-signalman, tablet loop in hand, is collecting parcels from the van to load on to a wooden platform cart. Beyond the small goods shed, there are sidings whose approach and that of the station is guarded by an LMS upper quadrant home signal, while the down starter is still a Highland Railway lattice post lower quadrant. The huts in the background are old Highland Railway company's wagons removed from their underframes and the corrugated iron building on the left is the engine shed (code 60C in BR days).

141

Dingwall, Junction for the Kyle line. With the signal arm 'off' for the main line ex Highland Railway Castle class 4-6-0 No 14677 heads the down 'Mail' – the 6.30am from Inverness, sometime in the late 1920s. The driver has slowed his engine with the cab almost opposite the signalman's wooden walkway. Note the shunt-ahead arms below the main semaphores and the train crew about to take the tablet hoop.

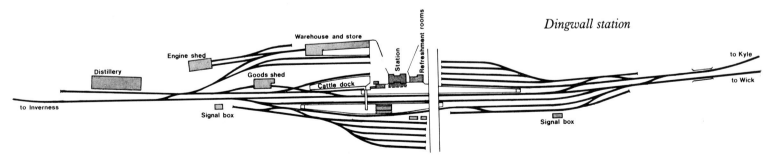

Dingwall station

But there are times when Dingwall really comes to life, even if everything is headed in one direction only. Such a one starts as darkness is falling on the Highland winter. There is a biting east wind off the Firth, with flurries of snow in it, and the staff thank their gods that they can get it over quickly and retreat to the warmth of the porters' room and signalbox to thaw out for the next spell.

It begins, incongruously, with one of Cumming's 4-6-0 superheater goods engines coming off Dingwall shed about half past three and running through the platform to the north end sidings, where it fussily catches in successive swoops four empty cattle vans, a wagon of coal for Garve and a brake van, and shoves them back into the downside bay platform, where earlier in the day a Travelling Post Office of Highland vintage had a long lay-over (as it would every morning well into BR days). Off it goes again to get the two coaches, one an old Highland corridor, which brought the overnight steamer passengers from Kyle and have been lying in the adjacent siding for the last six hours. These are now set back on to the wagons in the bay and coupled, the steam heat turned on. The 4.10 mixed to Kyle is in business. The driver watches the developing scene from his deep protective cab, his shape silhouetted against the glare as his fireman puts the finishing touches to his fire. Within five minutes of departure the engine will be working well-nigh flat out on the vicious four-mile climb at 1 in 50, briefly interrupted by the station stop at Achterneed, as it lifts its train from little above sea level to the summit at Raven Rock, 458ft up. The driver will need every bit of steam he can get for his tough little engine if he is not to stall.

Next comes the arrival of the 3.47 from Strathpeffer, which also runs 'mixed' to bring back the empties from the slim traffic in coal, fertilisers and whatever. It clatters in with its one coach, trailed by a couple of open wagons (one of them the engineering department's) and a brake. The tank engines have gone to Valhalla or Dornoch, and Dingwall has provided a 'Small Ben' for the job today. With no turntable at the terminus, the enginemen have taken it upon themselves to run tender first outwards, to get protection when running into the wind coming home, though they have also rigged a tarpaulin sheet for comfort. Only one passenger alights – maybe the threat to close Strathpeffer is real – the wagons are quickly propelled back into the yard before the engine cuts off, rounds its coach in the up platform and propels it to the South box.

While this activity has been breaking the silence, the Inverness–Helmsdale train has bowled into the down platform at four o'clock and stopped with the 'Castle' at the water column. A handful of passengers alight from the comparative warmth of the waiting rooms making for the steam-wreathed coaches, and there is a criss-cross conflict under the platform awning as they meet the alighting people (the day's largest number) making either for the town or the Kyle train. The fireman throws the bag out, puts another knob of coal in the water column cresset and joins the engine as the whistle blows and the driver makes his first two-handed pull at the regulator handle. The 'Castle' makes an energetic start to get speed for the bank, and the fireman has to be smart

---

Irregular Caravan

Stories about Englishmen taking to the Scottish moors for the Glorious Twelfth could fill several books. Let us stick to fact, and quote from Foxwell's *Express Trains, English and Foreign* about how part of the traffic was handled in the late 1880s. The train in question is the 7.50am from Perth:

'In July and August this 7.50 train is the unique railway phenomenon. Passenger carriages, saloons, horse-boxes and vans, concentrated at Perth from all parts of England, and intermixed to make an irregular caravan. Engines are attached fore and aft and the procession toils pluckily over the Grampians. Thus on August 7th, 1888, this train sailed out of Perth:

LBSCR ..	Horsebox
,, ..	,,
,, ..	Carriage van
,, ..	Horsebox
LNWR ..	,,
NER ..	,,
LNWR ..	Saloon
,, ..	Horsebox
Mid R ..	Saloon
,, ..	Luggage van
,, ..	Carriage truck
,, ..	Horsebox
LNWR ..	,,
NBR ..	Luggage van
,, ..	Horsebox
,, ..	,,
,, ..	,,
ECR ..	Sleeping car
GNR ..	Saloon
WCR ..	Composite
Mid R ..	,,
LNWR ..	Luggage van
LSWR ..	Horsebox
WCR ..	Composite
LNWR ..	Horsebox
,, ..	Meat van
HR ..	P.O. van
,, ..	Luggage van
,, ..	Third-class passenger
,, ..	First-class passenger
,, ..	Second-class passenger
,, ..	Third-class passenger
,, ..	Luggage van
,, ..	Third-class passenger
,, ..	First-class passenger
,, ..	Third-class passenger
,, ..	Guard's van

Ten companies, 37 carriages, 2 engines in front, 1 put on behind at Blair Athol.'

143

to catch the token from the signalman in his pulpit at the North box.

With the Helmsdale away, the South box signalman can now exercise his muscle to let the Strathpeffer engine and its coach come through the road into the down platform for its 4.17 departure. There are a few shoppers and a handful of children waiting for it; nobody off the Helmsdale. And the 5.5 and the six o'clock probably will not be any busier. The outfit has hardly stopped before the Kyle guard is whistling his train away on the Skye road. His driver pulls at the regulator handle, steam oozes from a piston rod gland, there is a snatch of couplings among the wagons, and the 'Superheater' is off on its 64-mile journey, coast to coast. No sooner is it past Fodderty Junction than the signalman at the North box is given road clear for the Strathpeffer, and off goes the 'Ben'. Once they have lifted the token and puffed round the curve beyond the river and town, the crew will huddle as best they can in the corners of the cab as they head straight for the little spa town, its former glory already much faded.

On the Dingwall platform, the muffled back-shift porter has nearly reached his warm room. Time for a bite to eat and a mug of strong tea to fortify him for the arrival of the up train due in three quarters of an hour, though his mate in the parcels office will want help to bring the barrows over. Dingwall people seem to be sending a lot of items today.

And so it is all over the British Isles, parcels offices taking in perishables and other goods for the evening trains to bigger places, the pace of activity at the uncentralised Post Office sorting offices accelerating in readiness for taking the mail bags to the station too.

Many junctions were between a straight main line and single branch; always a meeting of unequals. The Cinderford auto-car waited almost apologetically in the bay platform for its connection to arrive, more passengers leaving the station than switching to it. Where it was not a case of push-and-pull, however, at least the scene was enlivened by the branch locomotive running round its train. Where there was a run-round clear of the main line, this act could be performed while the main-line train was at its platform. Almost always the Prairie tank ran around the two-coach Wadebridge train while the up express was at Bodmin Road, passengers for 'England' hearing the three shrill Great Western whistles at each end of the loop. According to your loyalty, this was smart branch-line work or an inordinate delay for the express. As an example of the latter, on the same main-line, at Par, one up train connected with both a train to and from Newquay, the down branch train passing the up one on the short section of double track to St Blazey before it was signalled into the same platform.

In the country as a whole, if up connections were smart, down ones were loose – for the simple reason that managers liked to record a high percentage of punctual arrivals. Allow branch trains an extra five minutes at the junction before starting their leisurely-timed trips, and the chances of a punctual arrival were considerably enhanced. Sad indeed were those responsible for punctuality averages when the time came to close short lines like Fraserburgh – St Combs and Holywell

Junction (on the North Wales main line) – Holywell Town where it was hard not to run to time.

There were, of course, stations from which you could not escape to continue your journey by road even if the branch-line train were not ready. At one such, Bala Junction, the delay was frequently increased by a pact between signalman and porters. Down 'main-line' trains, instead of using their proper platform, would be sent via the branch one, usually signalled for such through working. This saved having to carry luggage across the line, but meant that the branch train had to beat a temporary retreat.

Exchange platforms, not serving the local population, such as at Cairnie Junction on the Great North of Scotland, were indeed lonely places outside their short periods of intense activity. Another North Wales one, still open, though now devoid of its refreshment room and much of its glamour, is Dovey Junction, on the marshes subject to occasional flooding. Here, perhaps more than anywhere else, in busier railway days the mood varied according to the traffic. If no connection were available between the Aberystwyth and Barmouth lines, trains ran through without stopping, only momentarily interrupting the song of the curlew. But in high summer, a pair of double-headed full-length corridor trains would suddenly arrive and exchange considerable quantities of passengers and luggage, while at other times there was just long enough for the refreshment room staff to serve a queue of passengers transferring routes.

Take the Barmouth line, and eventually you would come to another unique junction, still nominally open under the name of Morfa Mawddach, but still known to all railwaymen as Barmouth Junction. At the southern end of Barmouth bridge whose footpath has so long been a scenic viewpoint, lovers walk and windy platform (havened by wooden shelters) for hopeful fishermen, it is a dramatic spot. At any time of day, the ebbing and flowing tides, and swirling river and the views of cloud-capped Cader Idris show nature at its most dramatic; but as the sun sets slowly the view up the valley towards Dolgellau (formerly Dolgelley) is supreme.

THE BARMOUTH JUNCTION SCENE

(i) Cambrian Survivor. Beyer Peacock built 3/08 0-6-0 No 894 heads a mixed goods into Barmouth Junction (Morfa Mawddach) in June 1952 ten months before her withdrawal from service. The bracket signal is pulled off for the coast line but the engine would have had more than trouble trying to take this long train of mixed freight up the Friog incline and under the landslip shelter. The clue is probably in the 8th and 9th vans – GWR brakes. The front portion (with a gunpowder van from the Penrhyndeudraeth factory third from the engine) will form the Machynlleth train while the rear will be dropped into the sidings at the back of the triangle for onward transmission over the hilly road to Ruabon, closed on 25 January 1965.

Barmouth Junction Layout. The Junction station and its triangle of tracks were built to deal with the interchange of traffic between the Great Western's route from Ruabon via Dolgelly (now Dolgellau) and the Cambrian Coast Line trains running from Pwllheli to Dovey Junction or Machynlleth. In Cambrian days the loop at the rear contained a siding for only fifteen wagons but this was increased in its capacity by the GWR on takeover. The loop was also used for turning engines particularly those coming off the Ruabon/Dolgelly line as most passenger trains, and all engines travelling this way, terminated at Barmouth. Before the second world war the Manors, 43XX Moguls and the occasional Aberdare 2-6-0s used on these services were not allowed over the Coast Line because of weight restrictions. There was no station footbridge and passengers needing to cross the tracks used the footboards at the north end of the platforms.

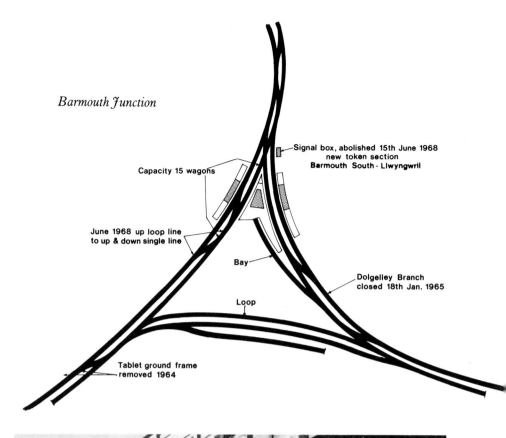

Barmouth Junction

Signal box, abolished 15th June 1968
new token section
Barmouth South - Llwyngwril

Capacity 15 wagons

June 1968 up loop line
to up & down single line

Bay

Dolgelley Branch
closed 18th Jan. 1965

Loop

Tablet ground frame
removed 1964

(ii) An interesting photograph showing the original timber section of Barmouth viaduct in good health in 1953. Below, at low tide, are the pools giving shelter to young flat fish, whilst the woodwork has yet to be attacked by a marine worm (toredo navalis). Even in its prime the bridge attracted a speed limit of 20mph for all trains.

(iii) Estuary View. A modern BR Standard 2-6-0 takes a Pwllheli bound train over the swing section of Barmouth Bridge on Whit Tuesday 1956 while in the background a Manor class 4-6-0 heads east from the Junction towards Dolgellau and Ruabon. Under the storm cloud to the left is Cader Idris, the highest mountain in mid Wales. The swing bridge was constructed to allow for traffic up the river but the railway killed this off in weeks. Note the treacherous current at high tide.

(iv) Engineman's View. Great Western 4-6-0 No 7800 Torquay Manor rumbles over Barmouth Bridge with a through train to London via Dolgellau, Ruabon, Shrewsbury and Birmingham in June 1953: the engine is spotless having been used on a Royal train the day before. Note the guard rails to the single track and the fixed distant signal on the edge of the sandstrewn stone embankment. To the left are the footpath (toll) and wooden wind shelters while on the right is a plume of steam from a coast line train.

Until the closure of the single line over the mountains from Ruabon and through Bala Junction and Dolgelley, Barmouth Junction, with its unusual triangle of tracks, was beyond reasonable doubt one of the loveliest country junctions in Britain. From its platforms, your back to the licensed refreshment room and the towering Cader Idris, it was possible to look down the coast to Fairbourne and the Friog incline with its avalanche shelter (built after a second train had collided with boulders and rolled into the sea) or round the curve past the great signalbox to the causeway, the trestle, the swing bridge to the green and grey sea, with Barmouth's small harbour just visible a mile or so away.

Inside the triangle, until the last great flood, when six feet of sea water swamped the area in 1938, were a gaggle of railwaymen's cottages. Just outside the tracks, a small community nestled against the hillside away from the direct force of the wind, its centre the hamlet's pub, the station refreshment room on the central island platform snug in a strong brick building. Here, in pre-television days, voices of the local lads gathered with the station staff would rise above the sound of the wind, and the singing was often one of those old Welsh hymns. If the last down, 'the branch' from Ruabon, Llangollen, Bala Junction and all stations via Dolgelley, was very late (it was the final connection from London) the coast train had to wait. Then it was not uncommon to see the driver descend from his Dean 0-6-0 or Cambrian goods, the storm sheet tied in place between open cab and tender, walk up and down the train for prying eyes and nip into the 'rooms' for a pint of ale. He was soon joined by the guard (discipline required the fireman to remain on the footplate) along with one or two passengers. After voices had been suitably lubricated, a good sing-song competed with the engine's safety valve, the driver assuring passengers that it would not leave without him.

However romantic it might have been changing from the main-line to the patiently waiting branch train for Saffron Walden at Audley End, or for Hythe at Sandling Junction, the climax of country railway enjoyment was undoubtedly to be found where single line met single line. No question here of an express, passenger or freight, racing through, showing as scant respect for local life and trade as the aeroplane overhead. Everything, everybody on the platform was of the country railway. To be sure, a branch off a branch might be more country yet, the engines less powerful, the trains shorter, older and no doubt more unprofitable. But there was a bond between *all* country railways, stations, trains and those running them and travelling by them. What it really said was that life was for living, that there was no virtue in rushing, and those who dashed about on expresses and spent their time in cities had only themselves to blame.

In the Border Country there were ample opportunities to consider your place in the universe, or hear about the local game or where a good crop of mushrooms had been seen, while changing trains at remote junctions. Reedsmouth was one such, on the North British Border Counties branch from Hexham to Riccarton, itself basically served by only three trains a day plus a freight. Here began the branch off the

Opposite below:
Midland Junction. Ashchurch station, a characteristically Midland Railway structure on 27 February 1966. Situated north of Cheltenham, Ashchurch was on the main line from Derby and Birmingham to Bristol and was the junction for the branch to Tewkesbury and Malvern (closed to passenger traffic in two stages – Malvern to Upton-on-Severn on 1 December 1952, and Upton-on-Severn to Ashchurch on 14 August 1961) and the loop to Barnt Green via Evesham and Redditch (closed as far as Redditch – now a Birmingham commuter terminus – on 12 June 1963). Once most trains stopped at Ashchurch but after the closure of the branches its usefulness was over and it closed on 15 November 1971. The Tewkesbury–Upton line was the last home of the Stanier LMS 0-4-4 tanks.

Making Ready. Ex Caledonian Railway 0-4-4 tank, her appearance spoilt by a stove pipe chimney, takes water at Loch Tay shed while being prepared for another quiet day: time is getting late for it is April 1961 and the Killin branch was to close on 28 September 1965.

Overleaf:
Summer Saturday Loading. A Cambrian Coast line express of over eleven coaches crawls up Talerdigg incline east of Machynlleth behind an ex GWR 43XX class 2-6-0 piloted by BR standard class 2 2-6-0 No 78005. Normally the train engine would have been a Manor class 4-6-0 but Summer Saturdays sometimes produced the Moguls. The date is probably the late 1950s.

branch to Morpeth, to be joined at Scotsgap by yet another branch, from Rothbury. Like many country railways, these had been built partly in the territorial wars between companies, and Reedsmouth was given an importance that it could never live up to. The solid station buildings between platforms on two sides of a triangle looked as though they had been built for eternity, while the substantial, elevated signalbox overlooking the actual junction would not have seemed out of place controlling a smaller London terminus. Apart from the few passengers changing trains, about the only users of the station were railwaymen, for Reedsmouth was one of those lonely railway settlements where everyone knew everyone and just what he and she did and the company provided everything except the church. And in fact it even provided that in the form of a worshippers special to Hexham alternate Sundays, a Sunday train on a North British branch and that in England being a real curiosity.

Long after the last regular passenger trains had gone, it was still possible to watch the signalbox in full activity. The steam trains at the two platforms together were the thrice-weekly freight from Morpeth to Bellingham (all that then remained of the system, involving reversal at Reedsmouth) and an engineer's special loaded full of cheery officials enjoying an afternoon's 'inspection', which also reversed on its return from Bellingham. Since all signalboxes had been retained and staffed, albeit for only one daily turn now, the pair of trains followed each other to Morpeth block-to-block. Though having an 'assistant' (a young lad who had been ill and sent to Reedsmouth for country air and light duties), the signalman complained that the number of lever movements involved in reversing two trains in each direction in sharp succession warranted an electrically assisted frame.

Ravenstonedale

I strolled onto the semi-derelict platform one fine afternoon early in June. The sidings of the little goods-yard were silent and empty and in the background the hills above Tebay stood out gloriously in the sunshine.

'Was there owt you were efter,' said a voice. It was the Ravenstonedale signalman, leaning over the rail of the steps leading up to his little box.

I hastened to explain I was just 'an interested spectator' of the railway scene and as a sharp hill shower came across, I was invited into the shelter of the cabin.

Ravenstonedale is the point where the double track of the former NER line from Tebay to Kirkby Stephen becomes single. 'Only coke trains to deal with nowadays,' I said. 'Aye, nobbut that; but we git military specials, and then there's Blackpool excursions in't summer.' 'We've eight coke jobs a day: double turns out and back from West Auckland to Tebay; double-headed.'

I observed that these coke trains seemed to move pretty smartly. 'They do that: you should see them go through yon cross-over on to the single line. Our stationmaster here's a young chap, and many a time when them coke jobs come through he'll stand and hold himself and say to me 'Do you think yon engines'll come off t'track Jim?' But them drivers know their job aw reet.'

Inside the box the walls were lined with coloured pictures of locomotives, many in pre-Grouping liveries. 'We work two shifts, 5.30am to 1.30pm and 4.30pm to 12.30am. Stationmaster fills in for us from 1.30 to 4.30pm, so as we don't do any overtime.'

'Come and see us agean, if tha's passing this way,' said the signalman. I said I would.
W. McGowan Gradon, *SLS Journal*, July 1957

He would have approved of arrangements at Heathfield, where the Teign Valley branch via Christow joined the Mortonhampstead branch and in the 1930s the GW installed an electric panel to aid control of the busy traffic, three passenger and a freight frequently being in the station at once. Expresses and through working from Exeter to Bovey Tracey were not resumed after the second world war, but then a lignite mine was opened, and with heavy general freight and traffic for the tile factory, the layout was fully used hours on end. If the afternoon freight from Exeter (run straight through to Newton Abbot solely for driver familiarisation – ready for the next time the sea washed ballast from the track at Dawlish and the inland diversion was needed) did not leave Trusham on time, it had to be held for at least two hours before Heathfield could cope. But, here too, BR wasted money after passenger trains had been withdrawn. Not only was the signalbox retained for the by now only occasional freight, but when a siding was laid in to a banana ripening plant, it was fully signalled and added to the panel.

Many junctions, of course, are places at which tracks diverge well out of sight of passenger platforms, signalboxes built specially to serve them, their signalmen leading lonely lives doing a pretty mechanical job, though occasionally having to exercise discretion in accommodating the slower-moving trains off the branch. Certainly the signalman at Harpenden Junction had quite a challenge with the trains off the Hemel Hempstead branch – and a unique train it was at one time before the first world war, a small 4-4-0 tank, formerly Eastern & Midlands Railway and in its maroon livery, coupled to one of the Midland's first Pullman cars. It replaced an early Midland rail-motor after it failed to cope with the long 1 in 37 gradient that began immediately after the sharp curve in a

cutting at the branch's divergence. The train, and its later successors, never more than a single coach, had to travel main line to and from Harpenden, the cross-overs between main and relief lines being beyond the branch junction. Up trains of course had to cut in front of down expresses, fast lightweight expresses handled by Midland Compounds, and then potentially delay up ones – and always struck the onlooker as a kind of slow-moving obstacle.

Conversely, at places like Habrough on the Cleethorpes line, away from any physical junction, passengers have always had to be directed into the train for the appropriate route more carefully than at any London terminus with its clear departure boards. At nearby Barnetby is an example of yet another junction type, common in the industrial north: acres of track, still dozens of semaphore signals to be seen from the expansive though inevitably run-down platforms, two long islands, connected to the booking office in a large building beyond the rails by a substantial footbridge. The passenger usage per metre length of platform must always have been lower at places like this than more remote but compact country stations, and never can such places have felt cosy.

The Southern still has a further type of junction – where portions of

Unusual Combination. Harpenden station, Midland Railway around 1906/7. The train consists of an ex Midland & Great Northern Joint Railway 4-4-0 tank No 10 (one of four transferred to the MR in exchange for three 0-4-4 tanks and repainted at Kentish Town though retaining M&GN numbers) and an ex Pullman car fitted for auto train working.

Great Eastern Shuttle Service. The afternoon 4.28pm push and pull service to Saffron Walden at Audley End on 15 April 1952. The wooden bodied clerestory coach is a Great Eastern vehicle fitted for auto train working, while the engine unseen at the front is ex NER Worsdell (LNER class G5) 0-4-4 tank, No 67279 of 1894, one of several rebuilt with larger tanks.

155

End On Junction. The former LSWR Torrington station on 20 May 1949. This was where the branch from Barnstaple Junction met the North Devon and Cornwall Junction Light Railway head on. Two trains are in the platforms; on the left is the goods brake van of the mixed which has just arrived from Halwill Junction behind ex LB&SCR E1/R (Southern Railway rebuild) 0-6-2 tank No 32696; on the right heading a Barnstaple stopper is ex LSWR class M7 0-4-4 tank, still numbered 247 of Barnstaple shed (72E from 1950). Closures were ND&CJLR on 1 March 1965, Barnstaple line on 4 October 1965.

trains serving different destinations are joined and attached, often at the same time every hour throughout the day, and far more rapidly than anyone on the Great Western would have thought possible. Most such junctions are perhaps more suburban than country, but the Southern's tradition of sharp work benefitted passengers on its West Country branch network while it was still open. Indeed, but for smart shunting, attaching and detaching, 'portmanteau' trains like the Atlantic Coast Express, with through coaches serving not only up to ten terminal points but dozens of country settlements en route, would have been much slower. Barnstaple Junction saw perpetual attaching and detaching, almost all Waterloo trains being further split there – as they were at that more remote outpost of railways that still gives its name to the village built up around it, Halwill Junction. Another example was Tipton St John's, though here perhaps the work was more varied. Generally only one daily train, which in the down direction was the Atlantic Coast Express, carried through carriages for both Exmouth and Sidmouth, detached from the rear of the main train at Sidmouth Junction, and then split at Tipton St John's. But summer Saturdays brought extra through trains, including in some pre- and post-war years that from Cleethorpes, routed down the Somerset & Dorset to Templecombe (incidentally one of the few examples of through passenger working between the two railways that met at that idiosyncratic junction where, after waiting it seemed for ever, your S&D train *backed* out of its curved platform, engine at either end). But even when through coaches were not being handled, Tipton's work was varied. Usually, though not always, it was the Sidmouth train that went up to the main-line junction, that from Exmouth via Budleigh Salterton, having arrived first, disappearing into the yard on the up side where its locomotive could run round clear of the running tracks. There were only two platforms, strictly up and down, so that when the Sidmouth train had left to climb the gradient that began immediately outside the station, the Exmouth one crossed to the down side before taking a right turn over the double junction just beyond the level crossing. Often up and down Sidmouth trains, one of them perhaps a through service from Exeter, crossed here, while the Exmouth engine ran round in the yard; but there were also occasional through Exmouth–Sidmouth services, and an afternoon through train, mainly for children picked up at Ottery St Mary, to Honiton, involving reversal at Sidmouth Junction.

Finally, to Melton Constable, a country junction that lives on in the memory of many of its former users and admirers. Beyond the houses of the village, the gently undulating fields are beginning to change from

M&GN Stopper. Melton Constable on 23 May 1951 with D16/3 4-4-0 No 62523 heading the Kings Lynn portion of a Yarmouth to Lynn train which carried coaches for Cromer, via Weybourne and Sheringham. The works and shed were beyond the bridge to the right. The Cromer Line runs out of the left hand side of the photograph.

157

Opposite:
Colliers' Valley. Former LNWR 0-6-2 coal tank No 58933 of Tredegar shed (sub to 86K Abergavenny) leaves Bedwellty Pits Halt at the head of the 1.10pm from Newport on 19 August 1950. The Tredegar branch was a long shot enabling the LNWR to dig deep into the South Wales valleys via its joint line with the Great Western from Shrewsbury to Hereford (with running powers to Abergavenny Junction) and then on over the Heads of the Valleys route to Merthyr.

green to gold as the wheat ripens under a warm sun. But the stationmaster, on this August Bank Holiday Saturday, has no eyes for nature as he alternates between his office, the awninged island platform and the West Junction signalbox with its phone to Control at South Lynn. For today is the busiest of his year, with a host of special passenger trains from the Midlands and elsewhere to Yarmouth, and one or two to Cromer. It stretches the small M&GN locomotive fleet to the limit, since 'foreign' engines do not normally work beyond Lynn. A glance across to the works confirms that it is empty save for one 0-6-0 shunting tank. To the west, the double track stretches only the fourteen miles to Raynham Park, beyond which it is single line for much of the way to Saxby.

The through Yarmouth trains are fairly straightforward; stop in the down platform, six or eight minutes taking water, and they are away to a flying start down the five miles to Corpusty, where the single line starts again. The tricky ones are the regulars which involve a three-way split; the first portion for Yarmouth, while the remainder is divided and re-engined at both ends, for Norwich and Cromer. This blocks the platform for quite a while, and meanwhile the next special is coming along under 'Section clear but station blocked' from Thursford.

The Cromer engine – they are so hard pressed today that it is one of the elegant little outside-cylindered 4-4-2 tanks built at Melton Constable in the Beyer mould – is waiting out at the West Junction, its dark brown paintwork shining in the bright sunlight. The awaited train, running twenty minutes late because of the congestion, runs in behind a brace of 4-4-0s and has ten LMS corridors. The crew take care to stop with the train engine, a big Johnson 4-4-0 Class C, at the water column. As the assistant engine, a smaller Beyer of Class B, is hooked off and runs forward to the Norwich branch to stand, the Cromer engine is buffering up at the back end, the fireman already on the ground to throw on the shackle and couple the vacuum pipes. The shunter is three coaches forward, vacuum pipes already on the stoppers and the corridor connections uncoupled, signalling for a 'close up' to part the train. The starting signal is already off; the stationmaster blows his whistle long as a warning, the guard glances over his door handles and then checks his vacuum gauge and flags the train away. The little tank gives an acknowledging 'pop' on the whistle and chiffles out of the platform over the junction. At the other end, the fireman is throwing the bag out of the tender, and in a moment the five Yarmouth coaches are away.

The East Junction signalman has the road reset, almost before the tail lamp has cleared the crossings, to bring the Norwich engine back off the branch on to the rump of its train. A brief pause as an up train from Yarmouth rattles over the junction into the platform, and the road for Norwich can be set yet again. The little Beyer is gently blowing off, anxious to be away and out of the way as soon as the signal clears, and as soon as it starts to move the signalman is down the box steps to set the tablet catcher. At last the stationmaster has a free platform, but already the next special is whistling for the home signal at the West end.

158

THE HEADS OF THE VALLEYS LINE AND NANTYBWCH JUNCTION

Until the first world war the South Wales valleys with their many and profitable coal mines were eagerly sought goals for the two major railways serving the Principality, the London & North Western and Great Western. Most of these valleys also obtained Parliamentary Acts for their own railways, among the best known being perhaps the Rhymney, Taff Vale and Rhondda & Swansea Bay lines. The Great Western was a valley railway too but it also provided an outlet for the others, taking their non sea-bound coal eastwards to England. The LNWR infiltrated by other means, it built an isolated section of railway from Abergavenny Junction (reached by running powers beyond its North to West joint line with the GWR from Shrewsbury to Hereford) along the Heads of the Valleys to Merthyr, tapping most of the independents along the route. Two thirds of the way west along this line lay Nantybwch, an open and windswept junction with a branch tapping various coal mines and going through Sirhowy and Tredegar to Nine Mile Point where it met the Great Western again; the LNW had running powers, this time to Newport.

Nantybwch in the late 1940s early 1950s was a good place to watch trains, for although technically it was now in the Western Region, both the Heads of the Valleys route and the Sirhowy Valley branch were strongholds of LNWR locomotives, mainly in the form of Super D 0-8-0s and 0-6-2 coal tanks: both Abergavenny and Tredegar sheds were open then with allocations almost unbelievable today. In 1947 for example, Abergavenny had nine coal tanks, nine 0-8-4 tanks, ten Super Ds and one Stanier 2-6-2 tank, plus a couple of 18in Goods 0-6-0s. Tredegar had five 0-8-4 tanks and five 0-6-2 coal tanks.

Tredegar men worked the branch, and all passenger traffic was in the hands of the coal tanks, which made relatively easy work over the steep grades with three or four ageing ex LNWR vehicles, the colliers' trains being particularly disreputable. Today with a modern road running over the Heads of the Valleys line it is difficult even to find Nantybwch, certainly the once important branch serving the then prosperous Tredegar Iron Works, Bedwelty Pits and Holly Bush is gone with the ghosts of the North Western.

Heads of the Valleys Junction. A cold wind-swept Nantybwch on 19 August 1950 with coal tank No 58933 of Tredegar shed (86K). The train, the 1.10pm from Newport has just arrived stopping at all stations via the junction at Nine Mile Point where it left Great Western tracks.

Although now technically Western Region, this one time LNWR outpost still rates its pre grouping atmosphere, locomotives, ancient and decrepit stock and station buildings. All three coaches are ex LNWR including a double ended brake composite in the rear.

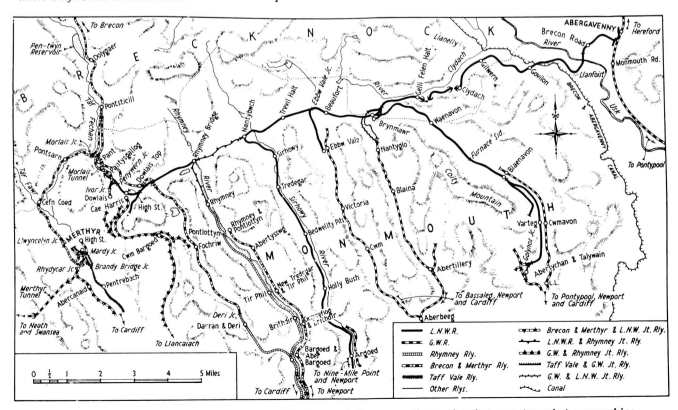

Map of the railway from Abergavenny to Merthyr and its connections, showing pre-grouping ownerships

KESWICK

The black Austin 12 taxi draws up in front of the station entrance and spills out father, mother and two boys at the end of their Lakeland holiday. The waiting porter takes note of the heavy suitcases strapped on the rear luggage grid and sidles up with his barrow. 'London train, sir?' He realises that he has guessed wrong with father's first word; 'No, the 10.10 to Leeds'. 'Right, sir. Platform 3. First or third class, sir?'. The taxi driver is unstrapping the cases as the group saunter into the booking hall and down through the subway smelling faintly of gas. The five-coach Leeds train is beginning to fill up, but they find a vacant table in a newish Fowler vestibule coach, whose wide windows will provide a good last view of the fells on their journey. (It has another attraction for boys, for the large windows can be pulled down and locked by a very tempting lever on the sill). The porter stacks the cases and a shilling changes hands. Once mama is settled, the boys are anxious for a look at the engine. As they march down the platform with father, the Workington section of the *Lakes Express* pulls in on the other side of the island, headed by an old LNW 0-6-0. The boys scoff; it does not seem right that an important train carrying nameboards on its crimson coaches should have such diminutive and elderly power. But they are further taken aback to find a similar engine at the front of their own train. The sun shines dully on the plain black paintwork on its slender boiler. From its tall chimney grey smoke curls lazily upwards, and there is a white feather at the safety valves. The cab is quite rudimentary, and its openness enables everything to be seen; the fire proves

particularly fascinating. So intrigued are they that the *Lakes* pulls out almost unnoticed.

The driver, one foot on the undulating footframing, is reaching between the frames with a long oil feeder; his job done, he straightens up and comes towards them. His overall jacket, well washed and faded, is buttoned at the neck but opens over a substantial paunch. His hair is silver under the shiny cap. 'Would you like to come up on the engine, lads?' The lads are eager, but before letting them up he wipes the handrails with his cloth. They feel the heat, smell coal and hot oil as the fireman makes room for them on the narrow footplate and chats to the signalman on the other side. 'What sort of engine is this?' asks the elder boy. 'It's what we call a "Cauliflower or 18 inch goods".' 'How old is it?' 'Oh, a lot older than you, fifty years or more.' 'Why do you have a goods engine on a passenger train?' 'How old have you got to be to drive a big engine?' And so it goes on until father decrees that it is time to get back. The boys are excited, but mama worries about whether their hands and clothes are dirty.

Whistles blow, the train eases forward over the points, and through the open window comes the sound of a thin, slightly irregular exhaust as the little 'Cauliflower' gets its train on the move. It is hard climbing for the first eight miles to Troutbeck, a lot of it at 1 in 62, and they have a stop at Threlkeld in the middle of it. The engine noises become more insistent, and because of the cinders coming in mama insists on the window being closed, causing great indignation. But the questions keep coming in a steady stream. 'Will we reverse at Penrith like we did when we came?'

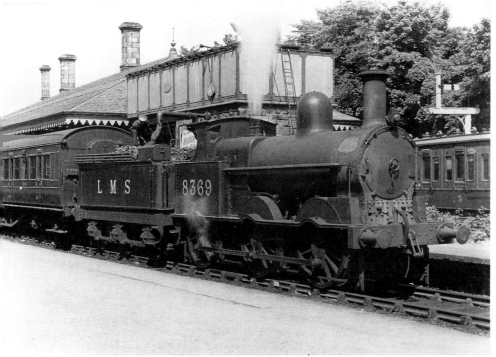

Water Stop. With its fire built up well for the heavy climb up through Threlkeld ex LNWR 18in goods 0-6-0 No 8369 takes water while waiting at Keswick with the 9.59am Lakes Express on 7 June 1939; in the background are the somewhat older coaches forming the 10.10 to Leeds. The engine carries the shed code 12B which was Carlisle Upperby, but around that time Penrith was a sub shed not having its own code.

161

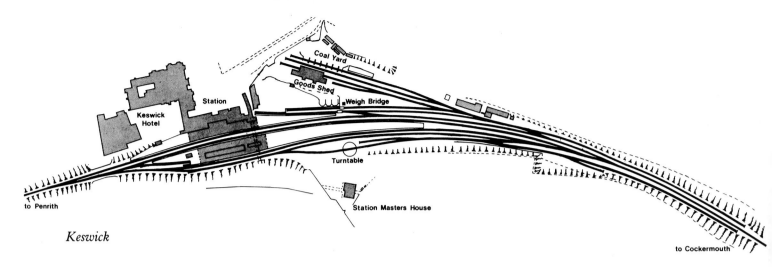

Keswick

BARNARD CASTLE

Funny set-up, muses the Barnard Castle East signalman as he nears the end of his early shift. You really would wonder how the experts came to build a station, at the 'crossroads' of four lines, with just one through platform, and not even a crossover in the middle. If only someone had thought through the shunting moves it would involve, all over the level crossing with the Stanhope road. Maybe last century they ran the Bishop Auckland and Middleton-on-Tees trains as shuttles from the east and west bays, but now you have through trains in fashion, and they are expected to interconnect at Barnard Castle, which makes precious little sense of this layout. So much for managers!

Such heretical thoughts are interrupted by the clang of a block bell; West offers a 3-1, the Middleton – Newcastle passenger, on the through road, and he accepts. It will be there in three minutes, so he wastes no time in getting the gates shut and clearing the road up to the starter. The 2 bells of 'Entering Section' have barely sounded when it rolls into the platform, stops briefly and then, after a slamming of doors, draws forward to come to a stand beyond the signal gantry. Set the road back into the east bay, pull off the peg, and it comes snaking back into the bay where passengers are waiting. He clears out to West, and immediately it is 3-1 again for the Penrith – Darlington passenger. He accepts, and gets the 'Entering Section' immediately, so he resets the through road and pulls off his outer home to bring the train right up the platform. Now there are cars waiting, so he opens the gates before offering the train on to Winston; when the cars are away, he closes the gates again and pulls off inner home, starter and advanced starter. But before the

E4 moves, there's a metallic jangle of buffers and couplings, and the brake van of the 4-1 in the Down South Mineral line, coke from Tyneside for the Millom furnaces, jerks forward and heads for the remoteness of Stainmore. As he restores the signal levers one by one after the departing Darlington train, he gets the 2-1 for the coke train clearing West box. Now he can set the road across from the bay to the Bishop Auckland line for the Newcastle, and pull off; if any more road traffic appears, it will just have to wait until that's away.

The passenger whistles off, and once clear of the connections goes off vigorously round the curve up to Coal Road. Signals back, open the gates, and wait for the 2-1 'Train out of Section'. In the up South Mineral line the engines on the empties have finished taking water, so they are ready for the away on the heels of the passenger. After two or three minutes the 2-1 comes, and he promptly offers 4-1, which is accepted. Set the road out of the Mineral line for Auckland, close the gates, pull off the signals, and with a whistle the two J21s take the slack out of the train in a clangour of rusty steel, clear the loop and go blasting up the bank. Tail lamp OK on the van, so he sends the 2-1 to West. Now there is just the shunt engine from the goods yard wanting to cross to the shed, a seesaw movement through the connections that again requires the crossing gates. It is all shoulder work, but the shift is nearly over and there will only be the down Middleton and Penrith passengers before his mate arrives at two. A chance to get a bit of polishing done on the already-bright levers as the railway settles down to half an hour of peace, broken only by the rattle and rumble of a lorry over the uneven crossing before it grinds up the hill into the town.

North Eastern Country Junction.
The 12.30pm to Newcastle waits in
Barnard Castle's east bay platform
behind ex NER Class G5 0-4-4
tank No 67298 on 8 August 1950.
This is the 11.55am from Middleton
in Teesdale which has had to
perform a complicated shunting
operation to make way for the 10.10
from Penrith to Darlington stopping
between 12.20 and 12.22. This used
the through platform and was
headed by a J21 class 0-6-0 No
65038 of Darlington shed (still
stencilled on buffer beam as
DGTON).

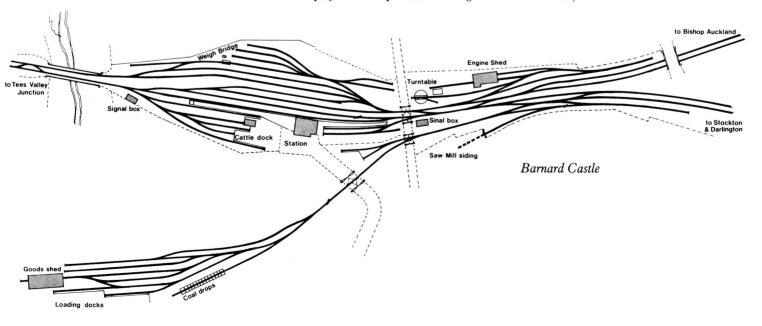

Barnard Castle

WATERHOUSES

It is one of those Indian Summer October days that people dream about, colour appearing on the trees to relieve the green of the Staffordshire hills, though a very different setting from that of Mother India for which the engine was designed. The driver whistles long for the crossing over the Ashbourne – Leek road and, as the attractive little 2-6-4 tank rumbles across a steel bridge over the River Hamp, sees that the Waterhouses porter has the crossing gates open for the valley train. With a wave he cracks the regulator a bit more and the engine responds as it squeals round the curve and up the steep bank. Regulator shut, a light touch on the brake valve, and the train stops neatly in Waterhouses narrow-gauge platform. From the two distinctive coaches a handful of country people alight, some to make their way up the few steps to the standard-gauge platform, where a single brake third waits for them, its tank engine simmering gently. The others make their way down the subway steps and into the village. The fireman also alights, mashing can in hand, followed by his mate's admonition to make it a strong brew.

Now the driver makes preparations for the return working to Hulme End. The first job is to dispose of the empty standard gauge 12-tonner on its transporter wagon. He draws the train forward from the platform into the loop and destroys the vacuum. After a few moments Bert the guard emerges from the van, after applying the handbrake, and disappears behind the transporter wagon; a hand appears to indicate that he's parted the brake hoses. The driver releases the brake, and the engine imperceptibly eases back on the grade, just enough to release the chopper coupling between the transporter and the leading coach. Out comes Bert and steps on to the end of the transporter, arm round the standard gauge wagon buffer, while the driver pushes open the regulator handle to take engine and transporter into the headshunt. Bert drops off to throw the points, and the little caravan eases down into the interchange siding nearest to the standard gauge line and buffers up

to the static coupler; as it does so there is a whistle from the Knotty tank and off she goes up the 1 in 40, her noisy exhaust audible for quite a while.

The driver brings his engine back to the loop, stopping alongside the coaches to take water from the little tank. The fireman has not returned with the tea, so he climbs up himself, puts the bag in and stands holding the chain, looking down into the village and deep in thought. A milk lorry passes through on its way to the Ashbourne creamery with the farm collections that once travelled on the Manifold train. How much longer can it last, and what will he do when the time comes? Move to Uttoxeter or Stoke? The tank full, he runs his engine to the loop end, sets back to pick up the coaches, and eases down into the platform again, now bunker first. A cup of tea is welcome as the little group of villagers and farmers' wives, laden shopping baskets on arms, climb on to the end platforms and disappear inside. The starting signal is pulled off long since, though it seems quite superfluous. Bert is waiting, watch in hand and an eye on the subway steps for Mrs White, who's been into Waterhouses to visit her sister and will be coming back on this, the last train of the day. At the last minute she puffs up on to the platform and exchanges a few bantering words before boarding.

The green flag waves, the driver gives a melodious toot and gives the engine a breath of steam to run down the 1 in 54 to the level crossing. He is soon rubbing the brake and applies it harder to stop clear. Down goes his fireman, red flag in hand, to place the gates across the road. Enough to release the brake for the little train to run forward down the bank and the fireman clambers on to the footplate. Another hiss of air as the driver brakes to stop beyond the crossing. Bert hops down and closes the gates over the narrow track, far one first. He climbs up again with a wave and bangs his door shut, and the driver is away to make his umpteenth run up the eight miles of the Manifold Valley. Behind the little train a great peace descends once more.

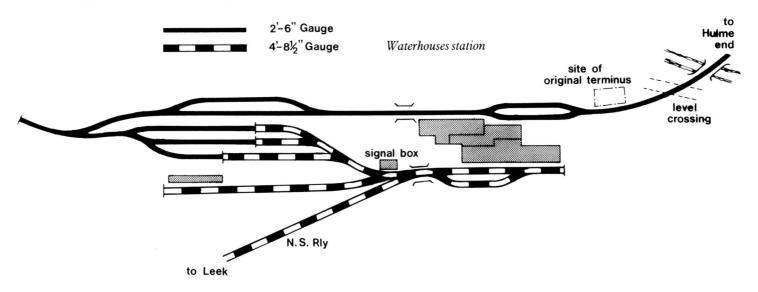

Waterhouses station

2'-6" Gauge
4'-8½" Gauge

signal box

to Leek

N.S. Rly

site of
original terminus

to
Hulme
end

level
crossing

North Stafford Mixture. Two photographs showing Waterhouses station in LMS days with opposite platform faces used by the standard and narrow gauge trains for which it was a terminus.

(i) Nothing could be more simple than the layout here. Ex North Stafford Railway Class D 0-6-0 tank of 1898 as LMS No 1597 of Stoke on Trent shed (40) simmers in the platform while awaiting the arrival of the Leek & Manifold Valley train whose signal is off at the right of the photograph. This single coach consist chuffed its way up from the junction at Leek three or four times a day (twice on Sundays) in the late 1920s. The engine carries an interesting but typical LMS piece of forgery – the cast iron oval plate on the sandbox sides states that it is 'LMS built Stoke'.

(ii) Leek and Manifold Valley. Kitson built 2-6-4 tank No 1 E R Calthrop with a Hulme End train on 22 July 1933 a year before closure. These large 2ft 6in gauge engines were similar in design to those designed by the same engineer for the Barsi Light Railway in India. Traffic does not seem to be heavy but there may still be the transporter wagon (carrying an empty milk tank wagon which has come all the way from London) to be picked up at the transfer sidings and dropped off at the creamery.

165

Carrying Pigeons by Train

Should a railway passenger sometimes overhear at a station such an expression as: 'We shall be returning with the pigeons to-morrow night,' he (or she) must not necessarily assume that 'pigeons' is merely a synonym for unsophisticated travellers who are to be 'plucked' by exponents of the three-card trick, for birds of the air are really meant and invariably those known as the homing variety. The expression in question is frequently used, in summer time, in connection with the homing pigeon traffic, of which the general public knows perhaps but very little, but which is, nevertheless, a lucrative feature of the railway companies' carrying trade, seeing that enormous numbers of the birds are despatched by train every week in various directions in order to take part in the championships and competitions which are organised by the pigeon fanciers and the legions of those interested in the hobby. Such is its importance that at this season of the year it is not unusual for special trains to be run entirely for pigeons and their guardians, especially on Friday nights, and that quite recently six pigeon specials were run, for instance, over the Southern Area of the LNER to and from certain specified points; whilst, in addition, on the same occasion, numerous vans, in some cases specially fitted for the traffic, were conveyed by ordinary trains.

The Railway Gazette, 9 June 1932

UP TO THE MOUND

In October 1950 the early morning train from Inverness to Wick on the further North line, rumbled slowly over the Caledonian Canal swing bridge just as dawn broke with the sun rising over Black Isle, and the steel grey waters of Beauly Firth sparkled into life. Breakfast was in an old Pullman dining car which had first seen service on the Caledonian; it had oval bevelled plate glass in the vestibule ends, movable chairs and a magnificent interior decoration of inlaid veneer. All this and the faint smell of gas emanating from the kitchen stirred nostalgic memories of railway journeys long ago.

Unlike its richer brother the North British Railway, the Highland with its poor terrain, had no money to fling great bridges across its coastal Firths, so from Tain on the southern shore of Dornoch Firth the line twisted no less than forty-four miles to reach Dornoch, the capital of Sutherland the smallest county town in Scotland, running via Invershin and Lairg, reaching a dizzy height above the gorge of the River Shin with a superb and wild prospect of mountain, loch and moor to the

westward. As the crow flies across the water the distance is but five miles. Mind you, passengers did not have matters that easily, they had to change trains at the Mound Junction if they wanted to go on to Dornoch.

All went sedately until the Mound was reached, but here the rare bustle of a country junction came into play for by now the ageing Highland Railway 0-4-4 tank had arrived with its connecting train from Dornoch, a single coach coupled to the odd van as traffic required, and would be waiting for the shunt. The dining car was uncoupled and the long journey north became bereft of food as the ex LMS Class 5 barked its way towards Helmsdale and Wick. Gently, so as not to wake the now dozing dining car crew, the little engine placed the old Pullman on a siding, ran back to get water and backed onto its short train for the journey home. In the afternoon, with the arrival of the southbound mail and the second train of the day off the branch, the procedure was reversed. A long day for dining car crew, they would have been on duty for nine hours by the time they got back to Inverness. No one grudged them their midday snooze.

Highland Junction. These two photographs show main and branch line activity at the Mound, junction for the county town and port of Dornoch en route from Inverness to stations Further North.

(i) The morning train for Helmsdale and Wick arrives at The Mound on a misty 19 May 1928 behind an ex Highland Railway 4-6-0 No 14676 Ballindalloch Castle designed by Peter Drummond. It is the 'Mail' bringing overnight post from the south to all stations which are few and far between in this wild land. On the station barrow are further sacks of mail from Dornoch to be taken forward. The station signboard reads 'The Mound Change Here for the Dornoch Line'.

(ii) Between Times. Ex Highland Railway 0-4-4 tank as BR No 55053, another Peter Drummond engine, at The Mound in October 1951. The coach is a one time Pullman Car and has been the breakfast car (three courses for 5s 0d [25p]) on the Further North train leaving Inverness at 6.40am. It is now being detached and will rest, with its crew, here until the southbound mail arrives at 11.25. The Pullman cars working on the Caledonian Railway were purchased by the LMS in 1933 and used as ordinary restaurant cars until withdrawal (the last in the early 1960s). No 219 was former Pullman car Queen Margaret built by Metro-Cammell in 1927.

166

8
SUMMER SATURDAYS ON THE M&GNJR

It is said that you cannot make a silk purse out of a sow's ear; this truism does not only apply to sows. You can't make a main line trunk railway – not a satisfactory one, anyway – by tying together a collection of rural branches with link lines, although plenty of people have tried. What you are apt to finish up with is the railway equivalent of a purse which is not big enough to hold all your change, with stitching that comes undone, with a zipper which is liable to jam, and is rough enough to wear holes in your pocket. Such a railway was the Midland & Great Northern Joint, a glimpse of which on the year's busiest day the last chapter ended.

It was a system put together piecemeal, and it showed. The constituent sections were built on the cheap, as befitted a railway in rural surroundings with few towns and little industry. The extremely fragmented gradient profiles gave the game away, and east of Lynn there were some difficult banks with a ruling gradient of 1 in 100. When the principal artery was finally assembled in 1883, from Little Bytham Junction (at the end of a single line spur from the Midland at Saxby), past Bourne, Spalding, Kings Lynn and Melton Constable to Great Yarmouth, it was a 125 mile route with pretensions to be a major traffic route for which it was ill-equipped to cater.

Eighty of those 125 miles were single track, in five bites ranging from 4 to 37 miles in length. The intermediate sections of double line were just about adequate for the operation of the necessary service of semi-fast and local passenger, fish and freight trains from Sunday to Friday, bearing in mind the seasonal nature of much of the freight – potatoes, cereals, market garden produce and fruit. An important factor in the equation was the Crosskeys swing bridge at Sutton Bridge, over which there was a severe weight restriction; as a result the M&GN owned no locomotive larger than 4-4-0s equivalent to LMS power Class 2P and 0-6-0s comparable with Midland Class 3Fs. To the last, when the line had come under full Eastern Region operating control, the biggest engines allowed on through workings were ex-GE B12/3 4-6-0s, Gresley K2/2 2-6-0s and Ivatt Class 4MT 2-6-0s. They worked wonders, but before the second world war many of the trains could only be described as under-powered. The frequent crossing moves on the single line militated against speed, and even through trains with no booked stops seldom averaged 30 mph. The M&GN did what it could to make the best of its inadequate infrastructure, improving the old engines to get better performance and standardising the Whitaker tablet catcher to give decent speeds through the loops. But it was still a difficult (and expensive) route to work.

In addition, Melton Constable, the engineering centre of the line, could prove an operating problem. As we have just seen, many of the regular through trains from Peterborough and the Midland carried portions for Norwich and Cromer as well as for Yarmouth/Lowestoft, requiring a three-way split (and a three-part join-up in the opposite direction) at Melton. The train engine worked through to and from Yarmouth; another engine lifted the Cromer coaches off the rear and went off, while the Norwich coaches in the middle had to await the departure of the Yarmouth section before they could get their engine. The whole procedure lengthened margins between trains and gave considerable potential for delay.

Last Year of Independence. Melton Constable station on 1 June 1936 with an eastbound train headed by Midland & Great Northern Joint Railway 4-4-0 No 1 in yellow ochre. The junction signals for the main and Cromer lines can be seen above the bridge. No 1 was built by Sharp Stewart (4001/1894) and became LNER Class D52 carrying the number 01; it was soon withdrawn, lasting only until November 1937.

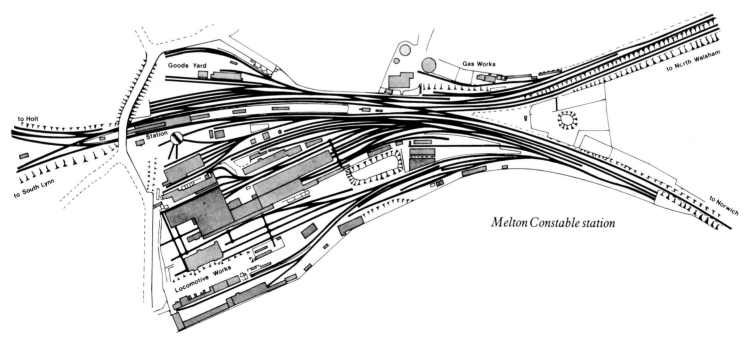

Melton Constable station

*Poster for the Broadlands. A
Midland & Great Northern Joint
Railway poster of 1914 advertising
its countryside delights: this
poster is a retouched photograph
crediting the Photochrom Co Ltd
of London. Below the pictorial
section is a route map showing (to
the left) the Midland Railway via
Bourne and the Great Northern
and Midland Railways at
Peterborough with the track to
the right terminating at Lowestoft
Central. The upper loop with its
junction at Melton Constable
takes in the coast line to Cromer
via Sheringham. (All marked
Poppyland). The line then runs
through Stalham, Potter Heigham
and Great Ormesby (Broadland)
to Yarmouth Beach
(Dickensland).*

But if it was not an easy line to operate throughout the year, summer
Saturdays during July and August could be a nightmare. Freight could
be cancelled – over the 37 mile single line out of Yarmouth only an
afternoon fish train would be allowed to shoulder its way westwards
against the tide – but on top of the regular passenger trains serving this
rural area it would be necessary to provide for anything up to 20 holiday
and day excursion trains to Great Yarmouth, mainly from Midlands and
Northern centres such as Birmingham, Leicester, Derby, Nottingham,
Sheffield, Leeds and Manchester.

They would roll in from Saxby, with a few through Peterborough and
Spalding, to fight their way eastwards, and enough paths for them could
only be provided by arranging it on a tidal flow basis – eastwards in the
morning and early afternoon, and westwards in the evening. It was not
just a question of line capacity, either. The M&GN never owned more
than about 90 locomotives, all of moderate power, and they were fully
stretched in the summer. Double heading was often needed. The holiday
and excursion trains were dependent for power on their originating
companies, and that meant LMS Class 4F 0-6-0s for the majority of

them. So until the eastbound trains arrived at destination and their engines had been serviced, there was little or no power available for westbound extra trains. The same applied to coaching stock (the M&GN was a six-wheeled non-corridor coach railway for its internal services), and there were extensive carriage sidings at Yarmouth Beach to hold it for the return journey.

The control of this inadequate artery was exercised until 1936 from the Joint's traffic headquarters at South Lynn, which was a sort of traffic watershed and was the site of the largest engine shed. According to the availability of power, some trains were re-engined here, or provided with assistant engines for the banks that lay ahead. Almost all special trains were re-manned there, because 'foreign' crews seldom knew the road beyond South Lynn, and even if they had, would have had insufficient rest at Yarmouth before working the cavalcade home again.

The traffic reached its peak on August Bank Holiday Saturday, and a look at the line between South Lynn and Yarmouth on a typical such day in the 1930s shows how it was planned and how it worked in practice. Most of the holiday extra trains were overnight, in a similar pattern to that traditionally used to the West of England. Between 02.00 and 04.10, five trains passed through South Lynn, and reached Yarmouth between 04.25 and 06.30. (Incidentally, what did you do when pitched out of a train at 04.25 on a summer Saturday morning?). They had good clear runs, chasing each other's tails and stopping at Melton Constable for water, with only the last of the group making a crossing at Ormesby with an early special. The next group of holiday specials, four in number, were from further afield and left Lynn between 05.40 and 07.05. The first got a good run through and was into Yarmouth at 07.50, but the other three got increasingly snarled up with opposing passenger trains. The 06.35 departure crossed four trains between Aylsham and Ormesby, but the following two were delayed getting on to the single line at Corpusty and then had to cross five and six trains respectively. The last one did not reach Yarmouth until 10.25, having had three waits of 15 – 20 minutes in loops waiting for up trains.

By now the control staff were in the thick of it. Between 08.10 and 13.25 they had to plan (and sometimes to replan in the light of events) ten specials and day excursions in addition to the eight regular trains, one of which branched off at Melton Constable for Norwich. Mostly they got good runs, but it was often touch and go. An interesting situation developed at Stalham one lunchtime, when *two* down trains had to cross an up excursion. The first down train was not running well, and limped to Stalham when it should have made the next loop, at Potter Heigham. The following regular train had to be held outside the loop until the up train arrived and the laggard down extra could go forward. One can imagine the Stalham signalman, unruffled, juggling his tokens in and out of his instruments and getting them to the drivers with an air of quiet urgency. He had probably seen all the variations from a whole storehouse of trouble – shortage of steam, failed injectors, dragging brakes, hot boxes, carriage doors open, the lot. And it only needed a

Opening of Signal Boxes, Market Rasen Branch
To the Editor
Sir,
It is high time the signalmen on this branch were put on a footing with other signalmen. Just fancy the 2am turn on Monday morning, a man having to walk two or three miles, and one I know even walks four miles, do about four hours' duty, walk home again another four miles, and then he is rewarded with one shilling. Some men having to sit up all Sunday night to make sure of being there to time after doing twelve hours duty on Sunday, all for that lonely shilling. If this is not a grievance I never saw one. This has been put before the district superintendent: of course it was the same old tale, cannot do anything for you. I say with others, shame.
Yours truly,
SHILLING
Great Central Railway Journal, February 1908

Sir,
I think it is time we went a step further, namely, draw a petition up and get it signed by all the signalmen affected and forward it to Grimsby and see what the result will be. If this has not the desired effect, then let them as lives so far away cease coming on Sunday nights and waiting for opening time, then I feel sure some of the boxes would get opened any time between 2.0am and 5.0am. In a circular issued by our General Manager a few years ago, it stated we were to study the stores, etc. as if the cost came from our own pockets. Now is it studying the Company's coals coming to the box at 10.30pm on Sunday nights. ·
Yours,
EARLY TO BED AND EARLY TO RISE
Great Central Railway Journal, April 1908

6 Miles A Penny

A recent LNER return excursion from Ipswich to London at 3s for the 137 miles is eclipsed by an LMS facility of 1 December last. In connection with a cattle and poultry show at Bingley Hall, Birmingham, passengers from Bath were provided with a special train in which they travelled to New Street and back – 187 miles – for 2s 9d, or very nearly six miles for a penny. A correspondent who sends us a handbill advertising the excursion remarks that on 6 August 1855, the Midland Railway is recorded to have conveyed 7,000 persons from Bristol to Birmingham and back for 1s 6d a head. No less remarkable, in that they were more regular, were the pre-war excursions of the Great North of Scotland Railway from Aberdeen to Boat of Garten on Wednesdays and Saturdays in the summer months – 202½ miles return for 2s 6d. For a short time, also, there was a Sunday excursion by the Great Central Railway from Marylebone to Cleethorpes for 4s 3d, a return journey of 446 miles by the shortest GC route. This worked out at 8½ miles a penny. – *Railway Magazine*, January 1935.

tablet catcher to muff the pickup and you could find yourself spending a quarter of an hour searching for it in long grass or a wayside ditch, while the trains queued up in both directions. Best to ignore the passengers' jibes.

Now the eastbound rush began to thin out, leaving only the regular trains from Peterborough and Bourne, and even they ceased soon after 18.00. But the carriage sidings at Yarmouth were full of hastily swept coaches, and it was hardly possible to move on Yarmouth Beach shed for engines, fires cleaned, coaled, watered, prepared and manned ready for work. Most of the weekly holiday-makers had already left on earlier trains; the first afternoon special, at 16.10, got a very poor road against the regular trains, waiting 15 minutes at Honing to cross two down trains and over 30 minutes at North Walsham to cross two more. One wonders how much the Norfolk scenery was being appreciated by the fuming passengers. Behind him came the Fish, threading an interrupted course through the same trains.

Three more day excursions left between 18.45 and 20.10, and only the first experienced any crossing delay, at Aylsham. The last of them was into South Lynn by 22.35. The first real rush of returning trains left Yarmouth at 21.50, followed at roughly 15-minute intervals by six more before midnight. These had no potential adversaries in their path, and all ran like clockwork one after the other, pounding through the loops at speed in the darkness and stopping only at Melton Constable for water on the way. The first of them was into Lynn at 23.55, 73 miles in 125 minutes at an average of 35 mph.

The war put a stop to much of this nonsense, and in the postwar years on this system, unlike some others, it never regained such volumes in the face of road competition which was usually faster and more responsive to the needs of passengers and families; more Midlanders still travelling by train were venturing further afield, too, to regions with more spectacular scenery and coastline.

In the middle of 1958, the Eastern Region announced that virtually the whole of the Joint system was to be closed at the end of February 1959. It duplicated much of the Great Eastern lines (to which some traffic had already been diverted); in this rural area the only four towns with populations of over 10,000 were served by alternative routes. Loadings had slipped to a point where the losses could no longer be sustained; it was estimated that closure would save at least £½ million a year, and avoid a major bridge renewal. Some 1500 men were affected, only a small proportion of whom could be absorbed elsewhere.

The closure proved to be a piece of clean surgery; only the line from Cromer to Melton Constable lingered on for a time, worked as an extension of the GE branch from Norwich. The rest was dismantled. Towns like Sutton Bridge and Fakenham were left rail-less. The Birmingham–Norwich service, successor to the 'Leicesters', now runs via Peterborough and Ely, four times a day, in a shade over 4 hours. A sprinkling of Saturday dated trains still makes for Yarmouth from centres like Chesterfield, Leeds and Manchester, but the total triumph

of car and coach is probably not far off. The collapse of freight traffic in Fenland is almost total in the face of lorry competition. After nearly a generation, the name of the Midland & Great Northern Joint is largely forgotten in East Anglia, though a few ghosts relive on busy days of the North Norfolk, which has brought back steam to a picturesque coastal section of the Cromer branch from Weybourne to Sheringham. But most of those who take that brief ride could not imagine what conditions were like on the hard-pressed main line half a century ago.

Country railways and single lines are virtually synonymous. Right from the early days of railways it was realised that however primitive the signalling might be on double lines, single lines needed an extra ingredient to prevent the real threat of head-on collision. The first form of protection was a man, a pilotman who had to ride on the engine of every train passing over a particular single-line section. This was expensive in manpower and it was soon realised that a token of some sort, provided that there was only one for each section, would serve the same purpose. First was the large wooden staff, in itself fairly restrictive, since it had to pass to and fro evenly so that trains had to run alternately one way and then the other. This was fine on a short dead end branch but on long through routes could not be guaranteed. So the staff system was developed into the staff and ticket, in which the drivers of a group of trains following in the same direction would be shown the staff and given a written ticket authorising them to proceed, all except the last of a group, that is, who would be given the staff as his authority to take to the other end of the single line section ready for the next train in the opposite direction.

Eventually by the 1890s an electrically controlled interlocked version of the staff system was evolved in which machines in the signalboxes at each end of a single line section were interlocked with each other and contained several staffs; the electrical interlocking made sure that only one could be drawn from either end at one time. The electric staff was a cumbersome thing, heavy and not easy to hand over between signalman and footplate crew on the move. The small round tablet, and later the key token systems, similar in principle, were much lighter, and since the tablet or token was strapped into a leather pouch attached to a hoop they were easier to exchange between fireman and signalman. Even so, changing tokens on the move was a skilled operation,

with the fireman leaning out of the cab of a swaying locomotive holding the token to be given up, hoop outermost, with one hand, while his other hand was stretched out and forward ready to go through the hoop of the token held up by the signalman. Both men had to watch two things – the hoop of the token they were holding to make sure they were aiming straight and the hoop being given to them to make sure the other man was holding it correctly.

Even then changing tokens on the move by hand was normally limited to 10mph and at that speed could give both men a thud on the inside of the elbow. Sometimes a token was missed, if by the fireman then the train had to stop. Sometimes a token would be dropped. It might go in the undergrowth and take some time to find, or it might bounce under the wheels of the train and be mangled so that it would not fit the token machine. That of course shut the job down until pilot working could be set up or until the lineman was called out to unlock the token machines and manually restore equilibrium.

Several railways with long lengths of single line and numerous passing loops adopted automatic token or tablet exchange in which lineside apparatus by the signalbox held the hoop to be picked up by token catchers fitted to the sides of locomotives working regularly over the route. Similar holders for setting down tokens were fitted to locomotives and catcher arms were mounted on the lineside to collect the token from a passing train. Automatic tablet catchers revolutionised the working of express trains on these routes since provided the geometry of the track layout permitted, automatic exchange of tokens could be carried out at up to 60mph or more. Some of the Scottish lines used the Manson and other types of catcher, but the Somerset & Dorset Locomotive Superintendent Whitaker devised his own type of apparatus which was also installed on the

Single Line Instruments. Unless worked on a one engine in steam basis, all British single trackage until the coming of modern technology was controlled by electrically interlocked block instruments containing large or small train staffs, tablets or key tokens, only one being available for any one section of line at one time. These were normally passed by hand to the locomotive crew by the signalman on duty; it was the locomotive crew's bounden duty to check the name of the section on the staff or tablet concerned. Often the exchange was carried out with the train on the move – special tablet catching

apparatus being contrived for both medium and high speed working, the former by means of a large hook or arm on a post and the latter by automatic means. The two photographs here show the methods of exchange used for staff or tablet.

Electric Tablet. Bury St Edmunds Junction on the one time Great Eastern line. A J15 class 0-6-0 No 65451 sets out with the 1.55pm train to Sudbury and Marks Tey and makes for the single line. The tablet is inside the leather pouch at the foot of the loop held out for the fireman by the signalman, the date is 13 August 1949.

Midland & Great Northern line. The M&GN found it especially useful for running the summer Saturday expresses from the Midlands to East Anglia. In an estimated total of 350,000 automatic tablet changes in a year on the M&GN the dropping rate was no more than 1 in 5000, roughly one a day.

Yet some lines continued to rely on hand exchange, not least on the Isle of Wight, where for example, Smallbrook Junction, situated just outside Ryde at the divergence of the Cowes and Ventnor lines, passed 10 trains every hour on summer Saturdays from breakfast to tea time. It was undoubtedly the most intensive

working with token equipment at one signalbox on the British railway system. Even then things did not always go to plan. On an inspection in post second world war years accompanied by a journalist, the manager instructed the taxi driver to the location of this remote signalbox: 'Oh yes' replied the taxi driver, 'I know just where it is; I had to take something called the token down there because a driver had taken it on to Ryde by mistake!' There was a stifled cough from the manager, but it was all part of the character of country railway operation. Of course there were incidents, but how many were actually reported to 'London' is anyone's guess.

Electric Train Staff. Rubery on the Great Western/Midland Railway's joint line in Worcestershire. Fireman and signalman are about to exchange single line staffs whilst the train is on the move, an action needing some judgment if the staff is not to be dropped. The Midland 2F's crew look on with some interest to see the result. The electric train staff apparatus can just be seen behind the left hand signalbox window. The engine on the left is an ex LNWR 0–6–2 coal tank No 58903 (Monument Lane 3E and usually New Street station pilot). It is heading a Stephenson Locomotive Society special train commemorating the one hundredth anniversary of New Street station on 2 June 1954. The 2F is No 58138 of Bournville shed (21B), the heaviest 0–6–0 allowed over the restricted Dowery Dell Viaduct on the Halesowen branch.

Single Line authorities. Examples of cardboard tickets issued by the signalman or other authorised person to train crews enabling them to proceed into a single line section having seen the requisite staff for that section. The staff and ticket form of operation allowed two or more trains to follow in the same direction.

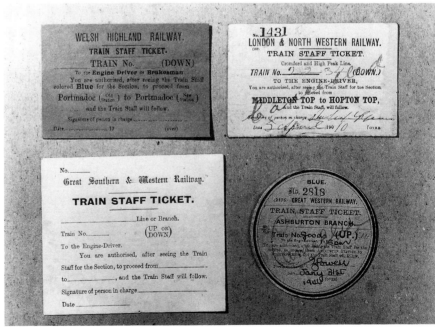

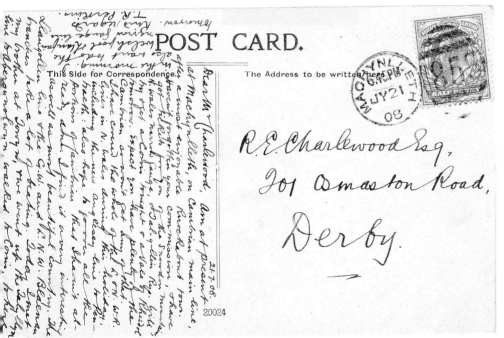

A pre first world war colour postcard, showing the 'Tal-y-Llyn Toy Railway' sent by that great traveller T. R. Perkins to railway author R. E. Charlewood on 21 July 1908. Somehow the un-named artist did not quite get the locomotive livery right since it should have been green but was depicted in brown.

T. R. Perkins, The Great Railway Explorer

From the early years of the century T. R. Perkins was known to readers of *The Railway Magazine* as the contributor of detailed and thoughtful articles on some of the lesser-known railways.

Quietly and without self-advertisement he approached the goal of an ambition – to have travelled over every passenger railway in the British Isles. In 1928 he had finished England, Scotland and Wales by riding over the new connection between the Taff Vale and Barry lines at Tonteg. In 1932, using a £5 14-day season ticket specially issued by the Great Southern Railway for the Eucharistic Congress – what a paradox for the Methodist Circuit Steward from Stratford! – and following an itinerary which had taken months to prepare in all its detail, he had completed the conquest of Ireland. His immediate goal was attained, but later years were to bring him an occasional rewarding excursion, usually in the company of a friend, over some line not normally available to passengers, such as the Bristol Docks, Willenhall to Darlaston and the Cromford and High Peak.

Many have since tried to emulate his feat, and were encouraged by advice in their planning or by racy anecdote of his adventures in far-away places.

G. J. Aston in the *SLS Journal*, March 1953

9
TROUBLE ON THE BRANCH

Black Dog Halt

Not in the public timetable, but with a stationmaster, Black Dog Halt on the Calne branch in Wiltshire had a special place among private and curious stations. The Marquess of Lansdowne was only prepared to co-operate in the building of the railway over his land if given a private station, complete with siding from which his racehorses could be despatched to various meets. The railway company went one better, providing a second siding designed to help the loading of his silverware when he transferred residence to or from London. He paid half the stationmaster's salary, any new appointment being subject to his consent. He did not object to passengers using the station, but since it did not officially exist you had to buy a ticket to the next stop.

In September 1952, however, the station suddenly appeared in the Western Region's timetable and a few weeks later workmen erected the first nameplate. It became an unstaffed halt in 1960 and closed in 1964, by which time the meat and other ingredients for the Harris sausage factory and the finished product which had once made Calne a particularly busy country terminus had long transferred to lorry.

The country railway was not always the peaceful place the picture postcards implied. There were upsets of all kinds, some as we will see in a moment, quite substantial; but the commonest – and then at otherwise happy times – were caused by rivalries between staff flaring into the open. Often little incidents in themselves, they nonetheless impaired the smooth working of traffic and tainted the atmosphere.

Thus, while it seems almost comic that the stationmaster at Cockermouth should refuse to give Right Away because the guard would not help him by carrying two motorcycles to Workington and back (to save them having to be carried down through the mini subway), the consequences were not such fun.

'They're labelled Cockermouth and they're here,' said the red-faced guard pushing them out onto the platform. 'I've got nobody to help me; I'll get a hernia,' complained the stationmaster. He refused to give Right Away, the guard threatened to go without it, to which the inevitable response was that that would be a punishable offence. So there the train sat until the signalman came to point out that another service was being delayed. For weeks afterwards, everyone on the branch took sides.

In a similar dispute, on a South Wales branch, a stationmaster 'got even' with a difficult guard by persuading the yardmaster at the main-line junction to put a stopping goods train together in the most perverse order possible. If the siding were at the front end of the station, the trucks for it were marshalled at the back, and vice versa. The slow freight ran seriously late, disrupting a passenger train. 'Delayed detaching, attaching and generally b----ing about' wrote the guard on his log, only to suffer further trouble in the shape of a reprimand and loss of wages for using unseemly language on a GWR document.

The driver of Scotland's only push-and-pull auto car train from St Combs to Fraserburgh refused to go into the handsome terminus built by the Great North of Scotland because the signal dipped only about 15 degrees. Only when the signalman reluctantly showed a green flag after a ten minute delay did the train proceed and then only to the signalbox where heated words were exchanged. 'Of course it's off man'. 'If I'd gone by it and you told me I shouldn't you'd have been right and where would I have been?' 'There isn't another train anyway'. 'So why do we need a signalman at all?'

Closed communities often produced in-fighting, and isolated railway settlements were no exception. On an exposed slope of the Cheviots remote from public roads, Riccarton Junction was where the Border

Counties branch from Hexham joined the fabled Waverley route from Carlisle to Edinburgh. The North British built a village of about thirty cottages to accommodate the station and signalbox staff, the linesmen, the engine crews for the branch and the Whitrope banking duties, the shop and one-teacher school necessary to make the community more or less self-sufficient. In his *Forgotten Railways: Scotland*, John Thomas tells of quarrels, especially among railwaymen's wives, and a particular vendetta against the *English* wife one young fireman had been foolish enough to choose himself. 'The people had done nothing but pull down my windows and throw stones into the rooms and bedrooms and use bad language,' the fireman complained. An inquiry resulted in four female viragos being ordered to sign a declaration they would not molest the English woman further.

Sussex Washout. On 19 November 1951 the 9.30am Chichester to Midhurst goods met with disaster near Midhurst after floods had washed away an underbridge. The engine, ex LB&SCR Class C2X 0-6-0 No 32522 fell into the river and was still there when this photograph was taken on 5 January 1952. This section of the branch never reopened, but passenger services had long been withdrawn, on 8 July 1935.

179

Picturesque though it was, the narrow-gauge seemed to encourage strife. Mention has already been made of Col Stephens' brusque manner when dealing with his consortium of assorted railways. The Leek & Manifold Valley, perhaps the railway above all that should not have been built at all, took itself especially solemnly. No unofficial footplate ride here. The driver, one Frank Salt, disliked the teasing by a group of schoolgirls who were standing on the open platform of the leading carriage. As they ran up to Butterton tunnel, he opened the fire door, threw in a bucket of water – and opened up. Frank, however, was better known for not having spoken to his son, the guard, for years, the fireman acting as go between when it was necessary to ease up or to shunt. The train looked fairylike, the atmosphere was devilish.

Relations between father and son following in his footsteps were usually good, but colleagues were always looking on to make sure there was fair play. Even if a son fireman were ordered (and father and son both questioned the instruction) to join his dad on a roster with extra mileage or other advantage, complaints would be bound to be heard.

Strikes often hit the country railway badly; at least, their aftermath was felt more seriously, especially in closed communities. Country railwaymen seldom initiated stoppages, but many were good union men, while others very independent and saw no point in disrupting customers

Irish Troubles. Troops guard a temporarily repaired bridge at Rochestown on the 3ft 0in gauge Cork, Blackrock and Passage Railway in 1923 – a Civil War problem. The engine is one of the CB&P 2-4-2 tanks of Class FN1 which were later (1934) transferred to the Cavan & Leitrim section where they remained until closure.

they personally knew for causes that could be fought out in the centres of population. So sometimes the branch line stayed in business when the main line was closed; sometimes only one pair of men at the terminal depot would keep going, religiously alternating between early and late shift each week, but still providing a service of sorts – like taking the daily supply of fresh water to signalboxes that lacked it.

Inter-union disputes were especially hard to handle in tight-knit communities, but sometimes a whole system – such as the Cavan & Leitrim's over Christmas 1950 – could come to a standstill for weeks on end because just one key man (in this case the steamraiser at Ballinamore) had been ordered out. One driver from a distant depot had the temerity to bring a train into this metropolis of the narrow gauge, where the three routes met and the engineering facilities were concentrated. He was quickly put in his place, given just enough coal to take himself back to his outpost and stay put there.

Sometimes, of course, country railwaymen knew only too well that any disruption might increase the chance of closure. Waterloo would still be in business even if for argument's sake a prolonged strike resulted in loss of some regular business. On the branch line it was very different, if only because the alternative means of transport was too obvious and the public as well as colleagues knew exactly who was working and who not. This was no doubt one reason why relatively more locomotive men were members of the NUR than ASLEF at country depots in Britain.

But this was all tame stuff compared with actual hostilities. Nowhere were these suffered more strongly than on the remoter lines of Ireland during the Troubles. Here are a few entries from the official records of the County Donegal Railways Joint Committee:

23 July 1920: Armed raiders searched and held two trains for Post Office mails, the 8.15am ex Ballyshannon at Bridgetown and the 7.55am ex Strabane at Ballinamore.

11 November: 8.30am train ex Killybegs detained for three hours as the driver refused to work.

20 February 1921: Train derailed between Fintown and Glenties due to malicious damage to track. The train ran down the embankment into Lough Finn.

13 May: Explosives used to damage an iron girder bridge over Stranabrottoge River near Fintown.

30 May: Fifty yd of track torn up at 26mp in Glassaghmore townland, between Cloghan and Ballinamore, carried away and thrown into river bed.

20 June: Three hundred yd of track and sleepers torn up near 24½mp.

28 June: Wagon load of coal for Letterkenny Shed seized by armed men and taken off the 5.35pm train ex Strabane at Raphoe.

31 July: Porter W held up by armed men at Mountcharles and robbed of £19 16s 10d, being the amount he had collected from traders for freight.

2 February, 1932: Armed men entered Mountcharles ticket office

West Country Tales

Villagers of Norton Fitzwarren, scene of two of the Great Western's most serious accidents, generally made little use of their inconveniently-sited station, a junction, with two island platforms. But a handful of shop assistants and school children went to Taunton, and had much fun in the process. There were simultaneous departures, usually at 8.28, of trains from Minehead and Barnstaple, the former using the relief line but going flat out in competition with the latter; though given the same treatment by the GW, the two branch lines and all who worked for them were seen as great rivals. Both trains were due at Taunton at 8.35 (when a third, from Exeter, left Norton Fitzwarren for anyone who was late), but, because of their one-upmanship, the Minehead and Barnstaple drivers, egged on by boys and girls sometimes holding hands between trains, they were usually early.

But the handful of passengers on a Totnes-bound train from Ashburton wondered why the driver was dawdling along that picturesque reach of the Dart, shortly before the main line is gained, especially as the day was most unpleasant. The weather was in fact the indirect reason. The usual Ashburton-based fireman was on his holidays, and the Newton man in the day that few owned cars was sent out by cycle, becoming drenched through in a thunderstorm. Such gentle firing as was necessary for the trip down to Totnes was done in socks and shorts, the driver easing up to allow the boiler suit longer to dry before arrival at Totnes.

Passengers on a train from Moretonhampstead were lucky to make their main-line connection at all. As at many country depots, the water supply at Newton Abbot became salty at exception-
continued overleaf

continued

ally high tides; usually the man in charge noticed this in time to take avoiding action, but not always. So off went the 'Prairie' tank with salt in her boiler, priming away, altogether a rough trip, and then a slight hiss from the plug as the troubled crew coaxed her into Moretonhampstead. The fire was reduced, Newton asked to have a replacement engine ready for the next trip, and the return done mainly freewheeling, fingers crossed. But at Newton the outer home was 'on' and they had to exert power to get her going on the slightly uphill approach: bang, the fusible plug blew. Mercifully the firebox door was closed. Just enough momentum had been created to drift over the complicated trackwork to the down relief and then over the scissors crossover half way down the platform, the fire totally out and not a whiff of steam, so that the replacement engine's first job was to remove the cripple.

One dark evening in 1952, the emergency services received a spate of calls from Eggesford to Ilfracombe. People wondered what calamity had hit them. The trouble was a stuck valve in the whistle of a West Country class light Pacific; the whistle sounded full blast the whole way, the fitter summoned on board at Barnstaple being able to stop the din only after they had come to a standstill at Ilfracombe. Peace; 'the all clear has gone,' said a Southern Region official. But prematurely, since on starting the return trip climb, off it went again, giving Barnstaple a repeat performance through Town and over the curved bridge across the Taw.

There has always been an innate sense of fairness among railwaymen. Fair, for example, that the signalman or crossing keeper should be given the occasional lump of coal to eke out his *continued opposite*

and compelled the stationmaster to hand over all the cash on hand, amounting to £2 2s 3d.

Almost randomly selected from the detailed, sometimes blood-curdling account in Edward M. Patterson's classic history of the Donegal, these do not include the most serious. They demonstrate, however, that the ordinary running of trains could never be relied upon, and you do not need much imagination to realise what operating morale must have been like, whatever your politics. It was substantially the same over much of the west and south of the island, the Dublin & South Eastern's rural lines being especially hard hit, bridges demolished, trains sent down embankments, while smaller concerns were very much in the front line. When the Tralee & Dingle closed, *The Kerryman* paid this tribute:

> The railwaymen were tested and found to be fine in troubled days. Often they refused to drive the British Army of Occupation at the point of the gun or the threat of imprisonment. They were despatch carriers and rendered remarkable service in this respect. Very often the Guard's green flag conveyed a message to the apparently uninterested passer by that something was about to happen or that an undesirable was on board. If the story of the railwaymen's part in the struggle for independence were ever written, it would be interesting reading.

The effect of the much wider, world wars varied dramatically between districts. Many branches ran so outwardly normally that they became security symbols, something you could depend upon when everything else was packing up. From the West Country, Cotswolds and parts of Scotland have come tales of how people under stress treated themselves to a regular trip to a quiet village station, where they enjoyed conversation around the fire in the porters' room before the return trip. In truth, the whole system was under strain; more passengers and freight had to be carried with fewer resources of every kind. So even the branch which never saw enemy activity and did not carry unusual military loads suffered from late trains, trains with inadequate seating, freight that could not be accommodated on today's and maybe not even on tomorrow's service. With more to do and most younger railwaymen away at the war, longer hours were worked than since the unions first became powerful, but wages were higher than ever.

Of the exceptional traffics, always first to mind is the strain of serving the then colossal British Fleet at Scapa Flow, and a ship-repair base at Invergordon, placed on the Highland Railway, with its long sections of steeply-graded single track over routes often far from roads.

Most glamorous of the many kinds of specials that congested the railway, even after many extra passing loops, signalboxes and other facilities had been added as an emergency, was the weekly 717-mile London to Thurso, allowed 21½ hours and usually consisting of fourteen corridor bogies – though sometimes split into two or three sections. Running non-stop from Carlisle to Perth via the Waverley route and Forth Bridge, it was the last word in wartime expresses, carrying a high proportion of VIPs. Imagine the scene at Inverness when 300 government officials, officers and men took advantage of the half-hour meal break. Further north, stops were made at Alness and Invergordon for passengers, and at Helmsdale and Forsinard for locomotive purposes. And, yes, the inevitable happened; on Sunday 13 January 1918, winter being no respecter of other conflicts, the snow was so deep that when the up train ran into a drift near Scotscalder, it was clear it would be there a long time. Next morning the 300 passengers abandoned train and tramped the eight miles back to Thurso. The line to the far north had not been reopened in time for the following week's special, which terminated at Invergordon, the journey on to Thurso being by a boisterous sea.

But however hard the strain on the rails, the rolling stock and the staff, in wartime, at home and overseas, it has usually been the locomotive position that became most critical. The Highland was reasonably equipped for its very different peacetime business, but simply could not handle a ceaseless flow of troop and equipment specials – and much heavier trains than the machines were normally expected to pull. Within a year of the start of hostilities, 50 of the company's 152 locomotives had had to be withdrawn from service, while another 50 were in urgent need of repair. The company's own workshops could not possibly cope, and engines sent down south were taking much longer to be returned than could be spared. An appeal to the Railway Executive Committee resulted in 20 locomotives and also fitters being drafted in from other lines, though the shortage of staff remained acute, crossing loops that the traffic badly required often being closed for want of signalmen. Then wagons ran out, and hundreds had to be loaned by other companies – and more obtained when those companies needed them back.

The emergency state lasted well after the war, when the rebuilding of tourism clashed with the still substantial naval business, albeit the fleet was being run down, and exceptional demand for timber. No railway in these islands has ever endured so prolonged agony of pressure as the Highland in 1914–20, and to this day, over a dram in the local hostelry, you can hear vivid memories of the exertions and excitements of some of those who helped keep the wheels moving.

No lines were quite so over-strained in the second world war, but its effect was felt far more widely. For a start, the emergency evacuation timetable, prepared by the Big Four in the 1930s, included distributing the evacuees from London and other big cities over most of the land – and hundreds of branch lines did indeed receive special train loads, in some cases the stationmaster thinking it wise to turn on the lights, the risk of East Enders who had never been in the countryside before breaking their limbs falling out of coaches not at platforms exceeding that of being attacked by the Germans in the war's early days. It was different when, after many of the children had returned home, there were renewed evacuation waves when serious bombing actually started and when the first doodlebugs hit London.

continued

official ration, but not that he should resell or even give away such supply. On one branch line an extra, unofficial rota was compiled. It was a line over which relief crews often found themselves – and found themselves halted by the signal at a particular crossing, the keeper making a grovelling appeal for coal. After it was realised that different crews had been stopped even on the same day, the enginemen agreed to limit their benevolence to once a month.

Enginemen always enjoyed the countryside they travelled through, and were particularly sharp in looking out when there was special cause to – as in the wooded country on the approach to Kingsbridge when a stag had run amok, killing and injuring lambs. One trip, his fire in good shape, the second man placed his head on the cab door, and as the train drifted quietly downhill, peered into the evening light, trying to catch sight of the rogue animal. Suddenly he became conscious of two bright sparks dashing toward him, jerked his head, and felt as much as a large hawk crash into the locker and fall stunned to the ground. It must have recovered – or at any rate was not there on the return trip.

Customs Examination. With the partition of Ireland in 1922 railways which owned lines crossing the border between North and South inherited time consuming customs examinations, something not calculated to improve their failing fortunes in the mid war years. One such railway was the 3ft gauge County Donegal Railways Joint Committee which had most of its trackage in the Free State (Eire) but its junction with the Great Northern Railway at Strabane in the Six Counties. Passengers fared reasonably well as they were carried in railcars, smaller numbers giving shorter examinations, but the daily freight was another matter. Painted in CDRJC geranium red 4-6-4 tank No 11 Erne waits at Castlefin in Eire one August morning in 1956, the last year of service. Note the jacks on the front of the locomotive, and the customs official examining the seals on the vans.

Unpopular Station

Only 193 passengers a day, and that in summer, were said to be using the whole Teign Valley branch from Exeter to Heathfield when in 1957 BR proposed to close it. By far the least contribution to the traffic receipts from any station (as opposed to unstaffed halt) came from Longdown, somewhat gloomily situated between a pair of tunnels.

Longdown's total outward freight for the previous year was ten tons, and that had involved a special extension of the goods which by those days ordinarily ran from Newton Abbot to Christow only. And if Longdown was unpopular with the commercial people, it was hardly an operational joy. A long loop through the curved one-platform station had been put in during the 1939–45 war to help with emergency diversions, but the ground frames controlling the points were close by them at each end of the loop – meaning that crossing was not possible in ordinary circumstances. So eight times a day when Christow's signalman sought line clear for the auto-car, Longdown 'blocked back' to City Basin Junction to prevent the signalman there having the idea of sending an unscheduled train down the branch.

The signalman at Longdown was not exactly stretched, and with few passengers to pass the time of day he quite naturally encouraged drivers to hang around talking a bit longer. When the foreman of the gang reported undue wear and tear on the permanent way, Control began taking an interest, timing trains on their dash back to civilisation,

until one especially dare-devil driver was brought to book.

When that loop line was put into service, however, there was nothing but crawling. Imagine the scene on a dark, wet winter's night in the middle years of the war. The wind is roaring through the woods in the valley between the pair of hills the railway tunnels through. Inevitably it is always at such a time that the sea stops traffic at Dawlish, and sheds that have got their 'Castles' and 'Kings' ready suddenly have to substitute 'Moguls' or tank engines.

Some traffic can be sent round by the Southern, but that is no good for Newton Abbot or Torbay, and Great Western passenger stock is mainly too wide anyway. So the American ambulance train that was to have gone down by Newton to its private siding at Stover, near Heathfield, is taking the road that in theory is more direct but in practice anything but. And there is a trooper already diverted at Newton Abbot.

Because of its emergency potential, this branch like various others is kept 'open' continuously, even at weekends, in these trying war years. Of course there is normally no traffic at night or on Sunday, and when there is the sole man in charge at Longdown cannot cope on his own. But relief is only coming on the ambulance train, so in the black-out (not that there would anyway be many lights showing around here) he has to trudge down to the up-end frame and yank the points. Then back to the centre of action to pull off the board – once

the driver has whistled and knows where he is. In fact there are two drivers, a 2-6-2 tank piloting a 'Mogul', and making heavy work of the ten bogies on the slippery rails. Thank goodness the procession is not quite halted at the home. It crawls into the loop, a sight and sound that in daylight a generation later would have been a sure crowd getter.

The relief man jumps off the leading engine, scrambles over the track and onto the platform to take instructions. He is despatched back to the up-end frame to return the road for platform working. The up trooper, two 'Moguls' in charge, is whistling for the home, and deliberately checked, then let slowly into the platform, the relief man not having arrived back. Four locomotives and twenty coaches stand together, the occasional soldier peeping out of a window wondering where in the name of civilisation they might be.

The relief man comes back, complaining that already he is soaked, but is told to press straight on to the down-end frame to set the road for the ambulance train to leave; and he might as well stop there till it has cleared so that he can restore it. The signalman pulls the starter for the trooper, and walks to the end of the platform and considerably beyond with the staff. As the outfit wheezes, unsteadily away, he returns to collect the staff for the ambulance train and sets off on another long walk; but at least he will be back before the relief man.

And now the newspaper train is waiting at City Basin Junction.

Omnibus Censor

Great was the consternation when women were appointed to positions of responsibility, such as signalman (nobody could bring himself to use the word 'signal-woman' and the idea of 'signal-person' would then have seemed ridiculous), in the second and third years of the 1939–45 war. The sheer unfamiliarity of it was enough to cause unease, occasionally resentment, and the women were often half apologetic, too readily admitting that they did not really understand railway work – and indeed had not spent their youth being brought up for it.

So when a signalwoman derailed the last wheels of one of those splendid GWR brake vans (which certainly gave GW guards a feeling of superiority over their kind on rival systems), she called up the next station and said: 'Please listen carefully. I changed the catch point too quickly and the end of the guard's van has fallen over. Please tell me what to do. I've got a pencil and paper to take it down.'

Some male staff were anxious not to offend. On one branch line a kind of precursor of Mary Whitehouse listened in to conversations between pairs of men on the omnibus telephone system serving all stations and boxes. When one newly-married signal-man was enquiring about a finer point of bed behaviour, a silent eavesdropper heard the other say: 'Now just stop that; suppose there was a *woman* listening in.' It of course brought a dual response: 'Mind your own ------ business and if she is it's her ---- fault anyway.'

The Kent ports were naturally exceptionally hard-pressed after the miraculous 'victory' on the beaches at Dunkirque, special trains again distributing the load over a substantial proportion of Britain's railways. Some country railways were of course themselves bombed, mainly in the south East, where the miniature Romney, Hythe & Dymchurch sported an armoured anti-aircraft gun train, but it was usually possible to patch and mend rapidly. Of a more lasting nature were the new streams of traffic to and from rural armament factories, to the many British and US air bases, especially in East Anglia (where large sections of country railways were transformed), and then to ports along several hundred miles of the English Channel in preparation for D-day. Cross-country routes, whose traffic by then would probably have declined to the point of no return had the war not happened, were suddenly provided with extra facilities of all kinds, especially longer passing loops such as on the Didcot, Newbury & Southampton and the Midland & South Western Junction.

Generally train services were curtailed somewhat over all country railways during the war, late-evening services being particular casualties, but extra cuts were made for some months starting just before D-day. Almost everywhere freight traffic was heavier, full loads becoming the norm and taxing ageing locomotives. Stalling was common, and frequently the tail of a train had to be left until the front portion had been safely tucked away in a siding. On one West Country route, the same locomotive stalled at exactly the same spot with its maximum of 28 wagons three days in a row, right by a farmhouse where on the last occasion the wife was prepared with a quick cuppa for the crew.

In Ireland things were dramatically different. The island was divided, one half at war, the other not; rationing in the north and a plentitude of the basic foods in the south. Cross-border traffic increased enormously, many compartments having a greater weight of meat, poultry, eggs and butter in them than of human beings. Here, especially, the war as it were came in the nick of time. The companies whose lines straddled the border were suffering acute declines in business by 1939, and since the governments did not yet acknowledge each other (years later the question of what to do about the Great Northern (Ireland) being the first on which Dublin and Belfast talked directly), massive closures could not have been put off much longer. As it was, the 1940s were the busiest in the whole history of railways in the Six Counties. In the south they became steadily more depressing, because of coal shortage. At times the system outside the immediate Dublin area, including the main lines, operated only three days a week. Even then there was only a single train from Dublin to Cork and vice versa, they and their branch connections having an almost spiritual meeting at Limerick Junction as a reminder of what things had been – and how important the railway still was, since if you did not catch a ride then you would have to wait several days.

But the fact that everywhere the railway had a renewed monopoly did help it in the difficult process of adjustment that was to follow. The war at once extended the life of many lines and made it even less likely that they would be adapted for a prolonged economically-sound existence.

186

'You remember,' said Arthur, 'coming with me not long ago on the 2.15 with a Swedie Brake?'

I did. Arthur had made a lot of a fuss about taking it at all; and indeed had got only half way when the examiner at Whittlesford had crippled it for a hot box.

'Well', he said, cocking an eye; 'You may remember that I mentioned the word "Tow-rope".'

Again I did. He had not refused in terms to take that brake without a tow-rope; indeed he could not have done so because they were not required equipment. But he had, so to speak, tossed the word lightly in the air and hoped. However, it had fallen on stony ground, the ears of Ben Mitchell. And no more had been heard of it. I was sorry because that brake was a stinker. Indeed all Swedie Brakes should have been grounded but in 1933 in the depression we were short of brakes and short of money to build better; so, as so often on the LNER, we were making do.

I said: 'Towing only where authorised; then only on adjacent roads when no other train is approaching; and a lot of other dum-dum-dum. They seem to be frightened of it. Funny it doesn't say, like fly-shunting, only to be done by experienced men.'

I had been looking it up.

Arthur said: 'Did you hear about Stephen and the Tow-rope?'

I hadn't but it was likely to be good. 'Well, we were, I being on late turn for the Fruit Working and being still single, collaborating on the 8.40am Whitemoor to Spalding Pick-up. And on a Pick-up you have plenty of time for gossip. You arrive at Guyhirne, place the empty vans for the fruit in the siding, take the road van into the shed, help to unload what is theirs, draw out and go on to Murrow. There you put the whole train aside, go through similar procedures and settle down while the passenger and a few empty trains warble by. Then the signalman may find you a gap to slip you on to French Drove to do it again and so to Postland and so to Cowbit.

A Pick-up is after all the Old Man's Home. When you are medically or domestically past holding on to Swedie Brakes with teeth and claws or lodging in hostels or private lodges far from home, then a benevolent yardmaster will talk his staff representative into putting you into the Old Man's Gang. This means that you go back to the young man's job of having some shunting to do.

Charlie Bunting regularly had the 7.10am Whitemoor to Lincoln. We used to make up his train, couple it, light the fire, see that he had his sidelights, tail lamp, shunting pole and sprags. We added to his sandwiches and tea if he looked short. Then we led him to his brake van, loaded him in, coupled on his engine and gave right away.

Then we telephoned Postland: '7.10am Whitemoor, Charlie Bunting; road van, six fitted empty for you, three coal, one cattle food.' And the goods porter at Postland would receive Charlie, do his shunting for him, put a new

list of his train in his hand, give right away to the driver and telephone Cowbit: '7.10am Whitemoor, Charlie Bunting . . .' Charles went along happily for years and came to no harm.

So, plenty of time, when Arthur said: 'Stephen was working the Shippea Hill Beet. Have you ever been to Duck Drove?'

'Only a foot note in the time table to me.'

'Well, Duck Drove is a siding on the down side between Padnal and Shippea Hill. Not much doing now except in the Beet season. You get the key from Padnal Box. Go forward with your train and stop short of the connection to the siding. You get down, walk to the ground-frame, unlock it and put the distant and home signals to danger. Then you can hook off your engine, pick up what's in the siding, put the empties in if you've brought any, back on to your train, pull the signals off again, lock the frame and go on to Shippea Hill.'

'Which' I said, 'gets the key at the wrong end. It's wanted for next time at Padnal.'

'So' said Arthur, 'the key goes back to Padnal on the next train, which may be yours when you have shunted Shippea Hill; or the porter may take it on his bike. 'But on this particular day there was a relief signalman on duty at Padnal. And he had had an idea. He said to Stephen: 'What's the load for your engine?'.

'37 of mineral.' He'd got a little old Black Goods, a J5.'

'So that's, say, 31 or 32 actual wagons, there being a lot of 12 tonners. OK Well, I've 25 Ely's here now and there's probably a dozen at Duck Drove. So you'd best do a trip to Ely sugar factory before going to Shippea Hill. Drop down to Duck Drove and bring them back facing road on the Down line. I'll give you a wrong line order.'

'How will I run round them?' said Stephen. 'There's no crossover'.

'Ah,' said Bobbie; 'I've found a Tow-Rope.'

So the Bobbie made out the wrong line order, signalman to driver: 'I authorise you to travel on the Down Line in the wrong direction from Duck Drove siding to this signal box.' And told Stephen where to find the Tow-Rope.

Stephen's plan when he got to Duck Drove was to go through the rigmarole of unlocking the frame and putting the signals to danger. He would then draw ahead over the points and knock his brake van on top of the loaded wagons so:

He would then bring his engine to point A and attach the rearmost wagon to it with the tow-rope. The driver would, at the word of command, set off rapidly for ten wagon lengths toward Norwich, thereby accelerating the brake van and wagons out on to the main line. The engine would stop short of the home signal. The train would come to rest. The engine would back on. Stephen

would couple up. And the whole would return facing road to Padnal under the protection of the wrong line order. That was the Plan.

'Stephen carried three quarters of it out to perfection,' recounted Arthur. 'He opened the frame, set back into the siding with the brake, closed the wagons together, coupled them up and on to the brake. He loaded the Tow-Rope on to the engine, came out of the siding, shut the points and set back. So far, so very good.'

By this time I was hugging myself with glee in the sure and certain knowledge of what would befall poor looking-at-his-boots Stephen.

'Stephen' said Arthur, 'attached one end of the Tow-rope to the tender. He took the other across to the last wagon, which happened to be a seven-plank Southern high-side. He couldn't find any towing lugs, so he debated to himself not whether to abandon the whole scheme and go on to Shippea Hill, which he could have done with only two shunting moves and square the

Wrong Line order somehow, he chose the drawbar hook. And gave the driver a fierce wave of the arm to go ahead.'

'The little old Black Goods started with a bang. In a minute Stephen was running hard to keep up, so as to nip the tow-rope off the drawbar hook as soon as they had got enough speed. He tripped over a pile of beet lying in the four-foot and fell flat on his face. The driver couldn't see what had happened till too late. The wagons trundled inexorably on. The Tow-rope was taut between engine and wagons. The whole enterprise arrived at the Home signal; engine on the down main; wagons in the siding; the home signal between the two. First the iron ladder buckled and caved in toward the post; then the post itself swayed, made to recover and fell athwart the line of wagons which was half way out on to the main line. Four derailed; beet everywhere; both main lines blocked.' – A personal tale by Gerry Fiennes, slightly shortened, from his final book *Fiennes on Rails*.

Highland Train in trouble. An accident at Killiecrankie on 17 November 1893. Nothing is known of this though there could have been no fatalities as no accident report is on record. The leading engine appears to be HR No 71 Clachnacuddin *built at Inverness in December 1883 and withdrawn in 1915.*

10
THE COUNTRY YEAR

Only in Scotland and, as time went on, steadily into Northern England, was New Year's Day anything special. And everywhere, once the last of the festivities were over, you faced the long, winter slog ahead – if you had not already been frozen in over the holidays. Traditionally there has indeed been a specially sharp spell around the turn of the year, occasionally cutting off people at their holiday retreats.

The emphasis on weather is right, for the country railway braved all the elements, and was especially vulnerable where it became the hill or mountain railway. The stationmaster at Alston, at the end of the steeply-graded branch from Haltwhistle, contemplating his previous years' traffic figures, knew that during the next few weeks it was likely that on some occasions there would be extra business, the trains keeping going while the roads were blocked, though there was always the risk of the railway having to shut up shop, too.

The epitome of a country station, Cricklade on the Midland & South Western Junction, on 11 September 1935. The locomotive has left part of its train in the platform while it goes off to shunt, but the activity is here with the GWR road motor standing on the platform while the staff unload crates from the solitary box van. Behind the van is a private owner coal wagon and the usual GWR brake van. On the opposite platform milk churns wait to be picked up by the next passenger train.

Milk

Two Rates are in operation for the carriage of Milk; one the Ordinary Rate charged when the Company accept the ordinary liability of a Railway Company with respect to the carriage of Perishable Merchandise by Passenger Train: the other a Reduced Rate, adopted when the sender agrees to relieve the Company and all other Companies or persons over whose lines the traffic may pass, or in whose possession the same may be during any portion of the transit, from all liability for loss, damage, mis-delivery, delay or detention.

The carriage must be prepaid.

Scale of Rates for Milk, conveyed by Passenger Train, charged (with a few exceptions) between any pair of Great Western Stations, at Owner's Risk, including the carriage of the Returned Empty Cans, but not including Collection or Delivery.

Distance	Rate per Imperial Gallon
Up to 20 miles	½d.
Above 20 and up to 40 miles . .	¾d.
Above 40 and up to 100 miles . .	1d.
Above 100 and up to 150 miles . .	1¼d.
Above 150 miles	1½d.

Minimum Charge, as for 12 Imperial Gallons per consignment.

Fractions of a gallon to be charged as a gallon for each consignment.

Fractions of a penny to be charged as a penny for each consignment.

Note – For the convenience of the public requiring Milk at Hammersmith, Kensington (Addison Road), West Brompton, Chelsea, Clapham Junction, Victoria, and other Stations on the Hammersmith and City, and West London Extension Railways, it has been arranged with the other Railway Companies concerned, that the above Scale shall apply to those Stations from the Great Western Railway, subject to an addition of *2d.* per Can.

GWR Parcels & Goods Arrangements, 1914

In moderation, snow was the railway's friend. In later days, when the local branch line came under threat, the first exclamation often was: 'But what *shall* we do when the roads are frozen?' Especially before the highway authorities finally came to grips with the need to invest in heavy equipment, a good white sprinkling and everywhere there would be small but unusual queues of people buying tickets. Even when the railway kept going, it was not always at its best, such people reverting to their car without question at the first possible moment. Meantime the revenue was useful, especially if the local big-wig usually driven to the junction bought his ticket to London or Manchester.

At Inverness and strategic points along the Highland system, snow-ploughs and other gear was at the ready, everyone knowing what to do if a blizzard struck, though it was not until very recent times, well after our Great Days, that it became mandatory to carry emergency rations on the trains themselves. The same on the West Highland and Oban lines. Those 'lighthouses of the land', isolated signalboxes not serving stations but breaking up the section, usually though by no means always with a crossing loop, were stuffed with rations and equipment. Not merely might the small communities at places like Gorton on the West Highland be cut off for a week or more, the school teacher unable to make her daily visitation and not even the necessary fresh water being delivered, but a whole train load, indeed two, might become stranded and need help.

Most years brought devastating blizzards somewhere, as often or not part of Scotland. Then the question was whether the trains should be allowed to set off at all, how they could be rescued if they got stuck, and how long the line would then remain closed. Which leaves out perhaps the most important consideration: how long could the locomotive keep up the steam heating if they ran into a drift? Even without heat, however, better to stay in the dry until the blizzard passed. Many lost their lives in losing their direction.

The occasional news picture made fighting snowdrifts look spectacular, but in reality, whatever the equipment it was a long test of endurance. And often pretty thankless, for as soon as the point blades were cleared, in the fiercest winds in they filled again. Townspeople might not realise that snowdrifts can build rapidly when there is no precipitation at all, but countrymen have always been well prepared. Not that blockages automatically meant gloom. There would be good overtime; if you were lucky, in later years, continuous overtime while you fed like fighting cocks at the station hotel, your train abandoned (that is to say its engine fireless) in the platform across the street. Some crews were able to afford their first television set this way.

Meantime the coal yards up and down the kingdom were at their busiest. Coal was king everywhere in Britain; in Ireland it was of course different and that difference the main reason why country railways were less profitable there. Allocated on a per capita basis, even the smallest hamlet had its own coal wagon, a street of twenty railwaymen's cottages a pair, and a village of a thousand or so souls a score. Even in the days that everything went by train, in winter by far the biggest inward load was

190

coal. There was hardly a goods yard without its coal merchant, the village of a thousand or two people probably having a couple; men who were very much part of the railway community, though not paid by the company – rather chivvied to empty their wagons so they could be sent to the colliery for the next load. All day long an incredible assortment of road vehicles were plying their way to and from the countryside's multitude of coal yards, the merchant naturally finding it more convenient to load direct from the rail wagon than create an intermediate storage heap, his customers desperate for their turn and sometimes forced to collect the odd hundredweight by barrow or pram.

And in winter, when cows were least productive, milk trains were making their longest runs. Especially in far flung areas like South West England, what would be turned into butter and cheese, or used for rice puddings, dried milk powder or whatever, at more productive times, would be needed in the cities (in the West Country's case that meant London) in winter. So when traffic was otherwise fairly quiet, long-distance milk despatches gave extra work.

As the evenings began to lighten, and the grass grew greener, and primroses adorned embankments, traffic increased pretty well every-where. Building projects were going ahead, which meant more demand

Deeside in Spring. A GWR Bulldog class 4-4-0 takes a Llangollen and Ruabon bound train out of Glyndyfrdwy in April 1934. The train has come from the Cambrian coast but the engine will only have worked through from Barmouth being too heavy for stations from Portmadoc and beyond. This is a through London train of four corridor coaches with polished brass door and grab handles; each compartment has its own side door as well as corridor door. Glyndyfrdwy station served a small hamlet half a mile away and up a hill; it had two platforms, a passing loop, a signalbox and a level crossing plus a stationmaster's house.

191

for bricks, tiles, road stone, paint, timber, mantlepieces and windows. And the farmers would be needing their fertilisers. So important was the fertiliser trade that the early weeks of spring saw extra freight trains running on most substantial country railways, and kept the railways' delivery lorries busy.

The last of the bulbs had long since been despatched from Spalding, and now came the first produce of the new season, daffodils from the Scilly Isles, and broccoli from Cornwall, once up to fifty trainloads a day, some starting from Nancegollan on the Helston branch where farmers had to be patient as they queued in their horse-drawn vehicles or tractors for their turn to load. Potatoes would follow, Cornish competing with Channel Isles and shortly after Pembrokeshire – the railways in 'little England beyond Wales' then being at their freight peak.

As the season progressed, too, the carriage of livestock became heavier, managers juggling when or not to release cattle wagons usurped for the broccoli and potato business for their rightful purpose. The first of the quarter days coming up, farm removal trains made their appearance; it was amazing how tenant farmers steadily improved their lot by moving up one, or suddenly took a liking to a quite different part of

Cross country link. A Marks Tey – Cambridge train headed by GE Class E4 2-4-0 No 62786 in early BR livery is seen amidst the spring flowers near Cavendish on 21 May 1951.

Britain. Machinery, feed, livestock from cattle to geese, a favourite gate, the furniture: everything was brought to the nearest station and somehow fitted onto the special, usually consisting of a passenger coach, a few horseboxes and cattle wagons, a low-loader or two for the container with the furniture in it and the tractor and mower, and a box van for the odds and bits. Always a one-off operation with excited dramatis personae, it could never be exactly efficient but was always fascinating to watch – as the driver and firemen did from the warmth of their cab. One of those millions of pieces of paper issued by headquarters gave the running details, including the stops at which the livestock were to be fed, the cows milked.

The approach of Easter also meant greater activity on the religious front, more people going by train to church (it happened in many places despite the paucity of Sunday train services) and in Ireland on pilgrimages. The pilgrimage traffic was very important to Irish lines, accounting for more than half the annual number of passengers on some. Centred on places like Claremorris, it attracted town and country people alike, sometimes giving them both a unique rural experience – mass at the village church en route. Where several specials followed each other (and this is not all in the past), each stopped at a different station for worship, the railway effectively closed, crews praying with passengers, until it all came back to life together.

The last frost hopefully behind them, the permanent-way gangs had their busiest season. As those who have actually worked on the track will know, the words Permanent Way are misleading. Nothing has ever been free from the deterioration process, though excess water and frosts especially attack lines laid on clay. After a severe winter, quite substantial remedial works might be needed, particularly if snow and ice blocked the normal free passage of excess water. Men were ever being extolled to improve the drainage; only ballast that would run dry quickly could do its job properly. And if the winter had been exceptionally wet, almost certainly there would be a slip or two on embankments that needed attention; take away the excess soil and probably build a small retaining wall.

Now was also the time to replace a few worn sleepers, to top up the ballast where necessary, and perhaps undertake a more major section of replacement. By the 1950s, the average section of rail and the average chair had probably served at least half a century on most branch lines, rather less long on cross-country routes or others with even occasional expresses. Money was spent extremely sparingly between the wars, especially after 1930, and something had to be pretty seriously wrong to warrant replacement on a branch line during the war. The linesman, perhaps patrolling one length daily by foot and the other by motor trolley (at first in some cases by pedal-operated one), of course alternating them, had to work hard to keep it all in order, but usually succeeded. On his patrol he replaced the occasional chair and noted what required more serious attention, next day perhaps taking his trolley off the track at a plate-layer's hut with an intermediate block token instrument. There he,

---

Prisoners of War – Whittington to Porthywaen and back

Every weekday until further notice, special trains will run as under:

UP	2 Empty Train am	4 Pass'ger Saturdays only pm	6 Pass'ger Saturdays excepted pm
Porthywaen ..... dep	...	...	4.45
Dolgoch Quarry Siding .... ,,	...	...	4.48
Llynclys Junction....... ,,	...	...	4.50
Oswestry.......... arr	...	...	
Oswestry.......... dep	6.25	2.45	5.05
Whittington ...... arr	6.32	2.52	5.12

DOWN	1 Pass'ger am	3 Empty Train Sats. only pm	5 Empty Train Sats. exc't. pm
Whittington ..... dep	6.45	3.00	5.30
Oswestry.......... arr	...	3.08	5.38
Oswestry.......... dep	6.53	...	...
Llynclys Junction....... ,,	7.08	...	...
Dolgoch Quarry Siding .... ,,	7.11	...	...
Porthywaen ...... arr	7.13	...	...

To be worked by Porthywaen engine and guard.

The 6.50am Nantmawr Goods, will leave Oswestry at 7.10am.

On Wednesdays No 14 Tanat Valley Goods must not leave Blodwell Junction before 4.45pm.

Inspector Evans to provide accommodation for about 55 passengers.

On Saturdays the passengers will return by No 10 Tanat Valley train, which will pick up the two coaches next to engine at Porthywaen, and work same through to Whittington and back, as shewn above, the Porthywaen train working from Llynclys Junction to Oswestry as usual.

Empty Wagons and Basic Vans for Porthywaen to be worked to Llynclys Junction by the Nantmawr goods, which will stop to detach same, but must not be detained to shunt.

These instructions to be preserved for reference.
Cambrian Railways weekly train notice, 3 March 1918

RCs On the Branch

Restaurant cars on single lines always brought a special touch of magic. Some routes, including the cross-country Midland & Great Northern and the Somerset & Dorset, had time-honoured daily restaurant-car expresses. The S&D's was of course called the *Pines Express*, which in its last days became famous for the bone thrown out for a dog near Blandford Forum. The last bone before the express was diverted via Reading made television.

Scottish Highland routes were famous for their culinary delights: Helmsdale and The Mound on the Far North line and Achnasheen on the Kyle of Lochalsh route saw the ritual of the restaurant car being transferred from a down to an up service as part of the 'crossing': Achnasheen usually had a couple of freights on hand at the same time, one having to shunt through the station to make the crossing of the passenger service possible. The ritual of changing the 'car' from a down to an up train happened even at South Molton every day during the summer timetable in the 1930s.

Summer Saturdays of course brought a big extension to the map of restaurant-car routes, especially in the West Country. Perranporth was a traditional starting point for a summer Saturday restaurant car service to Paddington, the car being one of an entire train of catering vehicles despatched from Paddington to West Country junctions to Truro. The Southern's 'withered arm' west of Exeter enjoyed up to half a dozen restaurant-car services instead of the normal single Brighton–Plymouth one on other days.

Undoubtedly many 'cars' were provided more for prestige than expectation of profit, though it has to be remembered that the *continued opposite*

and possibly a mate, would light a fire that would be ready for tea before venturing on the job. The biggest jobs, and ballasting, obviously required an engineer's train. Ballasting and small re-railing jobs could be fitted in between weekday trains, but a quarter of a mile of track to relay would mean special opening up of signalboxes on Sunday. Welcome overtime.

Though at its peak in the spring, on some routes using labour that would go into running summer traffic, maintenance never ceased. Bridges had to be checked, culverts cleared, and then grass cut. What an army of manpower that consumed, but how miserable those who maintained the grass swards through which the primroses and bluebells popped would be to learn that from mid-1960s British Railways would give up this practice, allowing railway verges to become one of our few habitats in which woodland is spreading. And the signalling department; a law unto itself. Always something to adjust in the point rodding and signal wiring even when not requested to ease the pulling of the distant – and always seeming to take so long about it. Track and signalling were generally both improved in the twenty years after 1945, BR being far more liberal in its engineering than had the private companies, because after nationalisation the engineers succeeded in making themselves more powerful in the hierarchy. And least in another way we can claim that the Great Days were relatively recent, many tracks being in fine fettle when the last trains ran over them.

Easter brought the year's first passenger flutter. More people went shopping beforehand, hotels and guest houses opened their doors, and excursions started in a big way. Some inland tourist spots actually received more trippers now than later in the season, when people would turn their attention to the beaches, while long-distance excursions (several hundred miles for a few bob) were run partly on the excuse that you could finalise arrangements for the summer holiday. Birmingham folk were perhaps best served: chance of getting to almost every tourist area in England and Wales on a day trip cheaply. The GW had pioneered the really long-distance stuff even before the turn of the century, Londoners being able to enjoy several hours on Dartmoor, or a sail down the Dart, between their fast journeys at bargain fares but in tightly-full trains. Specials ran to Spalding; from all six routes converging on the town, people came to see the bulb fields.

Now thoughts were increasingly concentrated on the season ahead. Good Great Western stationmasters would indeed not merely have sold their quota of *Holiday Haunts* but at least made a mental note of who extra should be advertising in the following year's issue. The season's tourist arrangements including special tickets, runabouts, day, halfday, evening, round trip, joint train and pleasure boat deals and for many years in North Wales the scenic land cruise, were distributed on their hundred-and-one separate handbills, posters displaying the more commercial offerings. Almost every country station had something available (though stationmasters might not always be satisfied with the range), and could expect to benefit from townspeople touring by train.

Some of these printed 'arrangements' would give clues about the forthcoming summer service, but even in the days when timetables arrived punctually (something that BR has never consistently been able to achieve), there would be anxious moments. The lord planning his trip eight weeks hence might have to be told that there would *probably* be a connection. Timetablewise, the country railway certainly has not enjoyed its greatest days since nationalisation. Many customers were lost through the staff's inability to tell what services would be offered sometimes even on the very morrow, even in tourist areas. And with the advent of diesels and general speeding up and re-arranging, there was an inverse ratio: the more you needed the timetable, the harder it was to get hold of. Worse than that, sometimes it was out of date even before it became current; worthless unless you could get the even scarcer initial supplement. Changes were now inflicted at almost any time, such as the end of June 1958, just as seasonal traffic was getting thoroughly under way, when swingeing cuts were made in many holiday areas. At least you could still check with the poster-timetables adorning the station notice boards. Pasting them up (along with other posters), and carefully underlining the individual station's times in pink crayon, was another of those multitude of station tasks once taken for granted and now forgotten.

The station garden would be coming into its own, the white lining along the platform edge sharpened up, the booking office and waiting rooms spring cleaned, and perhaps one year in eight or ten the painting gang sprucing the whole place up. How much cheaper he could have organised it himself, thought the stationmaster.

Summer. It was ever slow in coming. Easter was too early or Whit too cold. It might be beautiful weather in May and June but few visitors, or raining hard in late June and early July and keeping them away. The early ones always had the best attention, if not actually the fullest train service or best-aired beds in village catering establishments. They, in some areas, included the Camping Coach, another forgotten institution. Generous in size but always slightly behind the times in their level of luxury, they were rented by the week at quite competitive rates, but had the snag that you had to buy so many (usually the equivalent of four adult) tickets from your home station. Stationmasters organised welcoming provisions and daily milk and generally gave guests paternal attention, recommending places to visit and especially what trains to travel by.

The majority of country railways enjoyed at least a slightly fuller service in summer, the extra trains being greeted with some reverence. On some lines it was an extra early afternoon trip up the moors; on others a later evening service; on a few the running of extra trains missing the occasional stop as opposed to the winter all-trains-stop-everywhere routine. And on lines leading to the resorts, there were the Saturday extras. Some branches indeed justified having their total service printed separately for summer Saturdays, along with the main line's. If they did not, they could become extremely confusing.

continued

buffet car was a latecomer and that even in the 1950s the choice was usually a full meal or nothing. Scottish Highland routes often saw scant custom for main meals, but afternoon tea in a vintage carriage with wooden slatted sides was popular on the Oban run in the 1950s, even though the bread was stale three days in a row. The West Highland line, when still mainly patronised by workers from the Outer Hebrides, was culinarily uncertain; an LNER crew said that the eight lunches they had already served on a northbound service left only the three portions for the return, which they would need to eat themselves. Thanks be for the ten-minute refreshment stop at Crianlarich and its welcoming tea room.

You can of course still have a Scottish breakfast on the Highland south from Inverness and drink wine from the buffet in the observation car on to Kyle of Lochalsh.

Overseas visitors have often found the company and service in restaurant cars a helpful way of enjoying the British countryside. Back in 1951, the year of the Festival of Britain, one American staying with relatives at Hereford first visited London by restaurant car train, of course including single line at Ledbury. He enjoyed it so much that he spent his visit going to Paddington and back in the restaurant car every day. Many of us have repeated journeys over lunch from Leeds to Carlisle and afternoon tea in a former Pullman car between Crianlarich and Oban.

Summer Saturday Loading. Ilfracombe terminus Southern Railway one Saturday in September 1946, with newly built Bulleid Pacific then numbered 21C105 and appropriately named Barnstaple, *double heading a Great Western small Prairie tank No 5533. Two engines were needed to cover this hilly and tortuous route. No 21C105 was then shedded at Exmouth Junction (EXJ). The carriage stock appears to be LNWR and LMS suggesting the 9.25am to Cardiff via the GWR from Barnstaple; this probably accounts for the 45XX class 2-6-2 tank.*

Summer Saturdays is a big subject, not exclusive to the country railway. In the Summer Saturday chapter we have chosen to concentrate on the M&GNJ, but might note that there was a similar pattern, tidal waves of trains in different directions at different times of day, on that other major cross-country joint line, the Somerset & Dorset, and that many West Country and other branches that normally only enjoyed stopping trains now had expresses, destination boards and all. The Somerset & Dorset was even worse than the M&GN in one respect: its gradients. A whole line of locomotives was made ready on the centre siding at Evercreech Junction to assist the north-bound expresses over the Mendips. But here there was not the same weight restriction, and a much wider variety of motive power, at varying times in all the Big Four's tradition except that of the LNER, and eight-coupled locomotives designed especially for the S&D were often prominent.

Summer Sundays is another and less-frequently mentioned subject. Many lines closed for the the winter Sabbath of course opened for the summer, and large crowds were often carried, though on relatively few trains within relatively short operating hours. Even from villages and country towns well inland, the emphasis was on trips to the sea, perhaps involving one or two changes in each direction . . . business that was obviously vulnerable to road competition. Summer Sunday takings varied dramatically with the weather. But specials that had been pre-booked came in any event, the variable then being the state of mind of their passengers.

Weekdays and Sundays, there were always summer specials going the rounds. Long before a landslide prematurely closed the Callandar road, Glasgow folk benefitted from a service up the West Highland to Crianlarich and then to Oban. The North Wales Land Cruise (which did a circuit from Llandudno via Bangor, Afonwen, Barmouth, Corwen, Denbigh and so back to the North Wales main line, had various regional though regular counterparts. And for many years in the 1950s and 1960s 'City of ---' trains, the same seat guaranteed every Sunday to Friday for two weeks, every day from the city to a different destination, took in considerable country railway mileage. Nor must one forget the charter trains, notably the Sunday School Outing. Once virtually every major church reckoned to send its children, teachers and parents on their grand day by train, sometimes service train, but usually special. Churches on the same branch sometimes clubbed together, as did women's institutes. These might be the only originating trains from many villages in the

Sunday Excursion. An enterprising Scottish Region ran Sunday trains out of the ex North British Railway Queen Street Station, Glasgow, to Fort William and back until the late 1950s, though these were not shown in the post war timetables, being advertised on hand bills and posters. A variety of engines could be found hunting in pairs on this turn with former LNER K2 class 2-6-0s, B1 4-6-0s, LMS Class 5 4-6-0s, and sometimes, though very rarely, a Glen. Here are Class 5 No 45281 and K2 No 61784 on the return excursion, the 5.00pm from Fort William, near Spean Bridge on 2 August 1953.

whole year, though over a period it was surprising what stations did see trains starting up for some special occasion or other such as a Royal visit or carnival in the nearest town or works outing. And even into the 1950s, the occasional fair, certainly the circus, still went by its special train, demanding very special arrangements.

The peak fortnight straddling August Bank Holiday's traditional date at the month's start inevitably brought the greatest pressure, branch lines occasionally having to harbour passenger stock for which there was no room at the resorts or indeed on the nearest hundred miles of main line leading to them. All of August was busy, though the later the date the more the pressure depended on the weather. That applied even more to September, which if reasonable could bring some stations in inland tourist areas actually greater reward, for people patronising the moors generally wished to avoid the crowds. Walkers and anglers (sometimes especially from Birmingham whole angling clubs) to a variety of Severn destinations were much in evidence as children went back to school, the Scottish schools first, the season north of the border always having been earlier than in England, followed by Lancashire, then the Midlands, everywhere state schools before private ones.

The beginning of the boarding-school and university year brought the largest of the three annual rounds of passengers' luggage in advance (PLA). We forget how much baggage people of all ages reckoned to take before the age in which it became customary to lift it yourself and fit it into the family motor. In the week before term started, half the callers at

Waiting for the Train. A posed picture of staff and passengers waiting at Bradford on Avon in 1897. It is certainly a special occasion as a large 'Welcome' notice is hung over the exit and everyone is dressed in their best clothes.

stations serving well-heeled villages might be to deposit trunks – and often bicycles. PLA was also used in a big way by holidaymakers and also trickled in to most country stations throughout the season, the takings from miscellaneous charges, including pennies in toilet slots and cloakroom storage fees, being material.

Harvest was now gaining most attention. Strawberries had of course been sent by the trainload up from the West Country in late June and early July, followed by raspberries, especially big business in Fife, and summer vegetables and plums from the Vale of Evesham. August and September brought perhaps the most romantic harvest: Kent hops.

Whole families, largely from the Elephant & Castle area of London, moved by special trains to live in wooden shacks adjoining the hop fields, picking by day and providing their own entertainment by night. The main destinations for the specials from London Bridge Low Level were Maidstone West and Paddock Wood, the normally-sedate Hawkhurst branch also playing an important part in the annual tradition. The main movements took place in the early hours of weekend mornings, six or seven trains leaving just for the Hawkhurst branch between 3.30 and 6.30am. Made up of non-corridor and even non-cushion stock, the trains had to be away before the newspaper traffic. Special tickets were issued at bargain rates. Bill Ball, acting foreman in charge of the traffic at London Bridge, made quite a reputation for discovering those trying to travel without payment – and for keeping the exuberant spirits associated with the annual migration (a family tradition and economic necessity) within bounds.

In addition to the main specials at start and end of the season, Sunday extras were run during it, bringing dads for the one week they could afford to take off or friends just for the day. These Sunday trains were stabled at Hawkhurst until the evening, the crews operating the return workings becoming adept at keeping going even when the communication cord was constantly pulled.

Teazles and willows from Somerset, in later years sugar beet from much of the Eastern Counties, corn also from there and the Granary of Scotland, apples from Kent, Wisbech and Worcestershire, the Kent hops themselves to the breweries along with many trainloads from the maltings at Aldeburgh, still potatoes from Pembrokeshire and now also Wisbech – and time for the year's final round of cattle and horse fairs.

Most of the village shows have now been held, and earlier in the summer trains carried thousands of head of cattle, flocks of sheep, and all the new ideas in farm equipment to the big county and regional ones, while in Ireland the Great Northern and Great Southern have nearly driven themselves silly sending horses hither and thither, to races at the Curragh and everywhere else, and in England the stables at Newbury and Newmarket have pressed their usual unreasonable demands but paid well for the privilege. But nothing beat the day when a village or small market town had its annual do.

Passenger trains were strengthened not only on the branch but connecting branches; five or six instead of two or three coaches, most

Overleaf:
Country Station In Autumn. Dent on the Midland Railway's Settle to Carlisle route to Scotland in the early 1960s. Bleak and almost nowhere, the station here acted as a collecting point for the local community, sandwiched between Rise Hill and Widdale Fell. In earlier days with no proper roads in the area, the railway was a vital lifeline. Here there was no question but that the staff had their own accommodation as can be seen by the brick station house and cottages. Even at this date the whole place has a solid Midland Railway atmosphere, neat wooden fencing round the station area, horsebox or sheep van siding and plenty of coal around for the hard, hard winter. The engine working the train for the track gang is LMS type Class 4 2-6-0 No 43139. The shed plate looks like 12A, Carlisle Kingmoor.

199

Steam Special. As routes began to close and locomotive classes became extinct, a regular feature of the 1950s and 60s was the enthusiast sponsored special train. Travel on one of these excursions enabled passengers not only to ride behind a class about to be eliminated, but also to see it in appropriate surroundings. Often this was a way of exploring a branch long closed to passengers but sometimes it was for the pure joy of the occasion. Such trains were those arranged by the Talyllyn Railway Preservation Society taking members and friends to Towyn for a day out over the narrow gauge line and for the faithful to attend the Annual General Meeting. On 29 September 1962 the route chosen was via Ruabon, taking the old Great Western line from there via Bala Junction and Barmouth Junction. The two engines concerned were ex Croes Newydd (84J) Manors as clean as new pins. This photograph was taken shortly before crossing the River Dee close to Llangollen. All traffic over the section ceased on 1 April 1968 but through services and passengers had gone by 18 January 1965 because the line had been cut by flooding problems with the River Dee.

Midland Incursion. A Peterborough to Leicester train leaves the old market town of Stamford headed by a BR Class 4 4-6-0 No 75057 on 26 November 1960. This Midland built line gave that railway access to Peterborough and the Eastern Counties and to this day Birmingham to Norwich trains travel the route.

likely, and a much higher incidence of seats taken nonetheless. Normally unstaffed halts suddenly had someone issuing and collecting tickets, and signalmen and guards wore a carnation. And special trains; a long-distance excursion, maybe, and one or two rakes of cattle trucks. The excursion will probably have been advertised to go on to the terminus since it had to go there anyway; there was no room to stable it at the place whose day it was. Some of the cattle wagons will have worked down on previous days, leaving a light engine and van to come and take charge of the situation, another train following in reserve. Nobody ever knew exactly what business would be achieved, but unthinkable to turn custom away. Let us pay a visit, slightly earlier – say the late 1940s – than our passenger Great Days for it was alas such traffic as this that disappeared fastest.

The station and its yard are agog with activity. Such is the pressure on the gents that a keen porter takes it upon himself to bar it to those who cannot produce tickets, which sends – under the watchful eyes of a pair of railway policemen who have just arrived for what they hope will be a nice, gentle day out – several people to the booking office for platform tickets. That prompts the stationmaster to ask if they need parking tickets as well; as soon as the window is clear, he will pop out and assess the forecourt and maybe rake in a few more shillings. If he can lay his hands on it, there is a small supply of notices to affix to the windscreens of those who regard railway property as their own. 'Ah, hallo, had a good year?' A tall, gaunt dealer who has been coming many years, long before the stationmaster took up this job, will be needing help with his correspondence. A shrewd money-maker, and not a bad tipper, he is among a handful of those buying and selling today who cannot read.

The light engine and van stop outside, their crew's first priority to replenish their drinking-water; there might not be time to get to the station's only tap once shunting gets under way. But soon they are off down the yard, a couple of hundred people arrive by the excursion, briskly sent on down the line. The station empties as the auctioneer, in his pulpit among the pens a hundred yards down the road, takes up his position and addresses the world. The ordinary up goods stops in the up platform, its normal shunting work largely done by the engine that has already started to-ing and fro-ing collecting trucks in turn from each of the half-dozen sidings and tossing back those still to stay there, chased by the goods porter who pins their brakes down to prevent too much banging. The trainload of cattle empties arrives before this up freight can be on its way, which might delay the down passenger at the next station loop and in turn delay its crossing here with the next up passenger; but there is no alternative.

The empty cattle trucks are stowed where they can be in the yard, and soon the first animals (it might be cattle, sheep or horses; the crowds to be sure would be slightly different, but the railway work substantially the same) are directed to the small range of pens inconveniently placed on a short siding nearest the end of the headshunt. Only four trucks at a time can be cleared, so to-ing and fro-ing is going to continue all day.

There is a slight lull for lunch, which gives the station pub its busiest hour of its year, railwaymen who normally possess it hardly noticed among the noisy farming fraternity. But the pace quickens in the afternoon, when there is a crossing of passenger trains coinciding with the short down freight 'being about' as signalmen used to say. That means five trains at once on the simple layout of a crossing loop and goods headshunt off which the half dozen sidings lead.

Immediately the ordinary trains are away, the first of the specials starts to be made up in the down platform; whatever the running of the next pair of passengers, they cannot be crossed here. One of the special's locomotives runs round the first rake of loaded cattle trucks, its crew lingering for a grandstand view after the signal has been pulled off at the loop's up end. The auctioneer is in full flood and the fireman decides to put him down a peg. Just when it is important everyone hears what he is

Mixed Train in the Highlands. A winter scene on the Aberfeldy branch which ran from Ballinluig, north of Stanley Junction on the former Highland Railway main line from Perth to Inverness, to Aberfeldy close to the eastern end of Loch Tay. For many years this was the preserve of Caledonian Railway 0-4-4 tanks and No 55217 takes this mixed train through the snow in the late 1950s. The line closed to all traffic on 3 May 1965.

saying, the locomotive's whistle gives a long crow, all heads are turned, and the auctioneer realising he has been fooled has to repeat himself.

The first special is away about five, the second by half past six, but only has a dozen trucks. Business is down on last year, and for the first time several farmers have preferred to use lorries. What next? Until the last up, the passenger trains are busier than normal, arriving almost empty but filling up with the visitors, many of whom have been down to the town for fun and refreshment. That has given the station bus run by the hotel extra business; two trips for most trains, and delayed delivery of passenger train parcels which it contracts for the railway. Soon the day ends; in a few years possibly it will have ended for good.

The summer was unusually dry, October and November soaking wet. In several parts of the countryside there have been floods giving extra work to the maintenance men, but nothing on the scale that was to happen years later when the East Coast main line was effectively split into pieces and various branches in the North East and the Borders would have rendered yeoman service had some of their own bridges not also been washed away. There have been a few temporary diversions this year, but the most publicised incident was a branch-line train ploughing into a pack of hounds in the Quorn country. Each year the district offices reminded drivers to keep a sharp look out for hounds, as immediately unstoppable as a train itself, but if they came at you round a bend, what could you do?

Trainmen were noting that the last of the harvest had been delayed by the rains, but the mushrooms were good. And now Smithfield, extra cattle business but also passenger, indeed peak business for restaurant-cars in some rural areas as farmers and their families enjoyed a little of their hard-earned gains. And a quickening pace to Christmas, the great enemy now fog. Everyone remembered the year that it slowed the wheels down so badly in the days before Christmas that some trains full of livestock for the holiday table never reached the capital, emergency watering and even slaughtering arrangements creating much hard work and unpleasantness.

Decorations adorn the most-used parts of many stations, town and country alike, and Father Christmas is sent on tour of the 'lighthouses' on the West Highland, bringing his annual cheer to the small community at Gorton, where the provisions have again been topped up in readiness for winter. Christmas business is important everywhere, but especially in the country station's parcels offices (passenger and goods), and at this time there is no question of the railways taking a holiday of their own. Extra long-distance services leaving the cities on Christmas Eve do not reach their destinations until Christmas morning, when special branch-line connections are provided. Some branches then close for the rest of the day, and have a limited special service on Boxing Day, but the main lines keep going, the restaurant-car's seasonal fare written up in the Press which makes it sound as though the best place for Christmas lunch would be a Scottish express passing through the Lune Gorge and over Beattock. Or would the Midland over the Long Drag be even better?

Stationmaster's Thanks
Retirement of the stationmaster was a big event at a country town, thanks and testimonials (also contributions to the farewell gift, presented at a formal lunch) pouring in from traders and regular travellers. But by 1973 a passenger was right to be surprised on seeing a handwritten notice of thanks by the newly-retired railwayman at Hildenborough, Kent, placed under a bowl of flowers in the booking hall: 'To all my good friends at Hildenborough Station. I have been overwhelmed by your generosity to me on my retirement. I am sorry to be leaving as I have enjoyed meeting you each morning, passing time of day and exchanging little pleasantries. I hope in my humble way I have passed on a little pleasure and helped to ease some of the tedium of the daily journey up and down, and that you will be served in like manner by whoever succeeds me. I cannot fully express what I feel, but I am sure you will all understand. Thank you for everything. I am gratefully your servant. R. J. Hockley (Dick).'

ACKNOWLEDGEMENTS

Two former railwaymen have been untiring in their willingness to make sure that this book has come together in a form which is alive, and just as important, accurate, for each author is but an enthusiast for railways. John Powell who spent his working life with engines and enginemen has provided vignettes on the M&GN and Keswick summer Saturday traffic; he has looked at far away country junctions with a railwayman's eye, Dingwall, Melton Constable, Barnard Castle, Waterhouses and Farranfore, as well as taking a glimpse behind the scenes at a country junction shed along with a country terminus. John Edgington, now at the National Railway Museum but also with railway experience in the traffic and public relations departments, has checked the text and captions for accuracy; he has also spent countless hours looking up additional information, reading time-tables and delving into shed allocations. To both these friends we say thank you.

Others too, have provided specialist information, Geoffrey Kichenside on single line working, its whys and its wherefores (he also searched his collection of carriage photographs for some country gems) C. C. Green supplied information on things Cambrian, the Irish Railway Record Society, the Midland & Great Northern Railway Society, John Powell, and Colin Judge looked out station diagrams, while Ron Whateley gave willing access to his collection of printed ephemera. We have also referred to many books and magazines, and these are listed in the form of 'Suggested Reading'. Special mention must, however, be made of those erudite works on locomotive history carefully compiled and published by the Railway Correspondence and Travel Society. The editors of *The Railway Magazine*. *The Tenterden Terrier* (Kent & East Sussex Railway) and the *Stephenson Locomotive Society Journal* have kindly given permission for items to be reprinted from their periodicals, as has the Great Western Society. The National Railway Museum too has willingly answered requests for information and in particular Messrs Atkins and Edgington have been unfailingly helpful in their official capacities. Nor must the photographers be forgotten, as no authors can or should try to fill a volume such as this with their own work. Philip Alexander, Michael Mensing, Peter Gray, Eric Treacy, Jim Jarvis and Ron White of Colour-Rail deserve special mention. Lastly we would like to pay tribute to those who have unknowingly made this book possible, railwaymen of all grades, fellow enthusiasts and the compilers of books and journals; all have come together and made the whole. Alan Prior prepared the artwork for most of the line diagrams, information for the shed layouts being provided by permission of Wild Swan publications.

One of the joys of putting together the *Great Days of the Country Railway* has been looking back over the years and remembering the pleasures, not only of journeys made, but journeys shared with friends of like mind: the planning of the expeditions, the searching for photographic spots, the checking of timetables and the research to seek out this or that favourite class of engine, with the knowledge that any day the last survivor could go to a locomotive Valhalla. Both authors are fortunate in having many such friends, and would like to thank them for those days of adventure and exploration – well shared and never to be repeated: especially we would like to acknowledge the work of W. A. Camwell 'Cam' whose enthusiasm led so many along the path of country railway exploration. And to the railwaymen too, the driver who allowed a schoolboy a ride on a Cambrian 0-6-0 along the rocky Cambrian Coast line, the ticket collector who 'forgot' to collect those pieces of clipped card on a last train, the signalman who rang through to the junction to check that it really *was* an 18in Goods on the Keswick train, and the unknown benefactor who actually agreed to and sent off the lineside photographers permit. The shed staffs too, who moved engines just that wee bit to get the 'rods down' or to miss a pole, thank you.

The authors would also like to make acknowledgement to the following for the use of their illustrations.

P. M. Alexander – 26 (above), 26 (below), 38 (above), 48 (above), 60, 61 (above), 61 (below), 92, 113, 114, 136, 137 (below), 138 (above), 149, 156, 157, 175, 179, 192; *W. J. V. Anderson* – 205; *D. S. M. Barrie* – 165 (above); *Birmingham Post & Mail* – 67 (above); *British Railways, Western Region* – 119 (below); *W. A. Camwell* – 101, 172 (below); *H. C. Casserley* – 84 (above), 118 (above), 166 (above), 169; *The Colonel Stephens Railway Museum* – 37; *Colour Rail* – 45 (below), 148 (above), 152 (2); *Derek Cross* – 19, 82 (right); *P. W. Gray* – 55, 73, 77, 133; *J. G. Hubback* – 16; *J. M. Jarvis* – 45 (above), 79, 96; *R. G. Jarvis* – 25 (below); *R. L. Knight* – 129; *L&GRP* – 6, 10, 11, 17, 20, 118 (below), 119 (above), 120 (above), 123, 125 (below), 155, 172 (above), 188, 189, 198; *A. Looseley* – 104; *G. M. Kichenside* – 120 (2); *M. Mensing* – 51, 67 (below); *National Railway Museum* – 142, 170; *C. F. H. Oldham* – 103, 161; *Ivo Peters* – 97, 135; *E. S. Russell* – 116; *Arnold Stringer* – 25 (above); *Eric Treacy* – 72, 200/201; *P. H. Wells* – 203 (below); *P. B. Whitehouse* – frontispiece, 9, 15 (2), 21, 22, 23 (2), 26, 28 (2), 29, 30, 33, 34, 35, 38 (below), 39, 41/42, 47 (2), 48 (below), 52, 53, 54 (2), 57, 58, 59, 63, 68, 69 (2), 75, 78 (2), 80 (2), 81 (2), 82 (left), 84 (below), 85 (2), 86, 87, 90 (2), 91, 93 (2), 95 (2), 106, 111, 112, 117, 125 (above), 126, 137 (above), 138 (below), 141, 145, 146, 147 (2), 154, 159, 161, 163, 166 (below), 177 (2), 184, 191, 196, 197, 203 (below); *P. B. Whitehouse Collection* – 12, 41, 61 (centre), 87, 88, 98, 122, 140, 148 (below), 153, 165 (below), 178, 180. Maps 46, 160 courtesy *The Railway Magazine*. Painting by George Heiron from a colour transparency by *J. M. Jarvis*.

206

SUGGESTED READING

Literally hundreds of books have been published on country railways, most of them on individual lines and locomotive classes. Both of us have written rather more generally, *The Country Railway*, David St John Thomas (Newton Abbot, 1976), possibly being the bestselling railway title especially produced for the British (as opposed to international) market since the war, and *Narrow Gauge Railways of the British Isles*, Patrick B. Whitehouse and J. B. Snell (Newton Abbot, 1984), being the fullest introduction to that fascinating aspect. Many Great Western lines featured in our joint *The Great Western Railway: 150 Glorious Years* (Newton Abbot, 1984), uniform with the present work. Histories of individual lines are far too numerous to mention, but specialist railway bookshops carry a range of titles from

such publishers as the Oakwood Press (whose flexible-cover range of local histories is outstanding) and the Oxford Publishing Company. The extensive railway list of David & Charles includes two key series, *A Regional History of the Railways of Great Britain*, fourteen of whose ultimate fifteen volumes have now been published, covering the complete railway story in each region and also placing railways against the social and economic background, and Forgotten Railways. The key volume, *Forgotten Railways*, Pat White (David & Charles, 1986), like the regional volumes in this second series, tells of the building, traffics, decline and closure of yesterday's routes. The regional volumes each include a gazetteer of the most interesting remains and railway walks.

INDEX

INDEX